**PRINCIPLES OF FOREST POLICY**

## THE AMERICAN FOREST SERIES
HENRY J. VAUX, *Consulting Editor*

*Allen and Sharpe* · An Introduction to American Forestry
*Avery* · Forest Measurements
*Baker* · Principles of Silviculture
*Boyce* · Forest Pathology
*Brockman* · Recreational Use of Wild Lands
*Brown, Panshin, and Forsaith* · Textbook of Wood Technology
    Volume II—The Physical, Mechanical, and Chemical Properties of the
    Commercial Woods of the United States
*Bruce and Schumacher* · Forest Mensuration
*Chapman and Meyer* · Forest Mensuration
*Chapman and Meyer* · Forest Valuation
*Dana* · Forest and Range Policy
*Davis* · Forest Fire: Control and Use
*Davis* · Forest Management: Regulation and Evaluation
*Duerr* · Fundamentals of Forestry Economics
*Graham and Knight* · Principles of Forest Entomology
*Guise* · The Management of Farm Woodlands
*Harlow and Harrar* · Textbook of Dendrology
*Hunt and Garratt* · Wood Preservation
*Panshin and de Zeeuw* · Textbook of Wood Technology
    Volume I—Structure, Identification, Uses, and Properties of the Commercial
    Woods of the United States
*Panshin, Harrar, Bethel, and Baker* · Forest Products
*Shirley* · Forestry and Its Career Opportunities
*Stoddart and Smith* · Range Management
*Trippensee* · Wildlife Management
    Volume I—Upland Game and General Principles
    Volume II—Fur Bearers, Waterfowl, and Fish
*Wackerman, Hagenstein, and Michell* · Harvesting Timber Crops
*Worrell* · Principles of Forest Policy

Walter Mulford was Consulting Editor of this Series from its inception in 1931 until
January 1, 1952.

# PRINCIPLES OF FOREST POLICY

**Albert C. Worrell**
Edwin W. Davis Professor of Forest Policy
Yale University

**McGraw-Hill Book Company**

New York, St. Louis, San Francisco
London, Sydney, Toronto, Mexico, Panama

**Principles of Forest Policy**

*Library of Congress Catalog Card
Number 78–90025*
71891

1 2 3 4 5 6 7 8 9 0    M A M M    7 6 5 4 3 2 1 0

This book was set in News Gothic by
Brown Bros. Linotypers, Inc., and printed
on permanent paper and bound by The
Maple Press Company. The designer
was Merrill Haber. The editors were
James L. Smith and David Dunham.
Peter D. Guilmette supervised the pro-
duction.

**TO MY STUDENTS**

# Preface

This book is a direct outgrowth of a graduate discussion seminar in forest policy (now termed "renewable natural resource policy") which I have conducted during the past decade at Yale University. Early participants will find that their memories of the seminar bear little resemblance to the book because the content has gone through so much evolution over the years. A significant role in this evolution has been played by the students through questioning, arguing, and interjecting ideas into the sometimes heated discussions. I owe them a debt of gratitude for their patient support of my conviction that we were developing a viable and useful approach to the study of resource policy. To some extent this is really their book.

*Principles of Forest Policy* represents the latest step in a long effort to find a satisfying rationale for the complex relationships between civilized man and the natural resources. As a young and perhaps overly idealistic forester, I found my early career clouded by doubts about the real social significance of what I and my professional colleagues were doing. When I began to teach, the doubts intensified. Although I was reasonably sure of what my students were learning, I was not at all certain what they would be able to accomplish with their professional education.

I turned for help to economics, the social science which tries to understand man's efforts to satisfy his material needs. Because it proved most helpful, I devoted some years to helping make economic analysis a functional part of the professional forester's education. However, as my experience broadened, and as I became involved in such matters as the pesticide controversy, I began to realize that economics was providing only partial answers to many significant questions about man's use of the natural resources. I therefore began to grope my way about in yet other social sciences. This book is the result of my efforts to find, if not complete answers, at least fuller, more satisfying, and more useful explanations.

The approach I have taken in this book represents a departure from the traditional study of forest policy in the United States. I have in fact attempted a pioneer effort: a look at policy analytically rather than historically or descriptively. In doing so, I have not of course been able to build directly on the work of previous authors in the forest policy field, but instead have found it necessary to range far and wide in search of supporting ideas. My indebtedness to other writers is indicated by the numerous references. Further, since so many ideas in this book are theirs rather than mine, it has seemed only fair to present many of them in their own words.

My main moral support has come from Professor Henry J. Vaux, who encouraged me to continue when this project was in an early and somewhat disheartening stage, and who eventually read the entire manuscript and made numerous helpful suggestions. A group of colleagues and others read bits and pieces of the manuscript and offered helpful suggestions, but I claim sole credit for its imperfections. Finally, Yale University not only freed me of other responsibilities for a semester, so that I could devote full time to this book, but facilitated its completion in many other ways which I deeply appreciate.

ALBERT C. WORRELL

# Contents

**PRINCIPLES OF FOREST POLICY**

# Introduction

Forests cover more than one-third of the surface of North America—a forest-land area of some 1.8 billion acres. They vary greatly—from the tropical forests of southern Mexico to the boreal forests of northern Canada and from the coniferous forests of the Pacific Coast to the hardwood forests of north-central United States. They are so widely distributed that most North Americans have some kind of contact with them. And their potential as sources of wood, water, forage, recreation, wildlife, and aesthetic values is so great that what is done with them affects the well-being of every one of the 250 million people who live in this region.

How does such a large number of people go about using such a widely dispersed and valuable resource? How do they decide what to do with the forests? Is there a pattern to this use and to these decisions? If there is, how does it come into existence and how is it maintained?

This is the subject with which this book is concerned: the relation between a people and its forest resources. Our primary interest will be in society as a whole rather than in the individuals who make up that society. This does not imply that the individuals are not important in themselves, or that there are not significant mutual impacts between them and the forest resources. But these are not isolated individuals living in a wilderness. They spend their lives as parts of social groups, and these groups influence—and sometimes control—what their members do. We are, therefore, interested in how a society develops attitudes toward its forest resources and organizes itself to utilize those resources in the manner it deems best.

Before we try to come to grips with this subject, it will be important to

1

have clear definitions of what we are discussing and of the terminology we will be using.   The rest of this chapter will attempt to lay such a foundation for the book.

## POLICY AND POLICIES

In order for the members of a society to act together over a period of time in such a way as to achieve something which the social group desires, they must establish certain guidelines and agree to act according to them. Each individual will then know how the other members of the society are going to act under specific conditions and how he too should act.   In fact, there will be pressure on him to act according to the agreed-upon principles. Such recognized guides are necessary if the actions of the individual members are to conform and contribute to the achievement of the society's objectives.

This agreed-upon pattern is what we usually mean when we speak of a "policy."   Webster's Dictionary defines a policy as "a settled course adopted and followed by a government, institution, body, or individual."   We will not be much concerned here with the policies of individuals, but rather with the settled courses adopted and followed by society.   Boulding says that the term policy "generally refers to the principles that govern action directed towards given ends." [1]   We will be using the term *forest policy* with this meaning.   A forest policy specifies certain principles regarding the use of a society's forest resources which it is felt will contribute to the achievement of some of the objectives of that society.

Since both the ends which people desire and the actions which they direct toward those ends are numerous, a society must have many policies.   These are not all of the same kind.   There may, for instance, be one class comprising forest policy, agricultural policy, mining policy, and other similar ones.   In a different class would be economic policy, education policy, and development policy, among others.   Some of these policies will overlap each other and many times they will affect each other.   Once a society has decided on some broad economic policy, for example, its agricultural policy may be developed to conform to that economic policy.   Unless something like this is done, different policies will often conflict with each other.

Ciriacy-Wantrup, in his book *Resource Conservation Economics and Policies,* uses the term in the restricted sense of public policy after pointing out that private individuals, firms, and associations have opinions and attitudes about policies, aid in forming and executing them, and are always affected by them.[2] As a result of this definition, he limits himself to studying the actions of governments at different levels.   Government policies certainly play a major role in the use of forest resources, but they are not necessarily

---

[1] Kenneth E. Boulding, *Principles of Economic Policy,* Prentice-Hall, Inc., Englewood Cliffs, N.J., © 1958, p. 1.
[2] S. V. Ciriacy-Wantrup, *Resource Conservation Economics and Policies,* University of California Press, Berkeley, 1963, p. 223.

synonymous with the policies of the society.   We passed through a period in the United States, for example, during which the federal Forest Service was committed to and trying to develop a policy of public regulation of cutting on privately owned timberlands.   This policy did not conform to the feelings of a majority of the people and never was successfully established as a national policy.

We will try in this book to consider all policies regarding the forest resources, recognizing that these may be both public and private and that in addition there may be distinguishable international, national, regional, state, and local policies.   Since there are many possibilities for disagreement among these policies, one of our objectives will be to try to understand how society finally adopts and follows some particular course of action with respect to the forests.

What relationship is there between policy and economics and the other social sciences?   Certainly it is a close one but they are not the same thing. Each of the social sciences tries to explain some aspect of human behavior —economic, social, or political.   We will have to call on them for help in understanding policy.   But the settled courses adopted and followed by society in dealing with the forests are not a result of purely economic or political forces but rather of a combination of all kinds of social forces.

## FORESTS AND FORESTRY

A *forest* is defined by the Society of American Foresters as "a plant association predominantly of trees and other woody vegetation." [3]   However, when we use the word "forest" as it is used in forest policy we are usually thinking of the forest resource, including the land, rather than just the vegetation. The U.S. Forest Service defines forest land as "land at least 10 percent stocked by forest trees of any size, or formerly having such tree cover, and not currently developed for nonforest use." [4]   This is what we will be thinking of when we use the term "forest" in this book.

Since there is a field of human action and a profession called forestry, might it not be more exact to speak of forestry policy rather than forest policy?   The Society of American Foresters defines forestry as "the scientific management of forests for the continuous production of goods and services."   Even if this definition is broadened to include many aspects of the processing and consumption of forest products, it is still much narrower in its social implications than is the word forest.   Unless the definition of management is stretched enough to include "taking no action," limiting policy considerations to forestry would exclude some important forest problems.   It may be a policy in some cases to remove the forests in order to put the land to some other use.   Although this could hardly be called forestry, it certainly is a forest policy.   It seems best, therefore, to take forest

[3] Society of American Foresters, *Forestry Terminology*, Washington, 1958, p. 34.
[4] U.S. Forest Service, *Forest Survey Handbook*, Washington, 1963, p. 8.1–3.

policy as the focus of interest of this book.   There is such a thing as forestry policy and we will deal with it here, but we will also be concerned with other aspects of forest policy.

Is the forest a distinct enough entity that a society can have policies regarding it which are separate from those it has for other resources?   What a society does with its forests affects and is affected by many other things. Industry-owned forests are involved with industrial policy and farm woodlands with agricultural policy.   Watershed policy usually involves not only forests but also many other forms of land use since a single use does not ordinarily extend over an entire watershed.   It may appear, therefore, that it would be more logical to have policies regarding functions such as recreation, flood control, or industrial raw material rather than policies for specific natural resources.   We probably should define policies both ways, but there are good reasons for considering the forest resource separately for decision making.

Since the forest is a natural resource, might it not be logical to lump it together with other natural resources and establish policies that would cover all of them?   As soon as we try to define what we mean by a natural resource, we find ourselves in difficulty.   There clearly is such a category of things but they vary greatly among themselves.   They can be divided into two broad classes called *flow*, or renewable resources, and *stock*, or nonrenewable resources.[5]   The forest is generally a renewable resource, although in some situations if the existing trees are removed, they cannot be replaced— at least in kind.   Certainly for policy purposes the forest has little in common with stock resources such as metal ores and oil deposits.

Even within the category of renewable natural resources, however, the forest differs significantly from others such as solar radiation, precipitation, and streamflow.   It does not even have much in common with some of the other living resources such as ocean fishes.   Although there is a sufficient unity to the concept of natural resources that we find natural resource journals, government departments of natural resources, and even schools of natural resources, these often do not cover all of the natural resources and even so have usually had to departmentalize their programs in order to deal adequately with individual resources such as forests.

Since the forest has its base on land, it does have much in common with other land uses such as agriculture, range, and marshland.   It is possible to convert forest to pasture or cultivated fields to forest.   Might it then be logical to develop land-use policies with the forest included as just one of many land uses?   This has more to recommend it than the natural resource approach.   The dividing lines are not distinct between forests and cropland, range, marshlands, and other open lands.   But although they overlap on their margins, these various land uses are quite distinct in their centers. The forest is closely tied to one major segment of industry which cannot be ignored in policy decisions but has little to do with other land uses.   The gap between the use of land for cities and its use for forests is also too wide

[5] For a discussion of this classification, see Ciriacy-Wantrup, *op. cit.*, pp. 35–43.

to be bridged by any but the broadest policies.   It seems, therefore, that the forest is a logical unit for policy development but that forest policies must be closely integrated with other land-use policies.

What about conservation policy?   Forests have been linked with conservation ever since Pinchot gave that word the meaning it has carried since early in this century.   But conservation is a somewhat fuzzy concept and its proponents have so broadened their scope that ". . . it is becoming the care of the human habitat, which is the whole planet." [6]   Again, the class is too broad to be useful for forest policy in some respects and too narrow in others.

The forest resource is a physical-biological complex of great variability. It can be changed by man only over fairly long periods of time because change depends on the growth rates of the trees and other organisms involved.   It is not necessarily either natural or wild since large areas of intensively cultivated forests have been planted by man and in some cases could neither maintain nor reproduce themselves without his help.   But in general forests exist where the natural conditions are suitable for their growth and they tend to be quite persistent in spite of man's destructive actions.

Forests produce many goods and services which are valuable to man. The major classes are: wood products; other vegetative products such as maple syrup and Christmas trees; animal products such as beef, fur, fish, and game; water; suitable environments for recreation; and protection from floods, wind, and erosion.   While these are not necessarily all produced at the same time on any given area, most forests are capable of producing and do produce a number of different classes simultaneously.

The use of the forest to produce one product is not necessarily compatible with its use for other products.   Intensive management for wood production with dense stands of even-aged conifers may reduce the water yield in streams flowing from an area because of heavy water use by the trees for transpiration.   Intensive management for deer and other game animals may make it almost impossible to grow desirable timber species because of damage done to the seedlings by the animals.   Although multiple use is possible and desirable, there are many conflicts between uses that must be resolved.

Because of the multiple nature of forest production, management of an area for one product will ordinarily affect the other goods and services which the area might produce.   Very often the impact of these side effects is external to the operation itself.   That is, the person managing the land does not either benefit or suffer from the joint products he produces.   A man who reforests abandoned agricultural land for timber production may reduce water runoff and erosion to the benefit of people downstream.   Another man who clearcuts timber along a traveled highway may in the process destroy scenic values for many passersby.   These external economies and diseconomies from the use of forest land may affect large numbers of people and are,

---

[6] F. Fraser Darling, "Conservation and Ecological Theory," *Journal of Ecology*, 52 (supp.), 1964, p. 43.

therefore, also called <u>social benefits and costs.</u>[7] Since the operator of the forest is not directly affected by these benefits or costs, they usually have little or no influence on his land-use decisions. If they are to be taken into account, it ordinarily must be through some form of public action.

Some of the important forest products such as flood protection and aesthetic values do not pass through any kind of market where their value can be established by the reactions of producers and consumers. As a consequence, there are serious problems in determining how much to spend on producing these unpriced products.

A major characteristic of forests is the long time required to change the output of most goods and services. It takes from twenty to over a hundred years to grow a tree from seed to a commercially usable size. The full impact on soil stabilization and water yield of changes in the forest cover may not be felt for twenty years or more. It may take equally long to restore landscape values destroyed by fire or careless use. Many productive activities on forest land extend beyond the expected lifetimes of the current operators and some span several generations. The value to place on potential benefits far in the future and how to balance these with present investments and costs are serious problems.

These characteristics of the forest make it different from other resources. If it were a minor resource, these peculiar characteristics might not justify separate consideration, since what happened to it could have little significance for the well-being of society anyway. But the forest is not a minor resource—it occupies one-third of the land area of the United States. The value added in all the various manufacturing, transportation, and construction activities involved in the ultimate use of wood is estimated to have been 25 billion dollars in 1958, or some 5.6 percent of the total gross national product.[8] It is also estimated that some 3.3 million people were employed in those timber-based activities, or somewhat over 5 percent of the total civilian employment. Values for the other goods and services are difficult to estimate but it is clear that the forest resource forms the base for a substantial part of our total economy.

## FOREST POLICY

The preceding sections indicate rather well the major characteristics of the field of forest policy. It is concerned with the principles that govern the actions of people with respect to forest resources. Sometimes people from other countries ask: What is the forest policy of the United States? This question carries an implication that there must—or at least should—be a definite forest policy that is specifically written down somewhere, in perhaps a few concise paragraphs. If the people who ask this question have had much experience with forest policy, they do not really expect such a simple

[7] For a discussion of social costs and benefits in forestry, see Albert C. Worrell, *Economics of American Forestry,* John Wiley & Sons, Inc., New York, 1959, pp. 343–353.
[8] Dwight Hair, *The Economic Importance of Timber in the United States,* U.S. Department of Agriculture Misc. Pub. 941, Government Printing Office, Washington, D.C., 1963.

answer to their questions.    It actually is difficult to give any kind of brief answer that is at all meaningful.    There is no one forest policy for the country.    There is a set of policies which are interrelated, overlap, and change with time.    It is one purpose of this book to describe these policies, but in many respects a complete description is beyond the scope of any single book.

Forest policy has arrived at its current status in the United States through a gradual evolution over a long period of time.[9]    It has passed through broad stages which we can describe briefly.    The aboriginal Indians to a large extent lived with the forest, using it as a source of food and other materials and for shelter.    The white colonists by contrast followed a general policy of exploiting the existing timber to meet their various needs and of clearing the land for agricultural and other uses.    The forest was considered as a temporarily valuable resource but one that should eventually be removed in order to make way for more important land uses.    This carried over during the first century of the republic in a policy of dividing the nation's lands up among a large number of small private landowners.

After the middle of the nineteenth century it became evident that all forest land was not suitable for agriculture, the forest lands were not limitless, and the existing exploitative policies could lead to an eventual shortage of timber products.    A policy then developed of retaining a portion of the forest resource in public ownership.    This was followed by the gradual development of a policy of deliberately managing the forest resources for the production of goods and services.    Accompanying this has been the evolution of a policy of government intervention in the use of the privately owned forest resources.    Most recently, as some of these earlier policies have had their effect on increased forest yields, we have witnessed a shift in emphasis from wood, water, and forage as forest products to recreation and the environmental amenities.

The people of the United States have developed a complex set of policies regarding their forest resources.    Some of the details of these policies will appear as we proceed through the book.    At this point it is probably sufficient to point out that the forest policies of the United States are not necessarily the same as those of other countries.    Our nearest neighbors, Canada and Mexico, have different policies, partly because the conditions in the three countries are not the same.    Even within the United States we find that some policies vary between regions and states because of the diversity of forest and other conditions within the country.

## FOREST POLICY DECISION MAKING

Forest policy can be approached from a descriptive or a historical viewpoint. It is useful and interesting to know what the current policies are and the

[9] The most complete description of the historical development of forest policy in the United States is to be found in Samuel T. Dana, *Forest and Range Policy*, McGraw-Hill Book Company, New York, 1956.

chronological steps through which they have developed.    But the viewpoint taken in this book will be more an analytical one.    Forest policy is dynamic —it does not stay the same over any very long period of time.    We will, therefore, be more interested in how changes occur in forest policies than in what those policies are in a static sense.

 One of the reasons for having policies is that they simplify, or even eliminate, the necessity for decision making.    If we have agreed, for example, on a policy of suppressing every wild forest fire that is seen, we no longer have to decide each time we discover a wildfire whether we should put it out or let it burn.    But every policy itself is the result of decisions—society had to decide at some time in its history that all wildfires should be suppressed or the policy would not exist.    It is interesting, therefore, to find out how policy decisions are made.

Boulding says that any study of policy is concerned with three things: "what we want (the ends), how we get it (the means), and who are 'we,' that is, what is the nature of the organization or group concerned." [10]    All of these involve decisions, and we will want to try to understand the things which control them.

Our approach to the subject of forest policy will be made in three major steps: goals, means, and process.    The section on goals will analyze the problems a society faces in deciding what ends it wants its forest resources to serve.    Then the section on means will take a close look at various possible techniques which might be used by the society to implement the policies it has selected to achieve those ends.    Finally, the most important section on process will try to understand just how forest policies actually are formed and made effective and how they change over time.    The last chapter in this section will close the circle by considering ways in which forest policies and programs can be evaluated in terms of the achievement of society's original goals.

[10] Boulding, *op. cit.*, p. 1.

# GOALS

## II

In trying to work out a satisfactory and reasonably stable relationship with its forest resources, a society must adopt some courses of action which its members are willing to accept and follow. These agreed-upon courses are what we are calling the forest policies of that society. The decisions as to the kinds of policies to follow are conscious and even somewhat deliberate activities. Policies are not selected at random nor do they develop through some natural process which is beyond human control.

Policies also do not merely specify uniform behavior; the agreed-upon behavior is always directed toward some desired ends. A logical place to start our analysis of forest policies, therefore, is with a consideration of these desired ends. Of all the many things that modern man wants, which ones might be achieved or affected by forest policies? How does a society select its forest-policy objectives, rank them in some order of priority, and resolve the inevitable conflicts among them?

This group of four chapters will investigate various aspects of the selection of goals for forest policies. First we will consider the objectives that appear relevant to forest-policy decisions. Then we will look briefly at the problems and process of selecting policy objectives. This will bring us up against the question of what criteria to use in making policy choices. And finally we will have to take into account the fact that the objectives of forest policies almost always lie somewhere in the future and seldom can be attained immediately.

# The Objectives of Forest Policies

The purpose of a society in establishing policies about what its members do is to try to assure that their actions will contribute as much as possible toward some ends which the society deems desirable. Before the society can intelligently establish such policies, it must have a clear idea of the ends it wishes to attain. It also must understand the possible effects on these ends of the actions which it seeks to control through the policies.

A policy is thus a means to some end or ends, and its effectiveness can only be judged in terms of those ends. However, many of the ends toward which policies are aimed are desirable only because they in turn become means toward the achievement of other ends. For example, a society may have an objective of adequate wood supplies for all consumer needs. It, therefore, establishes a policy of increasing the growth of timber in its forests. One way of doing this is to reduce the occurrence and severity of wild forest fires. A second objective thus arises of keeping forest-fire damage to a minimum. In order to achieve this, a policy may be established of suppressing immediately all wildfires that are discovered. But if this policy is to be effective, it is necessary that the fires be discovered. So a further objective exists of discovering all wildfires as soon as possible. As a means of achieving this, the state forestry organization may put into effect a policy of manning all lookout towers on every day when the burning index is above some stipulated figure.

This example shows that in many cases there will be a hierarchy of policies as a result of the chain of ends and means. For society, the objective is to have an adequate supply of wood; for the state tower watchmen it is to discover all wildfires.   The two are linked together, however, and policies about manning towers are essential if broader policies about growing timber are to be made effective.   It is risky to say that one of these policies is more important than the other.   But in order to measure the value or effectiveness of any given policy, it may be necessary to look beyond its own immediate ends.

The objectives of forest policies are often not clearly stated and probably in many cases are not even clearly known.   We do not always go through a logical process of reasoning from ends to means in the development of forest policies.   This cannot be entirely overcome for reasons which will show up as we consider the policy-formation process.   But confusion about objectives leads to many difficulties, and it is desirable that the objectives of forest policies and of other policies which affect or conflict with them be made as explicit as possible.

## DIRECT BENEFITS FROM THE FORESTS

The most obvious objective of any society with forest resources is to obtain the benefits that it might from them.   These potential benefits cover a wide range, including: wood products, other vegetative products, animal products, water, recreation sites, flood reduction, soil stabilization, modification of climatic conditions, and environmental amenity.   Many of these benefits may be obtained in some degree at the same time from a single forest.

Wild forests, undisturbed by man, produce these benefits as a natural process.   The quantity and quality of each that is produced by any particular wild forest depends on the physiography and climate of the area where it is growing, the type of forest cover, and the history of the forest with regard to catastrophies, such as hurricanes, which may have upset the natural biotic balance in the area.   Not all forests are potentially capable of producing all of the benefits.   A river-bottom swamp forest, for example, cannot do anything to reduce floods.   It is also important to recognize that the benefits produced will not be the same at all times.   Even without catastrophies trees do not live forever.   When the large old veterans die, their place is taken by young trees and other vegetation which for a period of years may provide a much higher carrying capacity for deer and other animals than the mature forest did.   A forest cannot be preserved indefinitely in the same condition no matter how well it is protected from man.

Some of the potential benefits of the forest cannot be obtained without disturbing the natural conditions.   Wood in the trunks of trees standing in the forest has no value as such for man.   In order to obtain the benefits of wood products, he must cut the trees and remove the usable portions from the forest.   In the process he will make drastic changes in the vegetative cover on the area and perhaps also in the soil conditions.   If hogs are allowed to feed in an oak forest in order to eat the mast produced by the trees, they too will make changes in the vegetative cover and soil.   People can benefit from the forest as a recreation site only by using it for picnicking, camping, or similar activities.    Again, they will change conditions by trampling the soil and disturbing the vegetation.    The mere process of capturing many of the benefits is bound to affect the natural production of those and other benefits.    The magnitude of the adverse effects may be controlled to some extent, and this is one function of forest management.

The quantity and quality of the various benefits which a particular forest produces naturally are not the only possible quantities and qualities that it might produce.    Through manipulating the condition of the vegetation and site, man can change the output of most benefits in the directions that he desires.    The objective of a society, therefore, cannot be just a simple one of obtaining benefits from the forest resources but must stipulate something about the quantities and qualities of each desired benefit.    An objective of obtaining the maximum amount of each potential benefit is not a feasible one, as we shall see, and even the maximum amount of one benefit may not be a rational objective for society.

The yield of benefits from a particular forest can be increased through protection from fire, insects, and diseases; the application of silvicultural practices such as release cuttings or thinnings; the conversion to some other type of cover through removal of the existing vegetation and replanting or reseeding with different species; the construction of roads and camping facilities; and in many other ways.    All of them require the use of labor time, equipment, and materials.    These must be paid for, usually by hiring or buying them in the market.    The market prices of these factors indicate approximately the value of the other goods or services that might be produced with them in some alternative activity.    From society's viewpoint, using these economic factors to increase the forest benefits involves an opportunity cost equal to the value of the alternative benefits that might have been produced with these same factors.    Society has to choose between more benefits from the forests and the other goods and services which it might produce instead.

If one tries to increase the yield of a forest by managing it, he eventually will run into diminishing returns.    That is, it gradually will require larger and larger amounts of labor and capital to keep increasing the yield by additional cubic feet of wood, visitor days of recreational use, or cubic yards of water.    The opportunity cost per unit of these additional benefits may rise quite rapidly and eventually will become very high.    If the society is aware of these rising marginal costs, it probably will decide that the cost of additional units has become exorbitantly high long before the total yield reaches its potential maximum size.    A rational objective for society, therefore, is to obtain the optimum quantity of benefits from the forest or that quantity beyond which additional units would cost more than they are worth to the society.

Although a forest may simultaneously produce various benefits such as water, game, and wood, an attempt to increase the yield of all of these products will usually lead to serious conflicts.    The intensive use of a forest for one product is ordinarily not compatible with its intensive use for another one.    Water yield is increased by reducing the tree cover on a watershed but timber yield can only be raised by increasing the tree cover.    Even low intensities of use for some purposes may not be compatible.    Wilderness recreation, for example, excludes all other uses that require disturbance of the natural conditions.    A society, therefore, has to make choices among the benefits that it might receive from its forests.

A term long used by foresters and one which recently has become popular among other natural-resource interested people is _multiple use._    There has been a certain amount of debate as to what this term means and questions as to whether multiple use can be practiced on areas as small as a single acre.    This is really a footless debate since land of any significance to the nation is not likely to be managed in units this small.    Foresters usually have conceived of multiple use as a process applied to forest properties. In this sense, individual acres may be devoted exclusively to recreation or soil stabilization but the forest as a whole is managed to produce a number of different benefits.    Shanklin says "Multiple use is not a system of management but is a concept of management." [1]    For the entire forest resource of the country, multiple use definitely is a feasible and useful concept.

Multiple use is not a rational objective for forest policy unless it is accompanied by some recognition of the impossibility of obtaining a maximum yield of every one of the potential forest benefits.    That is, to be a feasible objective, multiple use must be defined as meaning the production of some amounts of the different potential benefits.    The term has not usually been used as implying that every one of the possible forest benefits must be produced.    For example, in the 1960 Multiple Use Act, Congress stated its policy to be that "the national forests are established and shall be administered for outdoor recreation, range, timber, watershed, and wildlife and fish purposes."    The definition of multiple use in the Act includes the following language:    "The management of all the . . . resources of the national forests . . . in the combination that will best meet the needs of the American people; . . . that some land will be used for less than all of the resources; . . . and not necessarily the combination of uses that will give the . . . greatest unit output." [2]    It has not always been made clear, however, that on individual areas some one use, or perhaps several uses, must be dominant and that the other benefits will be produced essentially as by-products.

Since it is not possible to obtain the maximum amount of every one of the potential forest benefits, society is forced to assign some sort of priorities to them.    This has not been a serious problem so far in the United States because of our great wealth of forest resources.    But as the population, national income, and consequent demand for forest goods and services all grow in the future, the problem of priorities will assume greater importance.

The positive efforts of the late ninetenth century to conserve the remaining forests and to augment them through tree planting were largely moti-

[1] John Shanklin, *Multiple Use of Land and Water Areas*, ORRRC Study Report 17, Outdoor Recreation Resources Review Commission, Washington, 1962, p. 3.
[2] Public Law 85–517, 74 Stat. 215, 16 U.S.C. 528, 529.

vated by fear of a timber famine.   Wood was widely used in construction and in the manufacture of many products.   The prospect of an impending shortage and perhaps wood's eventual disappearance was frightening. Even though the forests were producing or were capable of producing the other benefits then as now, the primary objective in setting aside the forest reserves and in developing public-forestry programs was to ensure a future supply of wood.

The forest policies developed during the past eighty years have made considerable progress toward achieving this objective.   The total wood growth increases every year and has been exceeding the amount removed each year by both man and the natural destructive agencies of fire, insects, and disease.   We may even be faced for some time with an overabundance of wood growth.   But two facts must not be forgotten:   The current situation is the result of large-scale efforts to increase net wood growth which already have extended over half a century and are becoming more intensive every year.   And, secondly, as our population and income continue to grow, we may reasonably expect the consumption of wood products to increase.

The basic conditions have not changed.   If we were to abandon our policies aimed at producing adequate supplies of wood, the specter of a timber famine would certainly arise again before many years had passed.   There has been a tendency in recent years to label professional foresters, and others concerned with producing wood, as "materialists" and to imply that the other benefits from the forests are now much more important than wood.   However, a nation which uses enough lumber each year to more than cover the whole state of Rhode Island and which depends almost entirely on wood as the raw material for the world's largest pulp and paper industry must assign a high priority to this material as an objective of its forest policies.

The improvement and stabilization of water flows—from the viewpoints of both usable water yield and flood reduction—were early objectives of forest policy in the United States.   The basic law of 1897 regarding administration of the forest reserves provided that such reserves should be established only to secure favorable conditions of water flows and to furnish a continuous supply of timber.   The first authorization for acquisition of forest lands by the federal government (in the Weeks Law of 1911) limited purchases to lands located on the headwaters of navigable streams, the objective clearly being to improve streamflow.

Animal products were also recognized early as an important benefit of the forests.   Grazing was one of the principal uses of the public domain, and the right of the Forest Service to charge a fee for grazing on the national forests was confirmed by the Supreme Court in 1911.   Wildlife, too, received attention with the Biological Survey extending its functions from research into administration in 1900.

While recreation was probably always recognized as an important forest use—at least in the forms of hunting and fishing—its specific inclusion in forest policies came later than that of the other benefits just mentioned. Yellowstone National Park was established in 1872 but it was considered more as a museum than as a recreational area in our present sense.   The first recognition by Congress of recreation as a use of the national forests came in 1915 when the Secretary of Agriculture was authorized to grant permits for summer homes and other recreation-oriented structures.

The remaining benefits of the forests have received relatively much less attention than the four already mentioned.   The other vegetative products are of minor significance except in some local areas.   Soil stabilization and water control are so closely related that they might be considered as joint products except for the case of wind erosion.   The modification of climatic conditions is seldom a primary function of forests although windbreaks and shelterbelts are important in some parts of the country.   Environmental amenity has been receiving much more attention in recent years with the growing concentration of our population in urban centers and the resulting urban sprawl into the surrounding countryside.   It may become the most important benefit the forests can produce in those regions.

What kind of priorities are assigned to these various benefits by our society?   Following an intensive study of American forest policy in 1950, Gulick stated that with regard to the public forests he believed that:

> Timber comes first. . . .   Water comes next, and ranks equally with timber in all primary watershed areas.   In some sections it comes first  . . .  furthermore, its importance is growing. . . .   Grazing comes next, but considerably below timber and water. . . .   Wildlife, recreation, and inspiration come fourth, and far down the line. . . .[3]

Gulick's classification is probably essentially still correct today.   Since he wrote, grazing has declined in importance as a forest-land use.   Outdoor recreation has undergone an "explosion" in the same period and most people would rank it much higher in the order of priority today than he did.   On a national basis it probably should rank above grazing.   So long as the forest resources are more than adequate to produce the wood, water, and meat that our people need, recreation may continue to improve its apparent priority relative to these other benefits.   However, recreation is largely a luxury item whereas water and food are absolute essentials and wood is the most efficient raw material for many products which come close to being essential.   In the event of a showdown, it seems almost certain that recreation would have to give way to these other uses.   The forest is not the only source of water and meat, however, and many other things are potential substitutes for wood as a raw material; so the decision may not be simple even in cases of serious conflict between recreation and the other benefits.

## OTHER POLICY OBJECTIVES

Our discussion of objectives has centered thus far around the direct benefits which a society might derive from its forest resources.   We now must

---

[3] Luther H. Gulick, *American Forest Policy*, Duell, Sloan & Pearce, Inc., New York, 1951, pp. 178–179.

recognize that any society will have other goals and that some of them will be more basic or fundamental than the kinds of benefits we have been talking about.   (The most fundamental objective of any society, for example, is probably survival.)   We cannot understand forest policy without considering these other objectives.   They may sometimes be the real ultimate ends toward whose attainment the apparent objective of forest benefits only provides the means.   And often they will influence forest policies because they conflict in some way with the more obvious goal of direct forest benefits.

In discussing economic policy, Boulding has suggested that its major objectives can be collected under four heads: economic progress, economic stabilization, economic justice, and economic freedom.[4]   If we remove the adjective economic, all four of these are clearly fundamental human objectives and not limited to economic policy.

Dahl and Lindblom state that "The important prime goals of human beings in Western societies include existence or survival, physiological gratifications (through food, sex, sleep, and comfort), love and affection, respect, self-respect, power or control, skill, enlightenment, prestige, aesthetic satisfaction, excitement, novelty, and many others."[5]   For purposes of analysis, they propose that these can be covered by seven instrumental goals: freedom, rationality, democracy, subjective equality, security, progress, and appropriate inclusion.   This is obviously a broader statement of social objectives than Boulding's.

Since not all of society's objectives are likely to be involved with forest policies, a more specific example may be helpful.   In a study of the pesticide controversy sponsored by the Conservation Foundation, I postulated that the basic goals relevant to the pesticide problem are material goods and services, health, comfort, leisure, aesthetic satisfaction, opportunity for recreation, and stability of existence.[6]   This is a mixture of direct and more basic objectives.   We have already considered the direct benefits as objectives of forest policies.   In the remainder of this section we will look at the other, more basic objectives which appear relevant to the consideration of forest policies.

A very basic goal of our society is *security and national defense.*   Whether this has—or should have—priority over other basic objectives would probably be disputed by some people.   In the following paragraphs the other basic goals will be presented in what appears to be a reasonable order of importance.   But part of the controversy which develops over policies is due to differences of opinion about which basic ends should have priority over others.

The relation between national security and defense policy and forest policy is fairly obvious but two examples may strengthen it.   Prior to the First World War, Great Britain followed a policy of importing its timber needs and no effort was put into growing wood in the islands.   During that war,

[4] Kenneth E. Boulding, *Principles of Economic Policy,* Prentice-Hall, Inc., Englewood Cliffs, N.J., 1958, p. 19.
[5] Robert A. Dahl and Charles E. Lindblom, *Politics, Economics, and Welfare,* Harper & Brothers, New York, 1953, p. 28.
[6] Albert C. Worrell, "Pests, Pesticides, and People," *American Forests,* July, 1960, p. 46.

the German submarine blockade effectively cut Britain off from its sources of wood with serious effects on the economy and the war effort.   With this experience vividly in mind, postwar Britain established a policy of acquiring and planting state forests and also stimulating private forest improvement and reforestation.   Germany, by contrast, had developed over the years some of the most intensive forest-land management in the world.   The German forests, in general, were managed on a sustained-yield basis with the further policy of maintaining high volumes of growing stock on the land in order to achieve a large annual yield.   However, during the late 1930s, the Germans began a policy of deliberately overcutting the forests in order to prepare for war, and once the war was under way they continued to deplete their forest resources in order to obtain the materials needed for prosecuting it.   In both of these cases, forest policies were aimed primarily at security or defense rather than at obtaining direct forest benefits.

Another fundamental objective of our society is the *health and welfare* of the people.   Its effects on forest policies are numerous.   Outdoor recreation activities are generally considered as conducive to health.   They also are assumed to add to the participants' welfare through the pleasure obtained and the favorable environment in which they are practiced.   Thus recreation becomes a means to the end of health and welfare, and the management of forests to provide recreational sites is a subsidiary means one step further removed from the ultimate objectives.   A somewhat more direct example is found in policies aimed at reducing logging accidents and making woods work less hazardous.   Welfare is difficult to define but policies of stabilizing forest-dependent communities, compensating workers during periods of involuntary unemployment, and improving the economic condition of low-income groups all have it as their objective.

Two basic objectives which become involved in many of our activities are the *maintenance of both a free-enterprise economic system and a democratic political system.*   It may be argued that even these are only means toward some more fundamental objective, such as liberty, but for forest policy they are clearcut objectives which cannot be ignored.   They control in many respects the political and economic processes through which forest policies are formulated and executed.   It seems odd to many European foresters, for example, that the managers of our public forests sell timber on the stump rather than harvesting it themselves and selling logs.   In the United States, logging has always been done by private enterprise, and a change to public logging would run counter to the basic aim of maintaining operation of the economy in the hands of private enterprise to the maximum extent possible. We also have traditionally limited the power of public-forestry agencies to establish regulations affecting private forests and to spend the income from public forests, insisting that such decisions be made in the legislatures where they are subject to greater control by the people.

*Economic development* is an objective which has received a great deal of attention in recent years.   This has been especially true with regard to the underdeveloped countries but there also has been much interest in the less developed regions of the United States.   Forests may occupy an important place in the development of countries which are well endowed with them.[7]  It has been proposed seriously that underdeveloped countries might liquidate their timber resources as a source of capital for investments of high development potential.  The relationship may also be reversed, with general economic development policies having a favorable impact on forest resources.

In the Employment Act of 1946, Congress stipulated _full employment_ as one of the basic objectives of national policy.  This continues to be a key objective of economic planning and one to which many other policies must conform.  Forest-based activities provide employment for a significant part of our population, and the stimulation or maintenance of such activities may be supported for their employment effects rather than for the goods or services produced.  The conservation camps and training centers established under the Job Corps program set up by the Economic Opportunity Act of 1964 present a good example of the relationship of the full-employment objective to forest policy.

A final basic objective is perhaps best described as _equitable distribution._  Although it is difficult to specify exactly what is desired in terms of distribution of economic and other goods among the population, it is nonetheless a real objective and an influential one.  Here we find the arguments against concentration of wealth and power and those for a minimum wage and social security.  Forest policy is affected too.  Proposals to charge for the use of public recreation areas are opposed on the grounds that this would keep the poor from using them.  And public timber-sale programs are designed to assure that timber will be available to the small business firms.

Other basic goals exist but the foregoing seem to be those most relevant to a consideration of forest policy in our society.

## CONFLICTS BETWEEN OBJECTIVES

The possibility of conflict between society's multitudinous objectives has been mentioned at various places in the preceding pages.  Such conflicts are inevitable, and part of the problem in policy formation is to resolve them satisfactorily.  Much of the rest of the book will be concerned with this problem of conflict resolution, but it will help at this point to become somewhat more clear as to the nature of these conflicts.

The simplest form is that in which one objective interferes physically with the attainment of another.  Wood products and wilderness recreation provide an example.  These two uses are not physically compatible on a given tract of forest land; in fact, by their nature they are mutually exclusive. This particular conflict can apparently be resolved only by assigning specific areas to one use or the other.  A society may be able to attain both of these goals, however, by designating some areas for wood production and

---

[7] See, for example, "The Role of Forest Industries in the Attack on Economic Underdevelopment," *The State of Food and Agriculture 1962*, FAO of the United Nations, Rome, 1962, pp. 88–128.

others for wilderness.   The policy problem then becomes one of the relative amounts of each use to strive for rather than the choice of one and the complete exclusion of the other.

In most cases, the attainment of one goal will not completely exclude the attainment of another but will physically interfere with it.   The policy problem then is to choose the best combination from among those which are physically possible.   Wood and water can be obtained from a single forest at the same time but the yield of one can usually be increased only by actions which reduce the yield of the other.   The conflict can be resolved by finding some optimum combination of the two products.

Objectives may come into economic conflict even when they do not interfere with each other physically.   The attainment of most goals involving forests requires the use of other economic resources such as capital or labor.   Since the total supply of these resources is limited and there are many other desirable uses for them, enough may not be available to attain all forest-related goals.   This conflict shows up in the appropriation of money by any legislative body.   It may be obvious that improved fire protection would increase timber growth and provide more raw material for local wood-using industries.   But at the same time there may be public pressure for an expansion of state parks.   Tax revenues are frequently insufficient to finance the attainment of both desirable goals.   The legislature may resolve this conflict by appropriating funds for only one program, or it may spread the available money over both with the knowledge that this will not permit the complete attainment of either goal.

The physical and economic conflicts just described can be resolved reasonably well in a society where everyone agrees on the relative importance of various objectives.   However, societies consist of individuals who are not likely to all agree about policy objectives.   One of the most common conflicts is between groups who consider different ends to be most important. When the forest resource is not adequate to satisfy the goals of both groups, there is conflict over whose desires should prevail.   An example of a conflict which probably will become more severe in the future is that between the people who want wilderness-type recreation and those who want more "civilized" kinds, such as motorboating, water skiing, travel by jeep or motor scooter, and campgrounds accessible by paved roads.

This type of conflict obviously gets mixed up with some of the more basic objectives.   Should the choices be made by majority rule?   Must the rights of minorities always be protected?   Will wilderness areas be used mainly by the wealthy and perhaps deprive the poor of simpler pleasures? There is no obvious way to resolve conflicts such as these.

Conflicts may not always revolve around situations in which everyone cannot get additional benefits.   The objectives of some groups may be attainable only at the expense of sacrifices by other groups.   The sacrifice may be quite clear, as in the case where zoning an area for watershed protection deprives an individual of the right to earn a livelihood by cultivating his steep and eroding fields.   This may represent a real sacrifice even though this individual is paid for his farm at going land prices.   In many cases, the sacrifices are less obvious but none the less real.   Opening up an area with roads for timber management or recreational use may destroy the solitude formerly enjoyed by local residents.   It is not at all surprising that the people who might suffer losses in such situations do their best to prevent other groups from attaining their objectives.

Still another source of conflict exists in the difference between the time perspectives of individuals and that of the social group.   The individual is primarily concerned with things which will affect him during his own lifetime.   Society may be concerned about timber supplies for the year 2100 but no individual now alive stands to suffer personally from any shortage which may exist at that date.   The older the individual, the shorter his planning horizon is likely to be.   Thus there are natural differences in the values which people of different ages and the social group place on various goals.

It is common knowledge that serious conflicts exist between the objectives of forest policy.   But it is not so clear to many people that these situations are not all black and white.   The advocates of conflicting goals are described as "moneygrubbers," "impractical visionaries," "ruthless exploiters," and even less complementary appellations.   The solutions proposed are to "throw the rascals out" and to "let the right prevail."   This tends to obscure the fact that most conflicts are not between "good" goals and "bad" ones. The answer is not a simple one of eliminating bad goals so that we may attain good ones.   There probably is no perfect resolution of these conflicts, and the function of forest-policy formation is primarily one of seeking the best possible forms of resolution.

## SOCIAL INSTITUTIONS AND POLICY OBJECTIVES

Throughout its history, every society has developed patterns of behavior for its members.   The patterns which survived and were accepted have now become social institutions.   For each institution, there has evolved a structure which controls or guides the actions of the present members of society. An example is the institution of private property and the complex legal, governmental, and social structure which exists to enforce compliance with it.

Originally, these social institutions developed as means of attaining some end desired by society.   The objectives of an existing social institution may be relevant only to some past situation which has changed with time, but the institution's structure may still keep it effective.   They are subject to change but are so firmly entrenched that people frequently do not even question them.[8]

Policies are concerned with future actions and therefore with future goals. But once policies have been established, they are likely to become institu-

---

[8] For a discussion of how policies differ from institutions, see S. V. Ciriacy-Wantrup, *Resource Conservation Economics and Policies,* University of California Press, Berkeley, 1963, p. 226.

tionalized.    The present generation may then inherit these policies without any serious consideration of them.    To some extent this is desirable since decisions can be limited largely to changing existing policies rather than developing entirely new ones.    But it has the danger that policies may be accepted blindly with little or no reconsideration of their objectives. In any case, it means that policies develop in an environment where there are many lags, changes are sticky, and clearcut choices or decisions are seldom possible.    In the real world, the ends and effects of actions often are not clearly understood, and it is not always obvious when maintaining existing institutions may not be the best policy.

## SOCIAL OBJECTIVES AND ATTITUDES

By now, it is clear that forest policies are closely related to the general objectives and attitudes of the society which forms them.    This explains some of the differences between the forest policies of different countries. Forest policy in the United States must be viewed in the light of the general economic, political, and sociological philosophy and organization of this country.

The way in which the people interpret their relationship to the forest resources is a matter of some concern.    Spoehr says: "To the degree that the Western world is composed of almost completely urbanized individuals, it not merely regards habitat, and consequently natural resources, as an entity that is to be dominated and manipulated . . . but tends to relegate the whole matter to a handful of specialists and . . . to place nature outside its immediate sphere of concern." [9]    Serious questions have been raised as to whether man can live as though he is separate from nature, or whether he must recognize that he is subject to the same processes and regularities as other parts of his environment.

We cannot deal with this controversial question here except to recognize its importance in policy decisions about the forests, which are both natural and environmental resources.    In general, we may expect the forest resources to be used in the ways which will further the social objectives of the people of the United Sates.    The general social attitude of the nation is therefore a prime factor in determining the objectives of forest policies.

[9] Alexander Spoehr, "Cultural Differences in the Interpretation of Natural Resources," in W. L. Thomas, Jr. (ed.), *Man's Role in Changing the Face of the Earth,* The University of Chicago Press, Chicago, 1956, p. 100.

# The Process of
# Forest-Policy Formation

Policies were defined in Chapter 1 as settled courses adopted and followed by society. Forest policies were separated out as defining principles regarding the use of forest resources. Since forest policies exist, there must be some identifiable processes through which these guiding principles were adopted and followed. The next three chapters will deal with the process of adoption—how a society settles on the courses of action to be followed. Later chapters will then consider the processes through which the society follows these courses or makes sure that they are followed.

It will be well to start by defining some terms. The subject matter of this chapter is policy formation—the way that policies take form or come into existence. The term *policy formulation* is also used. To formulate is to put into a systematized statement or expression. Policy formulation, therefore, is the process of preparing a systematic statement of the settled future course which a society has agreed to follow. This process takes place in legislatures and administrative agencies but also in the rules and resolutions committees of all sorts of organizations. It is an important process, but a narrower one than policy formation, which involves things that happen before a society gets around to actually formulating a policy statement and also changes in policy that occur while the formal policy statement remains unchanged.

Frequent reference is also made to *policy decisions.* These do exist, and they are important. But a society does not often adopt a settled course of action in a single decision. Even in the rare cases when this does happen, the decision is usually preceded by other actions and maneuvers which condition those involved so that they can make the decision.

Policy formation ordinarily involves many decisions by different people. These affect and reinforce or change each other.   The effects accumulate, and policy is formed and reformed in the process.   A policy decision is therefore probably better thought of as a decision about policy rather than as a decision which makes policy.

To decide is to arrive at a solution that ends uncertainty or dispute.   In this sense, society does make policy decisions, though often only after long and difficult efforts to find the solution.   To decide is also to make a choice or a judgment.   Decisions of this kind are involved in the formation of policies, but they do not ordinarily establish policies except in authoritarian or dictatorship situations.   In fact, the position is usually reversed, and policies function to save people from having to make these decisions of choice or judgment.

The difficulty with the word "decision" is that it has a sense of finality about it.   It implies that once a decision has been made, the policy is set. But we all know that policies change with time.   Sometimes the changes are made deliberately, and this is a most difficult kind of policy decision. More often, policies are gradually modified, eroded away or strengthened, ignored or stringently observed, without any overt decisions being made about them.   Policy formation, then, is usually a continuing process of further modifying policies which already exist.   The fact that the existing policy may be one of doing nothing tends to obscure this.   The passage of a law which prohibits people from burning brush without a permit, for example, does not mean that society now has a policy about brush burning where before it had none.   The policy before this law was to allow people to burn brush whenever they pleased.

A policy maker practically never starts out with a clean slate on which he can formulate the policy that concerns him.   In a country where people have been using the forests for some four hundred years, a completely new forest policy cannot be conceived of.   A host of policies about the use of the forests already exist.   They are not necessarily good policies, but people are following them and will continue to do so unless they are changed. They will not be changed by denouncing them as "bad" or by proposing new policies.   They may not even be changed by enacting laws against them. The intentional burning of the woods in the South was such a policy.   The accepted course of action was to burn off the woods every spring to improve grazing, make travel through the woods easier, kill ticks, and accomplish other objectives.   Changing this policy to one of using fire only as a controlled tool under specific circumstances has required almost half a century, and still is not completely accomplished.

As was pointed out in the preceding chapter, society has many other goals besides those which it can attain through use of the forests.   Policies aimed at these other goals are also a part of the environment in which forest policies are formed.   Many of them have developed into institutions which people accept without question.   These institutions so regulate and control behavior that it may be necessary to change them before changes in forest policies become possible.   With an objective of treating all taxpayers equitably, property taxes are traditionally levied against assessments based on other real estate transactions in the same area.    If one objective of forest policy is to maintain open space in suburban areas, the tax policy may have to be changed to give preferential treatment to owners of wooded land.    Otherwise their lands will be assessed at potential developed-real-estate values, and the resulting high taxes will force them to develop their lands as soon as possible for residential or business use.

## THE FORMATION PROCESS

It will help in analyzing forest policy formation to begin with a simple and somewhat abstract description of the process.    There is no point in starting from a hypothetical situation in which no forest policy of any kind exists and the formation process can begin from zero.    As far back in history as we would profit by going, human societies in forested areas have always had some kind of policy about their use of the forests.    Policy formation is always a process of evolution from some existing state.

Another stage in this evolution begins when some individuals or groups in a society recognize that some potentially valuable forest-related goals are not being achieved satisfactorily.    It may be that some possible objective is not being realized at all under existing policies.    They may not be achieving some objective as fully as it appears possible to do.    Or they may be achieving an objective in a manner which is not satisfactory.    Whatever the case, the first step is action by the concerned parties to try to bring about a change.    This may take two forms: criticizing the existing situation and demanding that some change be made or proposing and promoting the adoption of a specific change. The first form is more roundabout, since it involves passing onto other parties the burden of deciding what change to make, but it may not be any less effective in bringing a change about.

Part of the necessary action consists of getting enough people to accept the change so that it will be adopted by the group as a policy.    On most forestry issues the great mass of the people will be unconcerned or indifferent.    But there will always be a certain number of leaders or representatives who are able to speak for these people or gain their compliance.    The support of this small but influential group must be obtained before a change can be made.

It is also essential that not too many people oppose the idea of a change. There are almost certain to be some who will oppose any suggested changes. So some of the action must be aimed at reducing the number of these opponents.    Again it will usually be a case of winning over a relatively small group, because the apathy of the majority will keep them from actively opposing anything that does not obviously have a direct impact on them personally.    A substantial part of the opposition to any change in current policy may arise because it would conflict with the attainment of some other goals.    The resolution of such conflicts may well be the most difficult and important part of the action involved in changing a policy.    But unless they are resolved, the advocates of the conflicting goals may block the desired change.

It seems obvious that the problems of obtaining support and reducing opposition are less for small policy changes than for large ones.   The possibilities of making small improvements in an existing situation may also be easier to perceive.   The result of this is that policy tends to evolve in a series of small incremental changes.   This has an additional advantage in that it is easier to retreat from a small change if it should turn out to have been a mistake.   Action is therefore likely to take the form of a continuing program aimed at achieving a succession of small changes which have a common direction.

## THE EVOLUTION OF FOREST POLICY IN THE UNITED STATES

This section will present a brief summary of the formation of forest policy in the United States.   Its purpose is to show in broad outlines how present policies have evolved from those which existed when the nation was founded. No attempt will be made to go into details, and many important happenings will be omitted.   These are readily available to the interested reader in the authoritative book by Dana.[1]   The object here is not to give a complete history but to show through historical example how forest policy formation takes place.

The forest policy of the United States during the first part of its existence was a consequence of two broader land policies: that the country's land resources should be in private ownership and that the private owners should be free to use their lands as they saw fit.   The federal government found itself possessed of a large public domain which had been ceded to it by the states and then materially increased by the Louisiana Purchase.   Its dominant land policy for over a century was to transfer this resource to private owners for conversion into farms as rapidly as this could be done with equity and without conflicting with other public goals.   The only important exception made for forests was the reservation of lands containing live oak and red cedar as a source of timbers for the navy.

The policy of freedom of use reflected the general laissez faire philosophy of the times.   There was some concern over forest fires, and most states enacted laws intended to control them; but little was done to enforce these. To the relatively small population of those days, the forest resources appeared inexhaustible, and with improved transportation it was always possible to obtain sufficient wood even when local supplies ran short.

Around the middle of the nineteenth century, some individuals began to express concern about the depletion of the forest resources.   Gradually support was mustered among others who too became convinced that some change would be desirable from the policy of leaving future wood supplies entirely up to the whims of individual owners, many of whom were clearly not the farmers visualized by the early land policies.   The real change began in 1876 with the hiring of Franklin B. Hough by the Commissioner of Agriculture to write a report on forestry.   Congress then recognized the changing policy by continuing to appropriate funds in subsequent years for a forestry program in the Department of Agriculture.   By 1886 a Divi-

[1] Samuel T. Dana, *Forest and Range Policy,* McGraw-Hill Book Company, New York, 1956.

sion of Forestry had been officially established under B. E. Fernow and was conducting a program of research and education. The policy had now modified to allow for governmental action to influence the behavior of private forest owners but otherwise remained substantially the same.

Forest fires were early recognized as one cause of timber depletion that was not being curbed by private landowners. In 1885, the New York legislature passed forest-fire legislation, and by the end of the century practically all other states had followed suit. These laws were not very effective, but they were the first step toward a policy of public responsibility for forest protection.

The first major break in the policy of completely private ownership came in 1872 when Congress established the Yellowstone National Park in Wyoming. Pressure for reserving other forests from private exploitation then gradually increased, and in 1891 Congress authorized the President to set aside forest reserves from the public domain. During the next two years some 18 million acres went into such reserves. New York established its Forest Preserve in 1885, and Pennsylvania started to acquire land for forest reservations in 1897. By the turn of the century, the United States forest policy had changed to one of partial public ownership of the forest resources.

At first, these public forest lands were conceived of as "reserves" of timber. This persists in the New York Forest Preserve which, by provision of the state constitution, must remain forever as wild land. However, in the Organic Administration Act of 1897, Congress stated that federal reserves were to be established "for the purpose of securing favorable conditions of water flows, and to furnish a continuous supply of timber for the use and necessities of citizens of the United States." This strengthened the evolving policy that forest lands should be managed purposefully to produce goods and services. It was further reinforced by the transfer in 1905 of the forest reserves to the Department of Agriculture, whose Secretary specifically stated that all of their resources were to be for use. An important part of the new Forest Service's program was the regulation of grazing on National Forest range lands. Forest policy had by then recognized forage, water, and wood as vital forest products.

After Gifford Pinchot took charge of the federal Division of Forestry in 1898, it began to place more emphasis on assistance to private forest owners. By 1900, the forest policy of the United States had changed enough to provide in rudimentary form that the public should: own and manage part of the forest resources on a permanent basis; educate and assist private forest landowners; provide protection against forest fires; and do research on forest problems. Much of the policy that has formed since then has been extensions or modifications of these four lines.

The Weeks Law of 1911 provided for cooperation by the federal government with the states in forest fire protection on watersheds of navigable streams. This was an extension of the policy of public fire protection but also the beginning of a policy of cooperation by the federal and state governments in dealing with forest problems. In 1914, the Department of Agriculture and the land-grant colleges began to cooperate in agricultural extension, and forestry was included as part of this educational program.

The same Weeks law also provided for the purchase of forest lands in the headwaters of navigable streams.   Some of the states were already pursuing a policy of buying private land for public forests, but this was the first authorization for federal purchases.

A fourth use of the forests was beginning to assume importance at this time. The National Park Service was created in 1916 to administer the growing chain of national parks.   The states were also creating parks, and during the 1920s, recreational use began to develop on the national forests.   Forest policy was gradually broadening to include recreation as an important objective.

Despite the progress which had been made during the past fifty years, many people concerned about the forest resources felt that the United States policy was still inadequate to assure their proper conservation.   In 1919, both the Forest Service and the Society of American Foresters began a campaign to promote a policy of public regulation of cutting practices on private forest lands.   This was not a new idea, but it had not been pushed aggressively before this time.   This issue was debated bitterly during the next twenty years, with much of the controversy revolving around whether the states or the federal government should be the regulating body. No regulatory policies were formulated during this period, but the continuing threat of public regulation had a decided effect on the management practices of many private landowners.

The Clarke-McNary Act of 1924 provided for federal cooperation with the states in fire control on all forest lands, for similar cooperation in the production and distribution to private landowners of tree planting stock, and for the purchase of land to be added to the national forests specifically for timber production.   All of these were extensions of existing policy.   Similarly, the McSweeney-McNary Act of 1928 extended the existing policy of public forestry research by authorizing a much more comprehensive program.

By the 1920s, the timber had been cut from large areas of land which were unsuitable for agricultural development.   The owners of this land found the annual property taxes a burden at a time when they could derive no income from their property.   Taxes thus appeared to be a serious disincentive to desirable forest management.

The Clarke-McNary Act, therefore, instructed the Secretary of Agriculture to study "the effects of tax laws, methods, and practices upon forest perpetuation."   To carry out this instruction, the Forest Service established the Forest Taxation Inquiry in 1926 under the direction of Prof. Fred R. Fairchild of Yale University.   Its thorough and voluminous report was published in 1935.   During the 1930s, a number of states introduced yield taxes as alternatives to annual ad valorem taxes on forest properties, and others developed various modifications of tax rates or assessments to give relief to forest owners.   In 1943, the federal income tax law was modified to permit forest owners who harvested timber from their own lands for further conversion into products to treat the returns from holding or growing the timber as a capital gain rather than ordinary income for tax purposes. Since the tax rate on capital gains is half the rate on ordinary income and never exceeds 25 percent, this provided a definite economic incentive for people to hold and grow timber.

A large area of the public domain still remained in the category of "vacant, unappropriated, and unreserved" land in 1934. Most of this was range land which for one reason or another had not found its way into private ownership. The Taylor Grazing Act of 1934 provided that the major part of these lands be formed into grazing districts and managed by the Department of the Interior. Although the Taylor Act left the way open for eventual disposal of these lands to private owners, the long-run effect was to establish most of them as permanently in public ownership. Forest and range are so closely related in much of the West that such changes in grazing policy are obviously also changes in forest policy.

Forestry activity expanded tremendously during the New Deal era. A major policy change was the 1937 Cooperative Farm Forestry Act. This provided for direct technical assistance to farmers in such work as marking timber for harvesting. This policy was further expanded in 1950 by the Cooperative Forest Management Act to aid the states in giving technical assistance to private landowners and processors of primary forest products.

Pressure for public regulation continued and in 1941 resulted in the passage of the Oregon Forest Conservation Act. This was followed by similar acts in a number of other states. The constitutionality of such state regulation was upheld by the United States Supreme Court in 1949 in a test of the Washington state law. However, by this time, the larger private landowners had materially improved their forest practices, and considerable opposition had developed within the forestry profession itself to further extension of public regulation. The existing state laws present serious enforcement problems, and the United States does not really have a strong policy today of regulating timber cutting on private lands.

During the 1950s, the emphasis in United States forest policy gradually shifted from wood to the other forest benefits. It became apparent that existing policies were having beneficial effects and that the timber supply situation was improving year by year. This coincided with a period of unprecedented prosperity and leisure and a rapid population growth in all major urban centers. The resulting demand for water and recreation facilities directly affected the forest resources. Although the Forest Service has always tried to manage the national forests for all possible products, Congress felt it desirable in 1960 to make a clear policy statement in the Multiple Use Act that the national forests shall be administered for recreation, range, timber, watershed, wildlife, and fish. While this made little change in the current management practices, it did formulate explicit future policy for national-forest administration.

The relationship between the forests and water has been a continuous thread in the United States policy for almost a century. This was one of the prime objectives of a policy of permanent federal ownership and management of forest lands. Forest policies concerned with water have been strengthened and made more explicit with the passage of time. But there has been no "explosion" in policy formation such as has taken place with recreation.

The demand for outdoor recreation increased rapidly following the Second World War, and many people felt that existing policies were not adequate to accomplish the goals they considered desirable. Responding to this pressure, in 1958 Congress appointed an Outdoor Recreation Resources Review Commission which studied the matter thoroughly and reported to the President and Congress in January, 1962.   An immediate response to the ORRRC report was the establishment that same year of a Bureau of Outdoor Recreation in the Department of Interior, charged with cooperating with the states in developing plans and programs for outdoor recreation. Although an extension of the existing policy of federal-state cooperation, this also represented a new policy of a direct approach to outdoor recreation.   Its effects on forest policy are bound to be numerous.

Closely related to outdoor recreation but in some respects independent of it has been the development of a wilderness policy.   Its roots go far back in American history.   In the 1870s John Muir began writing for magazines and newspapers about Yosemite and other mountains and forests. Largely due to his stimulation, the Sierra Club was founded in San Francisco in 1892 and began its long campaign to preserve our wild land resources.   Action was slow until the late 1920s.   In 1930 the Forest Service adopted a policy of reserving portions of the national forests from road or residential development.   The Park Service was already committed by then to preserving most of its area in a state of roadlessness.   In the so-called Copeland Report of 1933, the Forest Service recommended that 10 million acres be set aside as wilderness areas and an additional 9.5 million as primeval areas (tracts of old-growth timber in which human activities have never upset the normal processes of nature).[2]

The Wilderness Society, which was formed in 1935, and many other interested people felt that the important objective of preserving land in wilderness condition was still not being adequately achieved and pressed for firmer policies.   The most recent step in the formation of this policy has been the passage by Congress in 1964 of the Wilderness Act, which establishes a National Wilderness Preservation System.

In somewhat over one hundred years, the general forest policy of the United States has evolved from one of laissez faire private ownership and operation, with a primary objective of wood, to one of mixed public and private ownership, with considerable public interference in management of the private lands and major objectives of wood, water, forage, opportunities for recreation, and environmental amenity.   Forest-policy formation continues through a process of incremental changes with the present trend of such changes emphasizing the non-wood forest benefits.

## THE PLACE OF PLANNING

The preceding section showed how forest policy has formed and modified over the years in the United States.   The process of change has been almost continuous.   These were clearly not autonomous changes which occurred in some random manner.   Rather, they were brought about by the responses of individuals and groups to the conditions which existed at the time.   In retrospect, we can see that some of the policies were not wise

---

[2] U.S. Forest Service, *A National Plan for American Forestry*, Government Printing Office, Washington, 1933, p. 1546.

even in their own time, and that others had undesirable long-run effects. Might the Lake States pineries not be more valuable today if the policy at the time they were first cut had been one of permanent forest maintenance rather than conversion to agricultural lands?   Hindsight is always better than foresight, but could we not have developed more clearsighted policies in the past?

Wengert points out that a fundamental conflict has existed and still does between two groups of people concerned with resource policy.   He describes them as: "those who sought to know and determine the future, to anticipate scarcities through rational analysis and calculation, and, on the basis of this knowledge, to determine resource allocation deliberately and thoughtfully" and "those who for many reasons preferred to continue relying on private action and drift to meet new problems on an ad hoc basis, improvising as the situation seemed to require." [3]   The first group consists of the planners and those who believe in planning.

It might seem odd that this divergence of opinion exists, since rational analysis and calculation followed by deliberate and thoughtful resource allocation appears such a sensible way to determine policy.   In abstract terms, it is hard to argue against planning.   But for policy purposes, planning must be concrete; or else it is open to all the criticisms leveled against other methods.   The difficulties in making planning effective fall into two broad categories: the environmental conditions within which planning must operate and the data which are essential to its function.

Meyerson and Banfield define a plan as "a course of action which can be carried into effect, which can be expected to lead to the ends sought, and which someone (an effectuating organization) intends to carry into effect." [4]   The most elaborate planning is worthless for policy formation unless it produces a product which meets these specifications.   But many things can interfere with this.   In an analysis of American agricultural planning, Hardin recognizes technological, cultural-psychological, and constitutional limitations on the planning process, plus others arising from pressure politics and inertia.[5]   The nature of the conditions which limit forest planning will become clearer as we proceed through this book.

Even more significant for forest planning are the weaknesses inherent in the available information.   Planning is essentially a rational process of determining the best means of achieving some given end or of making the best use of some given resource.   We have already seen in Chapter 2 some of the problems involved in deciding on appropriate objectives for forest policy.   But even if we were to assume that the ends of forest policy are clearly defined, the information needed for planning to achieve those ends would present many problems.   A rational analysis can be made only if there are data to use in the calculations.   The reliability—and even the validity—of such a planning analysis depends absolutely on the quality of these data.

[3] Norman Wengert, *Natural Resources and the Political Struggle*, Doubleday & Company, Inc., Garden City, N.Y., 1955, p. 4.
[4] Martin Meyerson and Edward C. Banfield, *Politics, Planning, and the Public Interest*, The Free Press, Glencoe, Ill., 1955, p. 312.
[5] Charles M. Hardin, "Political planning: Possibilities, Limitations, and Aberrations" in *Modern Land Policy*, The University of Illinois Press, Urbana, 1960, p. 258.

The problem is further complicated by the necessity of having two kinds of data.   These are what Simon has called _factual_ and _value_ elements.[6] There has been considerable argument among philosophers and social scientists about a distinction between facts and values.   But we need not get involved in this here.   It is clear that the information needed for planning or any other form of policy decision making falls into two broad categories which are reasonably distinct.   The first is "real" or "physical" data. For example: If a certain number of men use a certain amount of equipment and supplies to regularly perform certain specified operations on a certain-sized tract of forest which supports a specified volume of growing stock, it will be possible to harvest at certain regular intervals a specific volume of wood on a sustained basis.   These are facts.   The second category is value data.   What is the value of the productive factors used in managing this forest?   What is the value of the wood produced?   Is one "worth" more than the other?   These are not facts in the same sense as the physical data because of uncertainty as to how to measure them. Chapter 4 will go into this problem at considerable length.

Even the so-called facts are not perfect data, however.   The wood-growing example above is a typical case.   At the present time we do not know for sure how much wood can be grown per acre in the United States under any stipulated conditions of land quality, growing stock, and cultural operations.   We have estimates and opinions but that is all.   More is known about growing wood than about the other forest benefits, but the silviculturists are really just beginning to develop reliable data on what can be accomplished by various cultural practices and little is known about what may be achieved through tree improvement and genetics.

The situation is even less satisfactory with the other forest benefits. Our knowledge of the effects on water yields and stream flow which may be brought about by manipulating the forest cover is very imperfect.   No one knows for sure how much use the various forest types can sustain as campgrounds and picnic sites before deterioration of the soil and vegetation becomes serious.   We do not even know how to measure some of the important forest benefits.   What does a recreationist receive from a day in the forest?   How can one measure the aesthetic satisfaction produced by a landscape?

These information problems have two effects, which to some extent work in opposing directions.   It is almost impossible for a layman to get enough reliable information on the various forest uses to form satisfactory judgments about policy issues.   The natural thing to do under these circumstances is to turn for advice and guidance to those who specialize in forest use.   There is a tendency to delegate much of the responsibility for policy formation to the experts in the field—the forest scientists and professionals.

The other effect of the weak information is that it is very difficult for even the experts to do a satisfactory job of planning for the best use of the forest resource.   This does not mean that planning is not a useful activity and one which should be encouraged.   But it does mean that it is not the

[6] Herbert A. Simon, _Administrative Behavior_, The Macmillan Company, New York, 1958, p. 45.

straight and rapid road to forest-policy formation that it may at first seem. It is a difficult road with many obstacles, many detours, and many opportunities to go astray. Planning should play a significant role in forest-policy formation, but it needs to be supplemented in other ways.

## GENERAL APPROACHES TO POLICY FORMATION

We have now seen some of the problems which a society encounters in trying to arrive at satisfactory policies for forest-resource use. Many different people—perhaps all of the members of the society—are involved in one way or another. They have different ideas about what objectives are important and about the priorities that should be given to them. Information is not adequate to permit perfect advance calculation of the physical outcomes of following any particular policy. There are serious difficulties in determining the relative importance or values of the possible outcomes. Under such circumstances, how can a society go about adopting settled courses of action?

Students of this subject have recognized four broad processes which in various combinations represent the major possibilities. Dahl and Lindblom call them: the price system, hierarchy, polyarchy, and bargaining.[7]

Simon refers to them in the same order as: the price mechanism, mechanisms of authority and interpersonal influence, democratic political processes, and bargaining.[8] The names used are not important but Simon's are perhaps more self-explanatory.

We will start with a consideration of the second of these processes. In all societies, some individuals assume positions of leadership which are recognized and respected by the other members. These leaders play an important part in policy formation and may assume various roles in doing this. A modern society must have so many policies, and the issues involved in forming them are so complex that all of the members cannot understand or concern themselves with every individual policy. Instead, certain persons specialize in particular areas, develop knowledge about them, and devote a large part of their time to them. The other society members tend to delegate responsibility in varying degrees to these specialists and to follow where they lead.

This leader-follower role is never complete, for even an absolute dictator cannot completely ignore the opinions of his followers. The other three processes listed above are ways in which a society controls its leaders or uses them to form policies acceptable to the whole group. We will consider these other processes in order, but first let us see in more detail how the leadership process functions.

One way in which individuals exert leadership in policy formation is through the mechanism of authority. In any bureaucratic organization such as a government forest service there is a hierarchy of employees, each of whom must conform to the directions of those superior in rank to him.

[7] Robert A. Dahl and Charles E. Lindblom, *Politics, Economics, and Welfare,* Harper & Brothers, New York, 1953, p. 22.
[8] Herbert A. Simon, "New Developments in the Theory of the Firm," *American Economic Review,* Papers and Proceedings, May, 1962, p. 2.

The higher executives in such bureaucracies are in a position to actively participate in the formation of policies.   Of course, people in subordinate positions influence their superiors' actions by providing them with ideas, information, and advice.   The activities of the leader may consist to a considerable extent of comparing, combining, and choosing among ideas developed by his subordinates.   But once he arrives at a conclusion he has the authority to make his subordinates conform to it.   The authority of some leaders extends beyond their own organizations.   A state forester, for example, may have the authority to limit use of all of the forests in the state as a fire-prevention measure when weather conditions are extremely hazardous.   If he uses this authority to establish policies of closing down all logging operations or forbidding hunters and fishermen from entering the woods when the fire danger exceeds some particular intensity, the logger or sportsman has little option but to follow his policy lead.

A person may also achieve a position of policy leadership through interpersonal influence.   He may be a persuasive speaker or writer, a skillful manipulator of the opinions of group members, or a clever organizer of support among the membership.   Although he may have little real authority, individual members may find that the only alternative to following his ideas is to withdraw from the group.   To varying degrees, the leaders of the conservation and other associations concerned with forest resources fall in this category.   So do many of the nonoffice-holding local individuals who exert so much power over policy formation in their communities.   The members of society at large often delegate considerable responsibility for policy decisions to the professional foresters, forest scientists, and other specialists who they feel understand the problems better than they do themselves.

The leaders need ways of determining how their society feels about policy changes, and the society needs ways of transmitting its wishes to the leaders it has accepted.   In the United States, the price-and-market system plays a major role in this regard.   With a relatively free market system, people are able to demonstrate their desires by the things they purchase.   Because prices are free to fluctuate, they can also demonstrate their feelings about the relative values of different goods and services by the prices they are willing to pay for them.   Market prices thus serve as a signaling device for production policy, indicating both the desired goals of production and the relative importance of the different goals.   This process serves reasonably well in the case of wood, meat, Christmas trees and similar forest products.   But it can only function with things which are exchanged in a reasonably free market.   It does not work very well with such forest benefits as water and recreation and is practically inoperable with flood control and the forest amenities.   The market system has other weaknesses for policy formation.   Its signals are biased by the distribution of income and wealth, since the people with more money to spend obviously carry more weight in determining the kinds of goods purchased and the prices paid for them.   There is also a time bias because future consumers who are not yet born have no direct influence in the present market.

The price mechanism not only provides a way of determining goals and making choices but also serves as a means of achieving the goals.    In the United States, private productive activity is largely guided by the profit motive.    The price mechanism directs productive activity into those areas where the prices of the products and of the factors needed to produce them are such that attractive profits are possible.    In the case of forest re-sources, this function of the price mechanism tends to direct entrepreneurs and resources toward those products (such as lumber or beef) which are exchanged in the market and for which market prices are established.    Other forest benefits (such as environmental amenity) are ignored because there is no market through which the entrepreneur can receive a return for producing them.    Of course, price mechanisms are not limited to using prices which have resulted from a free exchange between consumers and producers in a market.    Prices may be set through some other process, such as bargaining, and the market then allowed to react to these prices. Although it plays a very important role in forest-policy formation, the price mechanism needs to be, and is, supplemented by other policy-formation processes.

Another important way in which society controls the actions of its lead-ers and informs them of the feelings of the group is through the democratic political processes.    Public policies are usually formulated by the legisla-tures, but administrative officials play an active role by submitting pro-posals, testifying before committees, and providing information.    Both legislators and elected officials are influenced by the attitudes of their constituents and by the fact that eventually they must stand for reelection. There thus exists a mechanism through which individual citizens can be-come involved in policy formation.

This may be the best process we have for developing policies about rec-reation, aesthetic amenities, and other forest benefits that are not ex-changed in the market.    The values placed by a society on these forest uses may be interpreted from the pressures brought on the legislatures and elected officials to do something about them.    In extreme cases, an election may hinge on the attitudes expressed by the candidates about forest policy.    Though forest policy is ordinarily outweighed by other issues, politicians have made capital of it in some states where the forests are an important economic resource.

The democratic political process has rather obvious weaknesses for pol-icy formation.    It seldom is feasible to vote for or against a candidate solely on the basis of his attitude toward some forest policy issue.    Usu-ally, it is only one—and often a relatively minor one—of the many issues with which the successful candidate will have to deal.    Once in office, he also is not likely to lose reelection solely on the ground of what he has done about some forest policy.    In some voting districts this is not true because of the local importance of the forests, and there the politicians lend a keen ear to forest-policy opinions.    But in the country as a whole, no for-est policy is likely to become a major political issue.    Incumbent politi-cians are influenced by what they hear from their constituents, however, and the process may work more effectively in this way than it does at the election booth.

In order to make the democratic political process function, it has been necessary to develop a machinery of political parties and nominating procedures which in effect prevent every citizen from having an equal say in who is elected to office.    No one individual can affect the outcome by his vote, and many people tend to be apathetic on this account.    However, if a number of people get together and act as a group, their effect is much more significant.    Such groups are common in our political system, and they play an important role in the formation of forest policy through the political process.    If a group becomes large and powerful enough, it may assume a dominant position in policy formation.

A third way in which the actions of leaders are influenced is through bargaining.    This obviously applies to situations in which there are differences of opinion about objectives or about means of achieving them. When leaders representing opposing viewpoints are able to muster approximately equal strength through their authority or interpersonal influence, a stalemate may develop in policy formation.    Or an opposing leader may be able to build up sufficient backing to enable him to challenge and prevent policy actions by a previously dominant leader.    In such cases, the leaders are forced to bargain with each other and to arrive at some kind of mutually acceptable compromise.

In forest policy, bargaining situations are most likely to develop between groups with divergent interests or between a government bureau or other agency and some opposing group.    The actual bargaining may take place between a few leaders, but each will usually be acting mostly as the representative of his group.    Such bargaining also takes place between different bureaus or departments in state and federal governments and in the large private corporations.    It is a rather significant process in the development of forest policy.

## A MORE DETAILED LOOK AT FOREST-POLICY FORMATION

We have now seen in brief and general terms how forest policy is formed in the United States.    However, some important issues have been brushed over very lightly and need further consideration.

In a number of places, we have discovered difficulties in the determination or measurement of what forest policy is concerned with.    We saw this in the discussion of policy objectives and of the conflicts which exist among them.    The problems of measurement were seen to loom large in any attempts at planning.    And the question of values appeared as a major uncertainty for leaders and for those who try to guide or control them.    The common problem in all of these cases is that of a satisfactory criterion or criteria to use in judging policies and in making choices and decisions among policy alternatives.    Because this is such a critical problem in both policy formation and the assessment of policy effects, we will devote the next chapter to it.    Eventually, we will return for a closer look at policy formation in Chapter 12, which deals with the politics of forest-resource use.

# Criteria for Forest Policy

# 4.o

Running through all of our discussion about forest policies, their objectives, and the processes through which they are formed has been a nagging question:  What should these things be?  What objectives should we seek in the use of our forests?  What policies should we follow in order to achieve those objectives?

These are normative questions.  In effect, when we ask what objective we should seek or what policy we should follow, we are looking for some principle of right action that we can use as a guide in making the choice or decision.  For example, if a particular society has decided it is important to strive constantly to improve the public health by every possible means, then that society's objective should be to use its forests to provide salubrious forms of recreation, produce pure water, and promote the public health in any other feasible way.  In this case no forest policy should be followed which might in any way damage the health of the public.

But this example deals with an unusually simple and clearcut situation. What would we mean by "right" action in a more general sense?  By definition, it is action that is in accordance with what is just, good, or proper, but these are difficult adjectives to pin down.  Although there often is substantial agreement about them among the members of a particular group at a particular time, they do not seem to have any universal meanings which can be applied under all conditions.  As a consequence, the concept of what is just, good, or proper varies from one social group to another and also changes with the passage of time.

In spite of this, policies do become established in every society, and behavior conforms to them.   The difficulty is that even though they have become firmly established, such policies are not always necessarily "good." For example, in many parts of the world, some form of shifting agriculture is the customary practice.   An area of forest is cut and burned, the soil is cultivated for several years until the fertility is depleted, the area is then abandoned, and the cycle is repeated on a new part of the forest.   In regions of heavy rainfall, the resulting erosion may be so severe that after an area has been cultivated several times, the soil is virtually destroyed. The long-run effect of such behavior might be the destruction of the resource base and starvation or forced emigration of the population.   It would appear reasonable, therefore, that forest policy should not include such practices.   The proper policy would seem to be to protect the forest from use by such shifting cultivators.

However, this would bring us up against two kinds of problems.   Suppose the local conditions are such that the only way these people can maintain themselves is by practicing this destructive type of agriculture? Suppose the resources of all kinds at their disposal are so limited that any other form of agriculture could not produce enough food, and their only real choice is between continuing to practice shifting cultivation or facing the starvation of a large part of the people?   Under these conditions, it is hard to call the existing practice "bad," even though it may eventually lead to disaster.   It would seem that any reasonable forest policy would have to allow the shifting cultivation to continue.   Any different policy for this area would somehow have to provide for transferring the people to some other area, supplying them with the means to practice some other form of subsistence agriculture, supporting them with imported foodstuffs, or using some combination of these measures.

What this example seems to indicate is that any policy or practice which has developed during the history of a society is likely to have sound factual reasons for existing.   It cannot be judged to be bad unless some superior alternatives actually exist and are feasible of attainment.   However, we must not fall into the trap of assuming that an existing policy is always the best possible one and that future forest policy should, therefore, always continue it.   Change is an essential characteristic of forest-policy formation.

This brings us to a second problem, which is perhaps even more difficult.   If the existing policy or practice is not good and it would be physically possible to change it, how do we decide what changes should be made?   In fact, on what basis do we decide that the existing practice is not good?   Since these are actions which the people apparently have considered to be just, good, or proper in the past, how do we decide that they are now wrong?   If we cannot use the existing policies as guides, what are we to use?   At the same time, if we should always do that which conforms to the existing policy, how can policies ever change or be changed?

Unfortunately, there are no definitive answers to these questions.   They are among the causes of the controversies over forest-resource use.   Such controversies cannot be completely eliminated.   But a clearer understanding of some approaches that are used or might be used in dealing with normative questions may help in resolving them.

## CRITERIA

Many choices and decisions must be made in connection with forest policy. These call for the exercise of judgment on the part of the people involved. Unless these judgments are to be purely haphazard or random, the people making them must have some means of determining what they should be. They need a criterion—or standard—on which to base their judgment or decision. This criterion may be anything that can be used as a test of quality. It does not necessarily have to be formulated as a rule or principle.

Criteria are needed for three fairly distinct purposes in connection with forest policy: for choosing between objectives, for choosing between courses of action, and for evaluating the effectiveness of the courses actually followed.

We can illustrate this with a much oversimplified example. Suppose a paper-manufacturing corporation owns a large forest property. What should be its objective in using this forest? A valid criterion for this choice would appear to be the maximum contribution to the company's profits. Upon analysis, the goal which satisfies this criterion turns out to be that of producing annually the amount of pulpwood needed to supply the company's mill. With this objective in mind, what policy should the company follow in managing its forest? An appropriate criterion for this decision seems to be minimum-average-cost for the wood produced. So a management plan is devised which will grow wood at a cost that satisfies this criterion. After the woodlands department has had time to put this policy into effect, the company officers will wish to evaluate its effectiveness. Satisfactory criteria for this evaluation would be twofold: production of the amount of wood required annually and minimum cost per unit. In order to be judged successful, the woodland-management program must meet both of these criteria.

The criteria used in this simple example were of an economic nature. Since the benefits produced by the forest resource consist in large part of material goods and services and since their production involves the use of scarce resources, economic criteria will usually be relevant to forest-policy considerations. However, in situations of any real significance, economic criteria are not as easy to apply as this simple example might indicate. We will consider this matter in more detail shortly.

Before doing that, it will be well to get some idea of the other kinds of criteria which might be useful in forest policy considerations. Edward P. Cliff, as Chief of the United States Forest Service, listed the principal factors or criteria considered by the Service when making judgments and choices as:

1. Compliance with applicable laws and regulations
2. National programs and goals
3. Compatibility of various resource and use developments to each other and to broad objectives for the area
4. Suitability of the land for a particular use or combination of uses
5. Maintenance of land productivity
6. Intangible as well as tangible values; social as well as economic factors
7. Future and current public needs or desires for particular resources or areas
8. Feasible opportunities to integrate orderly development of several resources and to place emphasis in accordance with specific objectives
9. Professional knowledge, research findings, and experience, as they relate to particular resources
10. Public attitudes, local economy, legislative climate
11. Programs and activities of other agencies [1]

This is quite a heterogeneous list. Some of the items appear to be more nearly limitations than criteria. But this kind of limitation criterion may be very important. Would the proposed policy comply with the applicable laws? If not, it is not an acceptable policy. Is the land in question suitable for the particular use proposed? If not, this objective is not feasible. Does the proposed policy make adequate allowance for maintaining the land's productivity? If not, are there other benefits which offset this eventual destruction of productivity? These may be useful and simple criteria to apply.

Some of these items relate a particular policy to the broader situation within which it will have to operate. Would this policy contribute to national programs and goals? Is it compatible with other programs and objectives, including those of different agencies? Other items relate more to feasibility. Is the necessary knowledge and experience available to implement such a policy? What would the public's attitude be toward it? Could it command support in the existing legislative climate? As Cliff pointed out, only a few of these criteria will be pertinent in any particular situation. But it is important that the pertinent ones be recognized and used in making the decision in each case.

It is significant that the Forest Service's list of criteria does not include such items as well-being, satisfaction, happiness, physical and mental health, or security. These are the kinds of things we are really concerned with, to be sure, but the problem is that we do not know how to relate them to the outcomes of different courses of action. "In practical problem solving . . . we have to look at some 'proximate' criterion which serves, we hope, to reflect what is happening to satisfaction, profits, or well-being. Actual criteria are the practicable substitutes for the maximization of whatever we would ultimately like to maximize." [2] The use of

---

[1] Edward P. Cliff, "Multiple-Use Planning in National Forest Management," in Harold L. Amoss and Roma K. McNickle (eds.), *Land and Water: Planning for Economic Growth*, University of Colorado Press, Boulder, 1962, p. 72.
[2] Roland N. McKean, *Efficiency in Government through Systems Analysis*, John Wiley & Sons, Inc., New York, 1958, p. 29.

"proximate" criteria is unavoidable in forest-policy choices, but we must recognize that it includes a danger of using erroneous criteria.  Maximum cash revenue is not always likely to be a good proximate criterion if our real criterion is maximum human welfare.

The most common failing of proximate criteria probably is a disregard for things outside of their immediate focus of interest.  Foresters have been accused of following a criterion of what is good for the forest rather than for people.  A criterion of maximum wood production ignores the costs of withdrawing the necessary capital and labor from other productive activities.  A criterion of preserving extensive forest areas perpetually in an undisturbed natural state does not consider their value and perhaps eventual urgent need for recreation or timber production.  Such criteria tend to be those of special interest groups.  They need to be combined, somehow in the process of policy formation, into more complete and useful criteria for broad policy decisions.

## ECONOMIC CRITERIA

Decisions about the use of forest resources are basically economic in nature.  Economics deals with man's attempt to obtain the material means of satisfying his desires.  The goods and services yielded by forests are among such means.  Men want water, wildlife, wood, and recreation sites to satisfy rather obvious desires.  But others, such as shelter from the elements, privacy, and even beautiful surroundings, can also be achieved with forests.

Obtaining the material means poses problems because the resources which can be used to produce them or which can serve as means themselves are not available in unlimited quantities.  Economic resources have utility to man but are scarce in relation to the many uses that he would like to make of them.  There are very few useful resources in the United States today which do not have this characteristic of scarcity.  Even pure air and water have become scarce items, as pollution of both has increased.

The basic problem with economic resources is this lack of adequacy to completely satisfy all the desires of all the people for all the various things that might be produced with them.  Because of this, we have to choose among the uses which might possibly be made of the resources that are available.  Since there cannot be enough of everything to go around, we must economize on the use of the resources we have.

The primary economic problem for forest policy is how to allocate the existing forest resources among their different possible uses and consequently to the satisfaction of the various possible wants.  However, forests cannot be used without also using other economic resources such as labor and capital; so the allocation decision must take into account all of the resources involved.

This is still not the total picture, because the forest goods and services not only have to be produced but also distributed among their possible consumers. This is not distribution in the sense of transportation and delivery but rather in the sense of dividing up the loot. The situation is not usually the simple one of rationing a short supply of one product among a number of consumers. Instead, some consumers may want water, others recreation sites, others lumber, and so on. If only some of these products can be produced at one time, some consumers will receive none of what they want. Which ones should be favored and which deprived? The allocation of scarce resources to production must consider not only what to produce but also for whom.

The economic problem of forest resource use is much easier to state than it is to solve. The fact of the matter is that economists have not yet been able to come up with a perfect solution to the problem of allocation and distribution in general. However, they have developed approaches which show clearly just what is involved in allocation and distribution decisions and which may provide us with some useable proximate criteria. It is important to understand the limitations of these approaches as well as their potentialities. The next few sections will consider some of them briefly.

## BENEFIT-COST ANALYSIS

Any productive economic activity produces benefits in the form of goods and services and involves costs in the form of materials consumed and the time of productive factors diverted from other useful employment. A comparison of these benefits and costs gives useful information for policy decisions.

A consideration of benefits and costs leads to a rather obvious basic economic criterion: An activity should not be undertaken unless its total benefits will exceed its total costs. For example, a policy of pruning every tree in forest plantations is not justified if the total cost of doing this pruning will be greater than the additional value which the timber will have at harvest time as a result of it.

This is a useful criterion for minor decisions, particularly those dealing with production. It is most helpful in marginal decisions; that is, in deciding whether to increase or extend an already existing activity. Suppose a state forest-fire control organization is now holding the area burned over annually by wildfires to 0.5 percent of the forest land. The state forester knows that with additional personnel and equipment, he could reduce this annual burn to 0.25 percent. Should the legislature increase the forestry department's appropriation enough so it can obtain the additional personnel and equipment? Not unless the average amount of damage that will be prevented by keeping fires off another 0.25 percent of the forest land will be greater than the additional appropriation required to do it.

There are problems in applying even this apparently straightforward criterion to any but very simple decisions. These center mainly around two points: all of the benefits and all of the costs must be included, and these benefits and costs must be measured in some units or terms that are comparable.

The first problem is a serious one in many forest-policy situations.  Suppose that in the forest-fire example just given, the only benefits recognized are the values from a wood-product viewpoint of the trees that would be destroyed or damaged if the fires are not controlled.  These fires may also destroy aesthetic values, do damage to the resident wildlife, and affect the quantity and quality of streamflow from the area.  Unless these are included among the potential benefits, the comparison will not be complete.  Take as another example a proposal to spray an extensive forest area with DDT in order to control an outbreak of a destructive insect pest.  The damage to the timber which will be prevented by the spraying may be much larger than the direct costs of the chemicals, airplanes, men and equipment required to do the work.  The project appears to be justified.  But now suppose that the chemical residues which find their way into the streams in the area will cause a high mortality among certain commercial fish species that use these streams.  Unless the resulting losses to the fishing industry are included among the costs of this project, the benefit-cost comparison will not be valid.

Economists have long recognized what they call *external economies* and *external diseconomies*.  These are benefits or costs which affect people other than those who are immediately involved in the activity.  The effect on the fishermen of the pesticide spraying described above is an example.  Many external effects are less obvious or more subtle than this, however.  The reforestation for purely wood-production purposes of some of the cut-over lands in the South has increased their scenic attractiveness to the benefit of both local residents and tourists.  The overgrazing of western rangelands has raised the cost of irrigation agriculture downstream by gradually increasing the silt load of the streams.  Because these external effects often involve large numbers of other people, they are frequently referred to as *social benefits* and *social costs*.[3]  In some cases they may be very large and of critical importance in comparing benefits and costs.

Sometime a complete benefit-cost comparison may require the inclusion of *secondary benefits.*  These are additional values added by an activity over and above those of the products or services produced directly by it.  Suppose, for example that a recreational complex is being considered for a fairly remote forested area.  The direct benefits to the potential users of this complex are estimated.  In addition, however, it is known that local residents will independently provide certain services to the recreationists, such as guides, bait, locally grown foodstuffs, and perhaps lodging.  The income which they will receive for these services is a secondary benefit from the project.  Such secondary benefits are commonly recognized in analyses of water-resource developments.

Care must be exercised with these secondary benefits, however.  They "are not attributable to the project from a national public viewpoint unless

[3] See Albert C. Worrell, *Economics of American Forestry*, John Wiley & Sons, Inc., New York, 1959, pp. 343–353.

it can be shown that there is an increase in net incomes in such activities as a result of the project as compared with conditions to be expected in the absence of the project." [4]   That is, in our recreation development example, the local people must actually have a larger income after the project is operating than they had before.   If they just shift from subsistence farming to selling bait and guiding fishermen at the same income level, there is no secondary benefit from the recreational development.   In general, secondary benefits only arise when there are unemployed or underemployed resources which are put to use as a result of the project.   If the local farmers have been shipping their vegetables to a market in town and now sell them directly to the tourists, no secondary benefit has been produced.   But if these farmers had spare time on their hands before and now use it to grow vegetables which they had not been growing, the payment they receive from the recreationists is a real secondary benefit and should be credited to the recreation development.

The other problem in benefit-cost analysis—that of measuring everything in some units or terms that are comparable—is perhaps even more serious in forest-policy situations.   Our ordinary way of handling such comparisons is to convert all benefits and costs into their equivalent value in terms of money.   This works quite well for many minor decisions.   I own a pine plantation which is ready for thinning.   A local man agrees to cut the trees that should come out and to stack the wood at the roadside for $10 per cord.   A local pulpwood buyer offers to pay me $12 per cord at the road-side for all the wood I will sell him.   Clearly the $12 benefit per unit from this thinning exceeds its $10 cost, and the undertaking is economically justified.

But even this case becomes rather fuzzy if we change a few of the assumptions.   Suppose that I cannot hire anyone to cut these trees, but I do have the necessary equipment and could do the thinning myself.   I work five days a week on my regular job and could spend the weekend in the plantation.   However, I like to spend my weekends skiing.   How much will it cost me to give up the skiing and produce pulpwood instead?   Will the $12 benefit from a cord exceed its actual cost to me?   The answer will depend to some extent on whether I am a $50,000-per-year surgeon or a $5,000-per-year millhand.

Now let us return to the original conditions of our example, but assume that the plantation is part of a state forest which borders on a recreational lake.   Should the state proceed with the thinning because the $12-per-cord benefit is greater than the $10 cost?   Here we have to consider the pos-sible detrimental effects on the pleasure of the recreationists.   How much, if any, will the sights and sounds of chain saws and logging equipment reduce this pleasure?   Will the changed appearance of the thinned planta-tion reduce its aesthetic value for these visitors?   What cost should be added to the $10 per cord to account for this cost to the recreationists?

[4] Subcommittee on Evaluation Standards, *Proposed Practices for Economic Analysis of River Basin Projects*, Inter-Agency Committee on Water Resources, Washington, 1958, p. 9.

For that matter, how does one measure the total value that these people are getting out of the time they spend on the lake?

In major policy decisions, the problem of measurability looms very large. An extreme case is the current emphasis on beauty and open space.   While there is widespread agreement that their value is high, no one really knows how to measure it in economic terms.   How much can communities justify paying for land to be reserved for greenbelts, parks, public golf courses, and other open-space uses?   The alternative value of such land for residential or commercial development is very high in the urbanized sections of the country.   Is the benefit a suburban community may anticipate getting from the future use of 100 acres of undeveloped second-growth woodland greater than the $150,000 the owner is asking for it?   The magnitude of these costs emphasizes the problem, but the benefits are no easier to measure in more remote regions where alternative costs are smaller.

Recreation and water are also difficult to value.   This is complicated by the fact that traditionally they have been considered as free benefits from forest lands.   Clawson has estimated that if the federal government followed a policy of administering the public lands to obtain a maximum revenue, it might receive between 125 and 375 million dollars per year for the water from these lands for which no charge is made at present.[5] Some charges are now levied for use of the national parks, and these will be increased in the future.   But Clawson also estimated that the annual income from these parks might be from 150 to 300 million dollars instead of less than 10 million.   The values of water and recreation as forest benefits can be determined to a much greater extent than they now are by use of the market, but there continues to be considerable resistance to any charge for such benefits from public lands.

Despite the difficulties that arise in making a quantitative analysis, the comparison of benefits and costs provides a helpful criterion for policy formation.   Even if all benefits and costs cannot be measured in the same units and totaled for comparison, merely arraying them with the benefits on one side and the costs on the other in whatever units are feasible will help in deciding whether the total benefits of a proposed policy are likely to exceed its costs.

Benefit-cost analysis can be used not only to decide whether a policy is economically justified, as in the cases above, but also in choosing between alternative policies.   Ordinarily, some constraint will exist as to the benefits it is desired to achieve or the costs that can be expended.   In simple terms, the problem is usually either to achieve some objective at a minimum cost or to obtain maximum benefits from the use of limited resources.   (It is never possible to minimize costs and maximize benefits in the same operation.)   A criterion that is applicable in all cases is to achieve a maximum net benefit; that is the greatest possible difference between total benefits and total costs.   "The most effective use of economic resources

[5] Marion Clawson, "How Much Should Users of Public Lands Pay?", *American Forests*, April, 1965, p. 39.

required for a project is made if they are utilized in such a way that the amount by which benefits exceed costs is at a maximum rather than in such a way as to produce a maximum benefit-cost ratio or on some other basis." [6]

There is a great temptation to use a maximum ratio of benefits to costs as a criterion because it appears to be a measure of efficiency.   The difficulty is that the efficiency it indicates may not be related to the real policy problem.   For example, in growing sawtimber a maximum benefit-cost ratio could be achieved by a policy of using only Site I (the most productive) land.   But since the area of Site I land is limited, this policy would not produce a very large volume of sawlogs.   A small amount of timber would be grown very efficiently while millions of acres of lower site quality land lay idle and millions of potential consumers made do without lumber. Obviously a policy of producing a maximum net benefit would bring more of the land into use and satisfy the demand of a larger proportion of the potential consumers.

## WELFARE ECONOMICS

In the previous section, we saw that benefit-cost analysis can be used to decide that a policy or project is not economically desirable when the costs will exceed the possible benefits.   But does the opposite situation where the benefits will exceed the costs always mean that the policy in question should be put into effect?   Clearly not, because we saw that benefit-cost analysis can also be used to choose between two or more alternatives, all of which will produce benefits greater than their costs.   But does the fact that one policy will produce a greater difference between total benefits and total costs than any of the alternatives with which it is being compared always mean that this policy should be put into effect?   The answer is still "not always" and we need to consider why.

Suppose that a state forestry department is developing a management policy for the public forest lands.   Three silvicultural practices appear to be desirable: reforesting open areas, releasing young reproduction from competing vegetation, and pruning young pole stands.   An economic analysis shows that the resulting increase in timber value would be greater than the cost of the cultural operation in all three cases.   But releasing the young reproduction would show the greatest total net benefit for the anticipated expenditure.   If the legislature has appropriated funds for cultural operations on state forests, the forestry department would do best to use these for releasing reproduction.   But should the legislature appropriate funds for any kind of cultural operation?   The alternatives available to the legislature are much more numerous.   Since the state's income is always limited, spending part of it on the state forests will mean less to spend for other purposes.   The benefits to the people of the state might

---

[6] Subcommittee on Evaluation Standards, *op. cit.*, p. 5.

be greater if these funds were spent on highways, education, or any number of other things rather than on the state forests.

This kind of problem is the subject matter of welfare economics.  Its objective is to find that arrangement of the economic universe that is best in terms of the welfare of the members of society.  Now welfare is a difficult thing to define, but we feel it is real and that we can recognize changes in welfare, at least in cases where the changes are fairly large.  Can this serve as a criterion for policy decisions?

The concept of optimum welfare is a difficult one, and the literature on the subject is voluminous, highly technical, and frustrating to peruse.  The description given here will have to be simplified but will suffice for our purpose.  The aspect of welfare economics which appears relevant for forest economics is that which deals with efficiency of production.  In order to be efficient, production must meet two standards: (a) achievement of the greatest possible output with given means or achievement of a given output with the smallest means and (b) conformity to the community's wishes.[7]  An increase in the efficiency of production will also increase the economic welfare of a society because (a) a greater amount of goods or services will be produced with the same means, (b) the same amount of goods or services will be produced but with less means so that the rest can be diverted into producing other things, or (c) the kinds of goods and services being produced will be more exactly what the community wants.

If all production were perfectly efficient, the economy would be in an optimum state, and it would not be possible to increase the total welfare by making any changes whatever in the way production is carried on.  That is, if an acre of land were shifted from watershed protection to timber production, or a workman were shifted from cutting pulpwood to maintaining picnic grounds, the total welfare would be reduced.  Clearly, we are not likely to ever be in this optimum state, and the relevant questions are: would shifting the acre from watershed protection to timber or the man from pulpwood to picnic grounds add to the total welfare or not?

We seem to be back to comparing benefits and costs.  But some things have been added.  All possible effects on total welfare are being considered.  Cost has now become the total alternative cost; that is, what must be given up somewhere else in order to carry out the action being considered.  And the comparisons are in terms of welfare rather than money or other physical units.

These pose some serious difficulties for anyone trying to make a watertight analysis; but if they are kept constantly in mind, they may prevent him from making mistaken or erroneous analyses.  It clearly is not possible to foresee every effect of a policy change of any magnitude; but if the attempt is made, it may uncover effects which otherwise would have been overlooked.

Except where the resources to be used are presently unemployed or underemployed, they can be employed only in a new activity by withdrawing them

---

[7] See Tibor Scitovsky, *Welfare and Competition*, Richard D. Irwin, Inc., Chicago, 1951, Chapter VIII.

from some other productive use.    Since practically all productive activity employs a combination of economic resources, some of them will almost certainly have to come from other uses.    For example, it may be proposed to reforest land which is now lying idle and unproductive.    Using the land will not stop the production of something else, but the labor and capital equipment required for the planting must be taken away from whatever they are now doing.    The real cost of reforesting the land is the value of the benefits which the labor and capital might otherwise have produced in their present employment.

Most policy changes of any significance will probably also bring about some change in the distribution of wealth or income.    Suppose it is decided to develop the recreational potential of a rather remote mountainous area.    The funds necessary for the development work will come from taxes which will be paid at least in part by people who never will use these recreation facilities.    Construction and operation of the facilities will provide jobs or other sources of income for local residents.    The result will be higher incomes for some local people and lower disposable incomes for the taxpayers.    This redistribution of income may have an effect on welfare, which is separate from the net benefits of the recreation services.    If, for example, the average increase in taxes is less than one dollar per taxpayer but a number of men who previously have been unemployed and living in abject poverty are now able to earn enough to support their families adequately, we would probably agree that total welfare has been increased by the redistribution effect of the recreational development.

This brings us to the question of how to measure welfare.    If, in the above example, one thousand dollars is transferred from the incomes of various taxpayers to that of an impoverished local resident, will the welfare of this individual increase more than the welfares of the affected taxpayers decrease because of their loss?    Welfare economists decided long ago that such interpersonal comparisons cannot be made in any exact manner.    The only case in which they feel a positive statement can be made is when a proposed change will make at least one person better off but will not make anyone worse off.    This change would increase total welfare.    However, there are not likely to be many forest-policy situations in which the comparison would be so simple and clearcut.    We are forced to conclude that welfare cannot be measured accurately enough to serve as an absolute standard of comparison between alternative policies.    Fortunately, the magnitudes of the welfare effects are often so large that there is really no question as to whether the change will increase welfare or not, even though it cannot be proven quantitatively.

In order not to leave the impression that benefit-cost analysis and welfare economics cannot contribute anything in the way of criteria for forest-policy decisions, it may help to look at several suggestions which have been offered in resource-policy situations.    In an attempt to develop criteria for judging pest-control policies and programs, it was proposed that if the benefits and costs used in testing the action were measured in terms of the relevant basic human goals, an action could be judged to be desirable if it met all of the following tests:

1. The total benefit that would result from this action must be at least as great as the benefit that could be produced in any possible alternative action by an expenditure of a sum of money equivalent to the value of those costs of the proposed action, which actually can be exchanged for money.
2. The total benefits that would result from this action must be greater than the total costs that the action would involve.
3. The total costs involved in this action must be less than the total costs of any possible alternative action which would accomplish the same objective or produce the same benefit.[8]

In discussing adequate criteria for water-resource projects, Garnsey has proposed that the decision makers be presented with four kinds of information about which he feels economists are now capable of giving fairly complete quantitative estimates.    These are:

1. The economic justification of the project in terms of output and input
2. The effects of the project on employment
3. Its effect on growth over time
4. The repercussions of the project on the distribution or redistribution of income [9]

The conclusion from the above discussion is that while economic criteria cannot provide a perfect measuring stick which can always be used to determine accurately, and almost mechanically, whether a particular policy is desirable or not, they can provide relevant information in the clear and complete form, which will be most useful in the process of forming policies.

## OTHER SOCIAL CRITERIA

The economic criteria basically assume that it is better to have more rather than less material goods and services.    In a world with scarce productive resources, a useful criterion is therefore one which measures the efficiency with which these resources are used in producing goods and services. Since the diverse forest products—such as water, wood, and recreational opportunities—cannot be added up in physical units, it is necessary to determine comparative values for them and to sum the values of all the products.    This does not change the basic assumption stated in the first sentence of this paragraph, however.    It merely says it is better to produce a greater total value of products than some lesser total value.
    Now the question may legitimately be raised of whether the policy that

[8] Albert C. Worrell, "Pests, Pesticides, and People," *American Forests*, July, 1960, p. 51.
[9] Morris E. Garnsey, "Welfare Economics and Resource Development," in Amos and McNickle, *op. cit.*, p. 200.

will lead to the production of the greatest value of forest products is always the most desirable one.   As an extreme example, it might be most efficient economically to produce with slave labor.   Or if we do not wish to go to that extreme, it might still be most efficient to have production decisions made by some kind of dictator.   It appears that some other criteria may be needed to supplement or modify the criterion of economic efficiency.

Dahl and Lindblom suggest four other criteria, and these might have relevance for forest-policy decisions.   They call them: freedom, democracy, subjective equality, and appropriate inclusion.[10]   As a starting point, they use Bertrand Russell's definition of freedom as "the absence of obstacles to the realisation of desires."   Under this definition, it is clear that complete freedom is unattainable, even for an isolated individual, because he has many desires, and some of them are bound to conflict with others.   In addition, individuals will run into conflicts with other individuals when each tries to realize his own special desires.   As a criterion then, freedom would have to be recognized as a relative thing with the test based on the idea that more freedom is to be preferred to less.

Lloyd recognizes what he calls "negative freedom," which is "concerned with so organizing the pattern of society, that despite all the restraints and limitations that are placed upon individual action for the benefit of society as a whole, there nevertheless remains as large a sphere for individual choice and initiative as is compatible with the public welfare."[11]   In this sense, freedom appears to be useful as a criterion.   But there remain some problems regarding how the individual is to express his choice and how to make sure the sphere is as large as possible.

In a theoretical, perfectly competitive market, the prices which developed as a result of the demand and supply actions of the large number of small, but perfectly informed and mobile, buyers and sellers would reflect accurately the relative values which the people in the economy placed on various goods and services.   In the real world, however, buyers or sellers or both may be few in numbers, poorly informed about the market, relatively immobile, and in some cases sufficiently large and powerful to dominate the market transactions.   Actual market prices may therefore be an unreliable indicator of how the people as a whole feel about the various goods and services.   When we add to this the fact that many important forest products such as wildlife, scenic beauty, and flood protection do not ordinarily pass through any markets and therefore do not have even unreliable prices developed for them, we see that it is difficult for individuals to express their choices perfectly through the economic criteria.   In fact, an economic criterion such as the benefit-cost ratio could lead to unwise decisions if, for example, the benefits were valued at monopoly prices, or the costs did not include external diseconomies such as stream pollution or the creation of unemployment.

Since we cannot depend on market prices as a universal and reliable in-

[10] Robert A. Dahl and Charles E. Lindblom, *Politics, Economics, and Welfare,* Harper & Brothers, New York, 1953, pp. 28–38; 41–49; 51–54.
[11] Dennis Lloyd, *The Idea of Law,* Penguin Books, Inc., Baltimore, 1964, p. 140.

dicator of individual choices, we commonly resort to the political process as a means of expressing these choices. The federal, state, and local governments take actions aimed at removing obstacles to the realization of the desires of their citizens. The basic criterion that we use in judging these government actions is that of democracy, which requires that control of governmental decisions be shared so that no one citizen's preferences carry more weight than those of any other. This is a criterion of political equality, and its realization involves majority rule in deciding on government actions. It seems obvious that in a country as large and complex as the United States, a perfect attainment of democracy is impossible. This criterion therefore also comes down to one which says that greater political equality is preferable to less.

Democracy or political equality is a useful criterion for judging decision-making situations or the process of policy formation, but it is hardly useful in judging a particular policy or in evaluating its effects. Here, a broader concept of equality may serve better. This cannot take the form of saying that things should be distributed equally among all of the people, because we know that people do not have the same preferences and do not place the same personal valuations on all goods and services. Dahl and Lindblom get around this by proposing a criterion of "subjective equality" which they say "exists wherever, in any specific situation in which more people rather than less can have the opportunity to achieve their goals, the decision is for the greater number rather than for any leser number." [12]  An example would be a case in which two policies are being considered for the management of public forest lands for recreation. One policy would reserve these forests in wilderness condition; the other would develop them for more intensive forms of use such as picnicking, camping, and skiing. Under the first policy, the forests would be used only by a limited number of wilderness enthusiasts; under the second they would be used by a large number of people who prefer less-primitive forms of recreation. The criterion of subjective equality would lead to the choice of the second policy.

But we now seem to have worked ourselves into a serious corner. In proposing equality as a policy criterion which would prevent the monopolization of the benefits from the forest resources by a few wealthy or powerful people, we have arrived at a policy of favoring the majority over any minority or minorities. We can visualize a situation in which this criterion would lead to a policy of developing an area for picnicking or camping by people who have only a mild and casual interest in such forms of recreation but who nevertheless outnumber two to one the enthusiastic and devoted wilderness explorers who prefer this to any other form of recreation. This is the reef of interpersonal comparisons on which welfare economics has foundered. A head count is not sufficient when people differ strongly in their appraisals of the values involved. We have in almost all other spheres of national interest a general policy of protecting minorities and minority

---

[12] Dahl and Lindblom, op. cit., p. 46.

interests.   Somehow, the minorities must also be recognized in forest policies.

Dahl and Lindblom present a further criterion which they call *appropriate inclusion* but do not define very clearly in their book.   This may, however, provide a clue in our present difficulty.   Part of the problem is to include the appropriate people in the process of policy formation or in the consideration of specific policies.   This is certainly more easily said than done.   But perhaps it can be dealt with if approached from the view of making sure that everyone is included who should be, rather than from the viewpoint of deciding who should not be included.

Appropriate inclusion may therefore serve as a criterion in judging policies or policy proposals by asking: has everyone who will be affected by this policy been considered, regardless of his wealth, power, or the degree to which he will be affected?   In judging a policy-making process, this criterion may ask: has everyone who will be affected by this policy been given an equal chance to take part in the making of the policy and an equal vote in finally deciding what the policy is to be?   If the answers to these questions should turn out to be no, it would not necessarily mean that the policy in question is wrong or undesirable.   But it would cast a cloud of uncertainty on it because we would not know what the outcome would have been if all of the appropriate people had been properly included.

Despite the conclusion by welfare economists that it is impossible to make valid comparisons between the welfare of different individuals, it is hard to see how democracy and subjective equality can be useful criteria for forest-policy situations if they insist that every person involved must have equal weight in the decision.   It would not seem reasonable to say that one individual whose future employment and support for his family depend on how a particular forest area is managed should receive no more consideration in arriving at a management policy for that area than another individual whose only contact with the forest is a casual impression of pleasant scenery when his other affairs cause him to occasionally pass that way.

Appropriate inclusion may be a helpful criterion with this problem also by limiting consideration to those who really are affected by the policy. However, even among those who definitely are affected, there will often be large differences in the extent of their involvement.   This is recognized subjectively in the actual process of policy formation, but unfortunately it seems almost impossible to find a criterion which is not equally subjective in nature.

This leaves us in a rather unsatisfactory state as far as the other social criteria are concerned.   But we do have some clearer ideas of what is involved in judging forest policies.   The criterion of freedom to realize desires serves as a useful limitation on the idea of producing a maximum value of goods and services and at the same time broadens our concept of the relation between forest resources and people.   The criteria of equality tell us that people must not be given different consideration in forest policies because of differences in wealth, power, origin, place of residence, or other factors which have nothing to do with whether they are affected by the policies in question or not.   The criterion of appropriate inclusion serves to include all who are affected by a policy but at the same time limits consideration to those who are affected.

## ENVIRONMENTAL AND ECOLOGICAL CRITERIA

The criteria which we have been discussing so far assume that certain biological and physical relationships are possible.   That is, they assume for example that a certain forest area can be managed for either timber production or recreation and then test the choice between these two uses by a criterion such as the benefit-cost ratio.   The difficulty with this is that it implies that man is able to do anything he might desire with the forest, and his only problem is to apply economic or other social criteria in order to decide what is best.

In actual fact, of course, we are all aware that there are limits on what man can do with the forests, and that his actions are therefore restricted to those which are physically feasible.   We know it is not possible to grow mahogany in Canada nor to produce sawtimber sized trees in one year.   But this is simplifying the problem too much.   Can you do it? is a form of criterion but not one that helps much with the policy questions of: Is it desirable? and Which course is best?

Any forest is a complex ecosystem in which many plants and animals have achieved a certain degree of balance with each other and with their common environment.   With the passage of time, changes take place in this ecosystem, but these are usually in the nature of successional developments or gradual readjustments in the balance rather than drastic changes, unless some outside interference such as a fire, windstorm, or actions by man are involved.   An undisturbed natural ecosystem is therefore likely to be in or approaching a dynamic equilibrium.

Changes can occur in many ecosystems without disturbing seriously the dynamic equilibrium.   Organisms possess to some degree a capacity to regulate their functions and structures in response to environmental changes.   But large or frequent changes due to severe fires or heavy defoliation by insects, for example, may upset the dynamic equilibrium enough to cause large fluctuations in other conditions within the ecosystem.   The system may then become unstable, and it may be difficult to predict what will happen in the future.   From man's viewpoint as a user of the forest ecosystem, a reasonable stability of the environment is very desirable. If conditions fluctuate greatly from year to year with consequent large insect outbreaks; sudden mortality of large numbers of trees; overabundance or virtual disappearance of game birds and animals; the forest is more difficult and expensive to manage and less productive on a sustained basis.

The problem for man is that in using the forest, he becomes a part of the ecosystem himself and is subject to the same restrictions as any other factor in the system.   Any actions he takes—be it cutting trees, killing game, occupying campsites—have some effects on the equilibrium of the system. An effect in one place always leads to a chain of effects and reactions in other places. If man makes large changes, he will very likely upset the dynamic equilibrium, and conditions may then fluctuate greatly before they approach another equilibrium.

Individual forest ecosystems vary a great deal in their susceptibility to and tolerance of disturbance. A cove hardwood forest growing in deep soil, well watered, and containing a mixture of tree species may tolerate very heavy cutting of the large trees with little change in the environmental conditions. By contrast, a high alpine meadow may deteriorate seriously as a result of only occasional disturbance by campers and their pack animals. The comparative fragility of various ecosystems must be recognized in developing policies for their use.

This is further complicated by the fact that some disturbances may result in changes in the ecosystem that are not reversible. When mature timber is harvested or many game animals are taken by hunters, a substantial change may be made in the ecosystem. But if adequate seed sources and breeding stock are maintained in the area and environmental conditions necessary to their development are not destroyed, the forest or animal population will rebuild itself in time. Under different conditions, however, the removal of the vegetative cover on a steep hillside may permit erosion which removes the thin layer of soil, and the reestablishment of the original ecosystem may then become virtually impossible within a time span of human consequence.

Nonreversible changes in the ecosystem may be of three kinds. First is the situation in which it becomes impossible to ever return to the original condition, as exemplified by the case where a plant or animal is destroyed to the extent that it becomes extinct.

In a second situation, it is physically possible to return to the original condition, but the time required to accomplish this is so long that it is of no interest. In an extreme example, the eroded hillside might eventually revert to its original condition if left alone, but the time required for soil formation to take place and for the vegetation to progress through all of the necessary successional stages would run into so many thousands of years that as far as we are concerned today, the loss is irretrievable. The recovery period may not have to be that long for people to consider the effect as irreversible, however. Most virgin or old-growth forests will probably return to their present condition in two or three hundred years if the timber is cut or killed by fire or insects, but the environment is otherwise not disturbed. As far as people living today are concerned, however, the change is not reversible within the time that is relevant for them.

In a third situation, it may be physically or biologically possible to reverse the change and restore the original condition, but the cost may be so great that it is economically impossible. For example, removing the forest cover from a wet area may permit the water table to rise enough that it becomes a permanent swamp, and the original tree species are unable to reestablish themselves even though seed sources exist. It may be physically possible to lower the water table through drainage works and to artificially replant the original kinds of vegetation.    But the cost of doing this may be so great that the value of the reestablished forest would under no circumstances justify it.    This indicates that certain ecosystems may be considered valuable today but not valuable enough to replace if they are in some way destroyed.

Another kind of situation appears to be very important but is only imperfectly understood at present.    It involves effects which may result beyond or outside of the immediate ecosystem in which a disturbance takes place.    The effects of some disturbances appear to resemble a chain reaction.    Some of the chemical pesticides are known to pass along the natural food chain—from earthworm, to robin, to hawk, for example—with the concentration increasing at each successive link in the chain.    The significance of this is clear: we must look beyond the immediate ecosystem which is being used in order to determine the full effects of an action.

In discussing flow resources—which include plants and animals—Ciriacy-Wantrup recognizes a *critical zone* which is "a more or less clearly defined range of rates below which a decrease in flow cannot be reversed *economically* under presently foreseeable conditions.    Frequently, such irreversibility is not only economic but also technological." [13]    He then proposes a "safe minimum standard of conservation" which is achieved by avoiding the critical zone.    This may provide a useful basic ecological criterion for forest policy, difficult though it may be to define this standard specifically and quantitatively.    We might say that for each forest ecosystem that would be affected by a forest policy an attempt should be made to determine the critical zone or amount of disturbance that would touch off changes in the environment which could not later be reversed.    Some forest ecosystems are probably always in this critical zone and consequently cannot tolerate any use by man at all.    The criterion of an acceptable policy might therefore be twofold: it must not disturb any ecosystems which are already in the critical zone, and it must not disturb any other affected ecosystems enough to push them into the critical zone.

This safe minimum standard is only a limiting criterion, however.    It does not help us to choose between two policies which would both be above this minimum.    A useful criterion for this appears to be stability of the environment.    In general, any use of the forest by man is going to involve some disturbance of the existing ecosystem.    Lutz says that "Disturbances of the forest ecosystem that seem to involve the greatest potential danger are those that are extreme and outside the evolutionary experience of the organisms involved." [14]    The criterion of stability would say that we should choose that policy which will disturb the existing balance the least; also, any policy which will require extreme disturbances of the ecosystem is not desirable because it will probably lead to serious instability.

Ecologists appear to be in rather general agreement that complex eco-

[13] S. V. Ciriacy-Wantrup, *Resource Conservation Economics and Policies,* University of California Press, Berkeley, 1963, p. 39.
[14] H. J. Lutz, "Forest Ecosystems: Their Maintenance, Amelioration, and Deterioration," *Journal of Forestry,* August, 1963, p. 567.

systems are likely to be more stable than simple ones. "The intricate checks and balances among the different populations . . . look inefficient and hampering from the point of view of any particular population, but they insure the stability and continuity of the system as a whole and thus, however indirectly, contribute to the survival of particular populations." [15]    The tendency in practically all land management is to simplify the ecosystem by eliminating plants and animals which compete with the desired crop or even to work toward a monoculture type of ecosystem, such as pure plantations of one tree species.    Elton has pointed out that "the balance of relatively simple communities of plants and animals is more easily upset than that of richer ones; that is, more subject to destructive oscillations in populations, especially of animals, and more vulnerable to invasions."    and warned that "there is something very dangerous about handling cultivated land as we handle it now, and even more dangerous if we continue to go farther down the present road of 'simplification for efficiency'." [16]

Goal    This suggests that "diversity" might serve as a proximate criterion for "stability" in judging the effects of a policy.    Bates has put it this way: "Diversity has a positive value in the ecosystem, or in the biosphere.    It is 'good' to have a variety of ecosystems; and it is 'good' to have diversity and complexity within any particular ecosystem.    Diversity tends to promote equilibrium within the system, and thus has utilitarian value.    I think it also has value from the point of view of aesthetics and from that of ethics." [17]    According to this criterion we should choose the policy that will maintain the greatest diversity of conditions in the forest, and avoid policies which require an extreme simplification of the forest ecosystem.

This is not a very satisfactory set of ecological criteria, but it seems to be about as far as we can go now.    It is quite generally recognized today that man is a part of nature and that he cannot make just any changes he pleases in the ecosystem without courting unforeseen disasters.    Still, the tendency is for man to expect too much of his environment; to try to get too much out of it or—in the case of pollutants—to put too much into it.    The criteria of the safe minimum standard of conservation and the maintenance of stability and diversity should serve as guides for living within the limits of the forest ecosystem.

## THE PUBLIC INTEREST AS A CRITERION

Our discussion up to this point has shown that there is no single clear-cut criterion which can be used in developing and judging forest policies.    In fact, we have found a number of criteria that appear to be relevant and useful in forest policy situations.    Is there then nothing we can use as a general, overall guide to forest policy in the United States?

[15] Marston Bates, *The Forest and the Sea*, Random House, Inc., New York, 1960, p. 261.
[16] Charles S. Elton, *The Ecology of Invasions*, John Wiley & Sons, Inc., New York, 1958, p. 145.
[17] Marston Bates, "Man and Nature," in *Proceedings of the Lockwood Conference on the Suburban Forest and Ecology*, Connecticut Agricultural Experiment Station, New Haven, 1962, p. 29.

One thread runs through the history of forest conservation in this country that has had a major influence on the profession of forestry and through it on the development of forest policies.    It is expressed in the letter Secretary of Agriculture Wilson wrote to Gifford Pinchot in 1905, giving instructions for the administration of the newly transferred forest reserves: ". . . all land is to be devoted to its most productive use for the permanent good of the whole people, and not for the temporary benefit of individuals or companies . . . . where conflicting interests must be reconciled the question will always be decided from the standpoint of the greatest good of the greatest number in the long run." This idea that the forest resources should serve all the people or the nation as a whole has not been restricted to the national forests alone.    Does it perhaps provide a basic criterion for judging forest policies?

The idea of a "public interest" as a guide to governmental actions and policies is not new, but in recent years there has been considerable argument as to just what it means.    Banfield has given the following definition: "A decision is said to serve special interests if it furthers the ends of some part of the public at the expense of the ends of the larger public.    It is said to be in the *public interest* if it serves the ends of the whole public rather than those of some sector of the public." [18]    He concedes that there are differences of opinion as to just what is meant by "the ends of the whole public."

Conceptions of the public interest appear to fall into two broad classes: unitary and individualistic.[19]    The unitary concept considers the "whole" to be a single set of ends which pertain equally to all members of the public.    It sometimes pictures the public as an entity or body politic which has ends of its own that may be different from those of any of the individuals who make up the public.    Part of the public interest with regard to forests seems to be of this nature.    The "public" or social unit has an interest in the long-run conservation and maintenance of forests, for example, whereas the individual interests of most people lie in extracting as much immediate satisfaction as possible from some current use of the forest.    Most conservation literature has construed the public interest in forests to be of this unitary nature.

A somewhat different form of unitary conception visualizes the "ends of the whole public" as common ends that are shared by the individual members.    In determining the public interest under this conception, more weight would be given to common ends than to unshared ends.    For example, if practically everyone agreed that scenic beauty was an important value of the forests but the other uses such as hunting, camping, and logging were each prized by only a small minority of the people, it would be considered in the public interest to manage the forests primarily to maintain their beauty and only secondarily for the other uses.    This concept of the public interest has been followed in developing some forest policies.    It

[18] Martin Meyerson and Edward C. Banfield, *Politics, Planning and the Public Interest,* The Free Press of Glencoe, Ill., Chicago, 1955, p. 322.
[19] Meyerson and Banfield, *op. cit.* This presentation of the unitary and individualistic conceptions is based largely on their pages 323 to 327.

does not seem unreasonable that commonly shared goals should carry greater weight in policy decisions.

An individualistic concept of the public interest considers the ends of the public "as a whole" to be simply the sum of the ends of its individual members. A decision is in the public interest if it is consistent with as large a part of the "whole" as possible. This is the concept which underlies the idea of "the greatest good for the greatest number." The relevant data for determining the public interest are considered to be the ends which the individuals have selected and ordered for themselves. This raises two problems: (1) is every man's utility considered to be of equal weight, and (2) is there any limitation on the kinds of ends the individuals can select?

We have already faced the question of whether everyone should be given equal weight in determining policies and decided that this is not always a reasonable procedure. Depending on the forest situation involved, greater or lesser weight might be given to certain individuals on the basis of residence, age, occupation, state of health, or other factors which would cause the impact of the policy on them to be different from that on other individuals.

In many cases, a completely free individual choice of ends would also be undesirable. This usually involves a situation where some unitary public interest conflicts with the private interests of individuals. As an example, some states have seen fit to prohibit the aerial spraying of DDT because its side effects are considered to be against the public interest. A satisfactory pest-control policy for these states might now consist of permitting individual people to decide for themselves which pests to combat and the techniques to use, so long as they did not resort to spraying DDT from the air. This concept also underlies the policies regulating cutting practices on private forest lands. The states which have such regulatory laws require anyone cuting timber to take certain minimum steps to assure regeneration of the forest. With this limitation, it is considered to be in the public interest to permit private timber owners to otherwise decide for themselves when and how to harvest their timber.

It appears that neither the unitary nor the individualistic conception of the public interest alone will fit forest-policy situations very well. However, a flexible combination of the two that can be varied for different situations may give us a usable version of "the public interest" for use as a policy criterion.[20]

The meaning of the term *ends* has been vague in the preceding discussion, and we need to firm up the content of the public interest before we can go any further with it. As a start, let us look at some propositions suggested by Pennock for dealing with the question of whether the public interest is more than the sum of private interests:

1. The public interest is not confined to interests that are recognized by those whose interests they are. recognition as such by the mass is not necessary.

[20] For an attempt to use such a combined conception of the public interest as a criterion in judging pest control policies see: Worrell, "Pests, Pesticides, and People," *op. cit.*, pp. 40–81.

2. The public interest includes the interests of persons who are not yet born. *yes!*
3. Private interests must be conceived as including the individual enjoyments, satisfactions, fulfillments, and so on that come only in and through society. [As an example, for most people satisfactory forest-based recreation requires the presence of other people; even most wilderness enthusiasts travel in pairs or groups.]
4. Anything that is part of the public interest must be capable of recognition by individuals as an interest that they share in the sense that they wish to see it furthered or think it ought to be furthered.[21]

Pennock's fourth proposition deals with a question that we have not yet asked: who determines the public interest?  His point is that a policy cannot be said to be in the public interest if most of the people do not think it ought to be furthered, even after they understand it completely. Mere opposition to a policy does not indicate it would not be in the public interest, because as the first proposition states the people may not recognize that it would be in their individual interests.  But if even after an intensive education campaign most of the people still do not recognize that this policy would be in their own best interest, then Pennock would say it cannot be in the public interest.  This question lies at the base of some of the controversies over forest policy.

Griffith has proposed some guidelines for decision makers who seek to discover and act in the public interest.  He says that other things being equal, decisions should:

1. Favor the consumer rather than the producer
2. Favor the future generations rather than the present, long-term rather than short-term goals
3. Favor freedom rather than coercion
4. Assume a basic equality among individuals in matters of rights and justice [22]

The public interest thus apparently comprises some of the other social criteria which we discussed earlier.

Leys says:

There are three meanings which can reasonably be attributed to "the public interest" as a set of criteria for judging proposed governmental actions.  Ideally, governmental action will:

1. Maximize interest satisfactions (utility)
2. Be determined by due process
3. Be motivated by a desire to avoid destructive social conflict (good faith)

In judgments of specific policy issues, it is seldom possible to find an alternative that satisfies all three criteria equally well.[23]

[21] J. Roland Pennock, "The One and the Many: A Note on the Concept," in Carl J. Friedrich (ed.), The Public Interest, Atherton Press, Inc., © New York, 1962, p. 180.  Reprinted by permission of the publishers. All rights reserved.
[22] Ernest S. Griffith, "The Ethical Foundations of the Public Interest," in Friedrich, op. cit., p. 22. Reprinted by permission of the publishers. All rights reserved.
[23] Wayne A. R. Leys, "The Relevance and Generality of 'The Public Interest'," in Friedrich, op. cit., p. 256. Reprinted by permission of the publishers. All rights reserved.

This presents some new dimensions to the problem.   Our discussion up to this point of the public interest has been based largely on the idea of maximizing interest satisfactions.   Now Leys says that the policy must also be determined by due process; that is, through a regular course of proceedings and in accordance with established rules and principles.   This means that people must be informed and be given a chance to be heard and to take part in the process of policy formulation.   It rules out any attempt to establish policies arbitrarily; instead there must be some regular procedure for developing policies, and some rules and principles must be established or adopted to guide that procedure.   A whole structure of legislative procedure, public hearings, appeals, and judicial review has been established to provide due process, and we will consider its application to forest policy later in this book.

Leys's third point also adds a new aspect to the public interest.   It is clearly in the public interest to avoid destructive conflicts among the members or groups in the society.   And yet we know that individuals and groups differ in the ends they desire and that often these ends conflict so that they cannot all be realized at the same time.   One of the major tasks of policy formation is to find acceptable resolutions to these conflicting interests.   A policy which would not actually resolve a conflict but instead would favor one group or give it an advantage over its competitors would merely postpone the resolution, prolong the conflict, and perhaps intensify and embitter it.   A policy can therefore only be considered to be in the public interest if its motive is to provide a reasonably permanent solution to the conflict of interests.   A proximate criterion for the public interest in this case is whether the proposed policy is presented and promoted in good faith.   If it can be determined that a particular policy proposal has an undisclosed underlying motive of favoring some special interest or of discriminating against competing interests, this alone would be strong evidence that it does not comply with the criterion of the public interest.

At this point, we had better pause to reconsider the apparent conflict between public and individual interests.   Hays has noted that "Emphasis upon the struggle between private and public interest has often transformed real conservation issues into spurious moral battles between the selfish capitalist and the noble public." [24]   If we go back to Banfield's definition, we find that a decision is in the public interest if it serves the ends of the whole public *rather than* those of some sector.   This implies that it has to serve one or the other.   But the first part of his definition says that a decision serves special interests if it furthers the ends of some part of the public *at the expense of* the ends of the larger public.   And this certainly implies that a decision could further the ends of some part of the public and still be in the public interest if it also furthered the ends of the larger public.   Conflict between public and private interests is not universal; it only exists in certain situations and under certain conditions.

This is well expressed by Cohen: "*All* conflict situations which call for

---

[24] Samuel P. Hays, "The Mythology of Conservation," in Henry Jarrett (ed.), *Perspectives on Conservation*, The Johns Hopkins Press, Baltimore, 1958, p. 44.

government action—no matter what the specific nature of the configurations —invite a consideration of community values, and hence of the public interest.  They *may* involve situations in which so-called 'special interests' are arrayed against the quantitative bulk of the community.  But to limit the concept to this conflict pattern alone would, in my judgment, place an unwarranted crimp upon its usage." [25]   If we are to use the public interest as a criterion, we will have to recognize that some policies which do not favor any particular private interests may still not be in the public interest. Completely free access to and absolutely unrestricted use of the national parks by everyone, for example, would obviously not be in the public interest. And we must also recognize that this criterion can be used to choose between two policies, neither of which favor private interests more than the public.

This means that there is no such thing as the public interest which can always be definitely determined.  As a result two kinds of conflicts may occur: one over the definition of just what the public interest is and the other between policies which it is agreed would be in the public interest.

We should not be surprised, nor concerned, that such conflicts exist. Barry says that, instead, we should expect them.  "Why are some logically possible proposals never advocated by anyone at all?  . . .  Obviously because nobody at all believes this would be in his interests . . . all proposals *which are actually put forward* meet opposition." [26]   A policy that no one feels is good will not come up for consideration at all, and a policy which everyone agrees is good will be accepted and followed by everyone without argument.  All viable policy issues can therefore be expected to involve what those concerned at least presume to be conflicts of interest.

It seems to me that Leys sums up the situation quite well when he says "no one can formulate an abstract principle, called 'the public interest,' which all intelligent men are willing to apply deductively to policy decisions . . . intelligent human beings will not find themselves 'of one mind' regarding 'the public interest' in some policy proposals [but] the improbability of complete agreement on specific public policies [does not] disprove the possibility of general criteria or standards, which are properly called 'the public interest'." [27]   And Griffith, in commenting on an article by Hays, expresses the optimistic opinion that "however much we may quarrel about the public interest and what it is—and that is the essence of the quarrel—I still say that there is a net gain insofar as today it is the *nature* of the public interest that is the battle, and not whether we shall conform to the public interest." [28]

It is plain that the public interest is a peculiar kind of criterion, and yet there is widespread agreement that it is a criterion that has meaning for policy decisions.  My purpose in quoting so extensively from other writers in this section has been to show how much thought has been given

---

[25] Julius Cohen, "A Lawman's View of the Public Interest," in Friedrich, *op. cit.,* p. 157. Reprinted by permission of the publishers.  All rights reserved.
[26] Brian M. Barry, "The Use and Abuse of 'The Public Interest'," in Friedrich, *op. cit.,* p. 198.   Reprinted by permission of the publishers.   All rights reserved.
[27] Leys, *op. cit.,* pp. 255–256. Reprinted by permission of the publishers. All rights reserved.
[28] Ernest S. Griffith, "Note by Mr. Griffith," in Jarrett, *op. cit.,* p. 45.

to this concept and how general the feeling is that it is useful. Bailey says, "It is no more than an act of faith, but I cannot help but believe that—in spite of operational dilemmas—'the public interest' is the central concept of a civilized polity. Its genius lies not in its clarity but in its perverse and persistent moral intrusion upon the internal and external discourse of rulers and ruled alike." [29] Schubert appears to be an exception. After a thorough study and analysis of the concept, he concluded that "there is no public-interest theory worthy of the name and . . . the concept itself is significant primarily as a datum of politics." [30] But Schubert was interested in analyzing political behavior and the scientific study of political responsibility. For our purposes the concept seems to be useful.

Wengert in his discussion of the search for the public interest in *Natural Resources and the Political Struggle* and his other writings presents what seems to me to be the sense in which the idea of the public interest can be and actually is used as a criterion in policy formation. "The usefulness of a concept like the public interest lies perhaps in the search for it, in the effort by administrator and scholar to make explicit the data and rationale behind particular decisions that are or have been urged as being in the public interest. . . . Like justice, the public interest is given meaning in the constant striving to achieve it, in the on-going effort to assess the impact of particular facts and to determine effects of particular situations." [31]

[29] Stephen K. Bailey, "The Public Interest: Some Operational Dilemmas," in Friedrich, *op. cit.*, p. 106. Reprinted by permission of the publishers. All rights reserved.
[30] Glendon Schubert, *The Public Interest,* The Free Press of Glencoe, Inc., New York, 1960, p. 223.
[31] Norman Wengert, "Resource Development and the Public Interest: a Challenge for Research," *Natural Resources Journal,* November, 1961, p. 220.

# Anticipation of the Future

Policies by their very nature are concerned with the future.  Decisions are never made about past actions—we are always deciding what to do now or in the future.  A decision which affects only a single current action is not a policy decision; it does not establish a settled course of action or provide principles to govern actions.  It might form the basis or precedent for a policy decision, but it is not a policy decision in itself.  A policy always involves decisions about a future course of action.

Since policies are concerned with future actions, the objectives of policies must also be in the future.  A forest policy is always aimed at some future end, such as adequate supplies of wood in the year 2000 or reduction of flood peaks during the next fifty years.  Since this is a characteristic of all policies, and not something unique with forest policies, why need it concern us here?  The reason lies in the magnitude of the time involved.  Because of the nature of the forest as a resource, many of the actions taken today will not bear fruit or produce their ultimate results until many years in the future.

Suppose it is decided that it is desirable to increase the amount of black walnut timber available for manufacture into lumber, veneer, and other products.  With this objective in mind, a policy is established of encouraging people to plant black walnut seedlings every year.  Even if this policy is successfully implemented, the resulting increased supply will not begin to appear on the timber market before the year 2050.  This policy must be based on an assumption about the desirability of increased walnut timber supplies almost a century from now.  How can we know whether there will be a demand for such timber in the year 2050 and thereafter? We cannot, for certain.  But in this case, we can be reasonably sure that unless some action is taken during the next several decades to start black walnut trees growing, there will not be adequate supplies of walnut timber in the year 2050, no matter how badly the people living at that time may want it.

Policies about growing timber are probably the extreme case.  Despite man's best efforts through silvicultural practices, fertilization, irrigation, selection and breeding of superior trees, and other scientific management practices, the production of wood remains a natural process which requires many seasons of growth for its completion.  Realistic objectives for policies about wood growth are therefore limited to that part of the future beyond the minimum time needed to bring about a change in the amount of wood available for harvest.  An objective of growing more wood next year is ridiculous—virtually nothing can be done now that will have any effect whatever on the amount of wood that will grow next year, unless it is to reduce it.  How far in the future the objective must be depends on the kind of product involved.  Current decisions can affect the number of Christmas trees available five years from now, the amount of pulpwood twenty-five years from now, the amount of southern pine sawtimber forty years from now, and so on.

The necessity for future objectives also exists for the other forest benefits.  In their case, the problem is not usually that of the extremely long production period that we find with wood.  But it may be a more difficult one.  Some kinds of forest use may stop or reduce the production of some of the other benefits.  As examples, clearcutting of timber with deliberate burning of the slash may destroy the beauty of a forest tract, and planting up all open areas with conifers may eliminate certain species of birds and animals.  These may be only temporary changes; if left alone, the area may in time revert to its earlier condition.  But there will be a period of time—and it may be fairly long—during which some benefits will not be produced.  The time at which these benefits are desired in the future thus becomes an important aspect of the objective.  If the area now being logged is remote and settlement by people is not expected to reach its vicinity for twenty years, the forest will have time to recover before many people are there to notice it, and a temporary destruction of aesthetic values is not serious.  A reasonable objective is to assure that the environmental amenities will be present when people are there to benefit from them.  However, if the proposed cutting area is in a heavily populated region where many people would immediately notice any defacing of the landscape, the objective must be to preserve the amenities for the immediate future.

In some cases, changes in the forest may be irreversible.  If cutting and burning open an area to erosion that destroys the soil mantle, it may be impossible to restore the forest cover within any foreseeable time, even through artificial planting.  If forest land is cleared and developed for housing projects or industrial sites, the potential amenities of open space may be destroyed forever.   Even though the benefits from these areas may not be needed by today's people, forest policy objectives must look to the future and the possibility of a time when people may want them badly.

## ANTICIPATING FUTURE DEMANDS

As we saw in Chapter 2, the ends which forest policies are designed to achieve are primarily direct benefits in the form of goods and services. (The other objectives which get involved in the formation of forest policies, and which may limit or conflict with the direct benefits, are not restricted to the use of forest resources, but are realized through many different kinds of policies.)   Rational policy formation therefore requires information about what people want in the way of forest-based goods and services.   But because of the time-lag required to change the production of these benefits, what is really needed is information about what people will want in the future.

Human wants are almost limitless, however, and policy can only be concerned realistically with wants that can be satisfied.   Basically, the quantities of goods and services that people can consume or use are limited by the amounts that are available or that can be produced.   Men therefore have to make choices between potential goods and services and sacrifice certain wants in order to fill others.   Choosing one particular benefit always entails a "cost" of the value of the other benefits foregone in order to have the one chosen.

This is the sense in which "demand" is used by economists.   It is not the amount of a good desired but the amount that people will actually choose to take, knowing that in order to have this good they must pay a price in terms of alternative benefits foregone.   When goods and services are bought and sold in a market, money prices are worked out at which people are willing to exchange.   Since money can be exchanged for any good or service offered in the market, the amount of money required to buy an item indicates the value of the other goods foregone in order to have the one actually purchased.   (Money is not absolutely essential to the functioning of an economic system, but it is a very convenient medium of exchange which makes it possible to engage in extensive and complicated economic relationships.)

The economist's definition of demand then is the amounts of a particular commodity which people would buy if it were offered to them at various prices.   A basic principle of economic theory says that at the same time and in the same place, people would buy more of a given commodity if it were offered to them at a low price than they would if it were offered at a high price.   The quantities that people actually want to buy thus vary with the prices they have to pay.   And forest policies have to aim at providing the amounts of forest-based benefits people will want at prospective future prices.

The overall demand for a good or service depends mainly on the number of people who desire it and the amount of money they have to spend. Since both our population and our disposable income per capita are increasing, the demand for most forest-based benefits seems likely to increase in the future. But it is not safe to assume that demand will increase in the same proportion as population, or income per capita, or even total disposable income. Demand also depends on the tastes and preferences of the people who desire the product, and these too may change with time.

The extent to which a change in price will cause people to increase or decrease the amount of the product they are willing to pay for depends on their tastes, their preference for this particular product, and the existence of acceptable substitute products at competitive prices. The demand for water may be quite inelastic, and people may want about the same amount regardless of whether the price they have to pay is high or low. By contrast, the demand for developed camping sites may be quite elastic with the number of people desiring to camp in a particular area, changing a great deal when the fee is raised or lowered. Since all we ever can actually measure is the amount of a forest product that people are willing to buy at the established price, there is always uncertainty as to the rest of the demand for that product and thus as to what the situation would be if the price were higher or lower.

The amount of a forest good or service that people will want to consume or use in the future will depend on how many people there are who desire this product at that time, the amount of money they have to spend, the strength of their preference for this particular product as compared to the other things which they could have instead, and the price they will have to pay for the product in question. But the future price is also a variable, because it will depend on how much it costs to produce the good and how scarce it is at that time. If the demand exceeds the supply, we may expect the sellers to increase the price and to lower it if supply exceeds demand. The quantity needed as a goal for forest policy is that which would sell for a price that would just balance supply and demand. This is the only quantity that realistically measures people's "wants" for policy purposes. But it obviously is a very difficult figure to obtain.[1]

In order to get around this difficult situation, practically all attempts to anticipate future demand have settled for an effort to estimate how much of the good would be consumed or used at a specified time in the future if certain conditions exist at that time. The forecaster specifically assumes some things such as no major war or other disaster, a continued high level of economic activity and employment, no unanticipated technological change in use of this and competing products, and no unanticipated change in consumer tastes or preferences. These assumptions imply that the nature of the demand will remain the same as it now is except for changes that can be foreseen with reasonable certainty. (We can foresee, for example, the further displacement of lumber by plywood and other panel

---

[1] Some attempts have been made to develop such estimates of future consumption for specific forest products. For a good example see Henry J. Vaux, *Economics of the Young-growth Sugar Pine Resource*, California Agricultural Experiment Station Bulletin 738, Berkeley, Cal., 1954.

products in certain construction uses.) He then makes specific assumptions about future changes in population and disposable income which will determine the magnitude of the future demand. These are still assumptions, because no one can know for sure what will happen in the future. Demographers have very accurate information on the makeup of the population, birth rates, life expectancies, and other data needed to calculate future populations. But the Census Bureau still finds it necessary to revise periodically its population projections as it discovers that changes have taken place in some basic factor such as the fertility rate.

Now, in order to estimate how much of the product people will consume or use under the assumed demand conditions, it is necessary to estimate what price they will have to pay for it. And this means that some kind of assumptions have to be made about the supply situation for the product at that future time. But the changes that take place in demand and supply over extended time periods are inextricably bound up with each other so that demand at any particular date is to some extent a result of the supply that was available in previous years. (In Connecticut, for example, the forests were so heavily depleted in the past that there was very little merchantable timber available for sawmills and other wood users. As a result, these mills moved away or went out of business. Today when the volume of standing timber has increased considerably, there is very little demand for it because there is virtually no domestic wood-using industry left.)

If we were interested in a forecast of the quantities of forest-based goods and services that will actually be used at some time in the future, it would be necessary to simultaneously project both demand and supply over the intervening period. (Gregory has proposed a "time-jointness" approach for doing this in which both supply and demand are projected and adjusted to each other interval by interval until the desired future date is reached.) [2] But this would imply a *laissez faire* forest policy that whatever happens to work out by itself will be best. And instead, we feel that the function of policy is to try to make things work out better. So for policy purposes, we are not interested in forecasts of what things will be like if nothing is done. Rather we want to know what things could be like, because this will give us a point of reference for developing policies, which in forestry are mainly concerned with supply rather than with demand. A national goal for the timber resource "is not a mere *descriptive forecast* of what is likeliest to happen, as in the absence of planning. Rather, it is a *normative forecast* that assumes special efforts to satisfy the public interest with respect to forest products." [3]

The idea of "requirements" estimates has developed from this viewpoint. It usually takes the form: If adequate supplies of the good in question are available at acceptable prices, what quantity will people want to use in some particular future year? The common assumption in estimates of future forest product requirements is either that prices will remain the same

[2] G. Robinson Gregory, "Forest Growth Goals in a Private Enterprise Economy," *Journal of Forestry,* November, 1955, pp. 816–821.
[3] William A. Duerr, *Fundamentals of Forestry Economics,* McGraw-Hill Book Company, New York, 1960, p. 525.

as they now are or that they will change in the same direction and to the same degree as prices of other relevant commodities do.   This simple assumption avoids the necessity for trying to estimate the effect of a change in the price on the amount people use.   It has been criticized on the grounds that it may not be possible to produce the quantity indicated at this assumed price under any conceivable policy and that therefore the estimated use is pure fantasy, since it cannot possibly be achieved.   This criticism may be largely academic, however, since so many assumptions and estimates are involved in any prediction of the future that reliability is unattainable in any event.

Since the outcome of any estimate of future requirements or consumption depends so heavily on the assumptions which were used, it is extremely important that these assumptions be clearly spelled out by the forecaster and thoroughly understood by the user.   Policy makers can then adjust the figures presented to them upward or downward according to whether they feel the assumptions are overly optimistic or pessimistic.

There will always be differences of opinion about the magnitude and composition of future demand for forest products, and these differences are bound to cause controversies over forest policies.   Much of the controversy in the past between the Forest Service and private forest owners has been of this nature.   The two have agreed in general on an objective of adequate timber supplies for the future but have disagreed on the amount of timber that would be adequate.   These controversies might be lessened —if not resolved—by achieving more general agreement on the demand forecasts which provide the basis for policy objectives.   Over the years, the Forest Service has made a series of detailed forecasts of future requirements for forest products.[4]   Each has been criticized severely by representatives of the forest industries and by some academic forest economists. In an effort to meet these criticisms, the Forest Service has steadily improved its projection techniques and has drawn more heavily on other informed opinions in setting up its assumptions.   Although the Service has properly maintained its right to have its own opinions and probably could not achieve complete agreement from all interested parties even if it did not do so, each successive study has received wider acceptance, and the area of potential controversy has gradually been reduced.

## OBJECTIVES WITH DIFFERENT REALIZATION DATES

Although all policies are concerned with the future, they are not all aimed at the same future.   Consider two policies which might be followed with land that is to be reforested: to plant and manage the land to grow Christmas trees or to grow sawtimber.   The obvious difference is that the Christmas-

---

[4] Earlier reports by the Forest Service included some estimates for individual products, but the most complete studies were: *A National Plan for American Forestry*, 1933; "Forest Resource Conservation," in *Yearbook of Agriculture 1940*; *Potential Requirements for Timber Products in the United States*, 1946; *Timber Resources for America's Future*, 1958; and *Timber Trends in the United States*, 1965.

tree policy will produce results in six to ten years, while the outcome of the sawtimber policy cannot be expected until fifty to sixty years from now. Assuming that there is an unsatisfied desire for both Christmas trees and lumber sufficiently strong to justify the cost of growing either product, how is a choice made between the two policies?

Even this simple example contains a number of complexities, and we will have to sort them out for separate consideration. To simplify things, let us suppose that both policies would have the same final outcome—$1,000 worth of product per acre—but with one policy this would be achieved ten years from now and with the other fifty years from now. The choice now seems clear: the policy which produces results in the shortest time will be preferred. "Time preference" may have a rational financial basis. For example, it may be possible to invest the receipts from the early-return policy and to receive interest or dividends from this investment during the intervening period until the late-return policy pays off. If the $1,000 which could be received at the end of ten years in the example above were invested in a savings account that paid 4 percent interest compounded annually, the principal sum would grow to $4,801 during the forty years before the $1,000 became available from the second policy. The choice between the two policies would be the same, then, as a choice between $4,801 fifty years from now and $1,000 fifty years from now. In this case the value of the outcome of the early return policy is much greater than that of the other policy.

Time preference exists even in cases where such additional financial gains are not possible. Suppose a group of people were offered the choice between a month's vacation in a forest camp this summer or an identical camping vacation five years from now. The majority and perhaps all of the group would probably choose this summer rather than wait. Impatience is a normal human characteristic which contributes much to time preference. For individuals, life expectancy also is a major factor in time preference. None of us are very much interested in things of personal benefit to us which we do not think are going to materialize before we die. Most people have some concern for the future welfare of their children and other descendants, and this feeling may even extend to nonrelatives. But it is not likely to change their time preferences materially unless there also are social pressures on them. The ruthless manner in which people have used and destroyed soil, forest, wildlife, and other natural resources for their immediate short-run benefit lends testimony to this.

Societies and social groups also exhibit time preference, though they usually do not discount the future as heavily as individuals. A society does not have the limited life expectancy of an individual; it is concerned for its long-run survival and for the welfare of its future members who are not yet born. The group is therefore likely to be less impatient than the individual. But even a society is not likely to consider that future benefits are as valuable as the identical benefits today because of the uncertainties surrounding the future benefits.

This brings us back to the Christmas tree and sawtimber example.

There are two kinds of uncertainties involved: how big the final crop will be (in terms of number of trees, size, quality, volume, and whatever other factors are relevant), and the value of this final crop.   There are many uncertainties about the physical outcomes of these two crops: how fast the trees will grow; what damage might be caused by fire, insects, drought, and other hazards; the quality of the final crop trees.   These uncertainties are likely to be greater with a crop that takes longer to mature.   Even more uncertain will be the value outcomes: what demand there will be for these products at the time they are ready for harvest; how much competition there will be at that time from other growers of the same crops and from producers of substitute products such as plastic Christmas trees and steel-construction materials.   These value uncertainties increase rapidly as one looks farther into the future.

Uncertainty as to the future results of policies are likely to bias choices in the direction of those policies which will produce results soon rather than in the distant future.   But choices will also be affected by the fact that all policy outcomes are not equally uncertain.   Purely for illustrative purposes let us assume an unrealistically simple situation.   A policy is to be established for the management of a public forest, and there are only two mutually exclusive alternatives: (1) recreational uses such as camping, picnicking, hunting and fishing for which fees would be charged or (2) timber production for sale.   Now let us assume that an acceptable criterion for choosing the best policy is the annual amount of net revenue the forest will return to the public treasury.   Careful studies of the potential outcomes of the two policies indicate the following possible annual net revenues:   Policy 1—$100,000, and Policy 2—$80,000.   There is some uncertainty as to future timber prices and possible fire and insect damage, but the study indicates that the income from Policy 2 is not likely to fall below $75,000 or to exceed $85,000.   By contrast, there is a great deal of uncertainty as to how many people would use this forest for recreational pursuits in any event and the kinds and sizes of fees which would bring in the greatest amount of revenue.   The study indicates that revenues from Policy 1 could be as high as $200,000 but with an equal probability might also be as low as $10,000.   Which policy would be best?

This example probably poses the most difficult situation.   If the possible range of outcomes for Policy 2 were the same but the range for Policy 1 were $95,000 to $105,000, the choice would be clear—the worst possible outcome under Policy 1 would still be better than the best possible outcome of Policy 2.   Even if the possible range for Policy 1 were from $80,000 to $120,000, the probability is very high that better results would be obtained with this policy.   However, in the example as given, uncertainty about the outcome of Policy 1 is very large and its results could be greatly inferior to the worst possible outcome of Policy 2.   But the results might also be vastly superior to Policy 2's best possible outcome.   There is no firm way of deciding in such a situation, but it is obvious that the policy makers must try to take into consideration both the size of the outcome and the certainty of realizing it.   In many cases, policy makers may choose the less attractive of two alternatives because of the greater certainty of actually achieving that end.[5]

## THE INTERTEMPORAL DISTRIBUTION OF USE

Our definition of policy as setting or guiding a course of action implies that policies affect resource use over periods of time.    But it does not necessarily imply that the use will be uniform or continuous over time.    Take the remaining stands of virgin timber, for example.    At least three policies are possible for the harvest of this timber: to cut it all as rapidly as the market will absorb it, to gradually cut part of it each year and thus extend the total harvest over many years, or to cut nothing now and reserve this timber for some future harvest.    Each of these policies represents a different intertemporal pattern of use for this same resource.

Ciriacy-Wantrup defines conservation as a change toward the future in the intertemporal distribution of resource use.[6]    In the virgin timber example above, the latter two policies appear to represent conservation as compared with the first policy of rapid liquidation.    But is the third policy of reserving the timber for some future time better conservation than the second policy of harvesting it gradually?    This would seem to depend on the condition of the timber.    If it is overmature and decadent, the usable volume may be diminishing each year as a result of death and deterioration of the trees.    In the course of the annual harvests of the second policy, trees may be salvaged which otherwise would be a complete loss by the time of the future harvest for which they were reserved by the third policy. In fact, if the forest is in a decadent enough condition, only the first policy of rapid liquidation might avoid the loss of much of the volume.    The latter policies might then represent only an apparent shift of use toward the future, because part of the volume will deteriorate if it is not harvested soon and therefore cannot be saved for the future.

A somewhat similar situation exists with all flow resources.    These are resources whose services cannot be saved or stored and which therefore must be used currently or be lost.    An example is a forest campground adequate for use by 20 families or groups.    If this campground is not used in the current season it will not be possible to make up these unused services by having 40 families camp on it next year.    It will still provide camping services for only 20 families next year; the 20 family-years of camping which are not obtained from it this year will be lost forever.

Now it is possible to overuse flow resources and as a consequence to reduce the future flow.    The growth of wood in a forest depends on the presence of growing stock trees.    If the forest growing stock is reduced,

[5] For further discussion of the uncertainty problem in forest management see Barney Dowdle, *Investment Theory and Forest Management Planning,* Yale University, School of Forestry Bulletin No. 67, 1962 and Robert Marty, *Analyzing Uncertain Timber Investments,* U.S. Forest Service Research Paper NE-23, 1964.
[6] S. V. Ciriacy-Wantrup, *Resource Conservation Economics and Policies,* University of California Press, Berkeley, 1963, p. 51.

the volume of wood grown each year will also be reduced. If the growing stock is built up again by planting trees or allowing the existing stand to grow larger by refraining from cutting for a period of years, the annual growth will also be increased. But the growth lost during the period of understocking can never be recovered. Because of this characteristic, forest management has usually aimed at maintaining an optimum growing stock on the ground—one that would use to the fullest the productive capacity of the site.

Traditional forest management has extended the idea of trying to capture the flow of forest benefits to the idea of sustained yield. The reasoning has been that it would be desirable to so regulate the growing stock that harvests of approximately the same volume could be obtained permanently at annual or regular periodic intervals. This concept of the forest as a permanent sustained producer of benefits for man occupies a significant place in the philosophy of forestry. It has been carried to its highest theoretical development in terms of growing timber, but is recognized as applying equally to the other forest goods and services.

An absolutely equal intertemporal distribution of forest use is not free from serious question. Economic conditions fluctuate and with them the demand for forest products. Population continues to grow relentlessly, and per capita purchasing power has been increasing almost as consistently. Changing technology has made wood obsolete as a fuel and increased many fold its importance as a source of fiber. The demand for outdoor recreation has increased at an explosive rate. How realistic, under such conditions, is a policy of sustained yield of forest benefits?

The apparent problem may be largely a semantic one of how the word *sustained* is to be defined. Certainly under conditions of increasinng population and demand, forest yields should not remain constant if it is possible to increase them. Certainly changes must be made in the product mix to reflect the changes in demand. But continuity and permanence still appear to be valid policy goals for forest management.

## DYNAMIC FOREST POLICIES

Much of the preceding discussion of anticipating the future in policy formation has revolved around the problem that things will be different in the future than they now are. The world continues to change, and these changes are probably now occurring at a more rapid rate than at any previous time in history. Policies concerning the forests must therefore look to a future that will be different from the present, and they must be susceptible to change as the true nature of those future conditions becomes more apparent.

In commenting on the increase in population, Clawson has said "The present population-resource balance in the United States is neither equilibrium nor is it rational dynamic; the trends which grow out of our very culture carry the seeds of their own destruction." [7]    It is perhaps too much to expect a truly rational balance between population and resources.    But if the balance is sufficiently dynamic, perhaps the trends in population and resource use can be modified gradually and intelligently rather than proceeding inexorably to their own destruction.

In their study of the economics of natural resource availability, Barnett and Morse note that "the exceedingly varied natural resource environment imposes a multitude of constraints—social no less than physical—upon the processes of economic growth.    This presents expansionist man with a never-ending stream of ever-changing problems."    But they then go on to say:    "Flexibility, not rigidity, characterizes the relationship of modern man to the physical universe in which he lives.    Nature imposes particular scarcities not an inescapable general scarcity.    Man is therefore able, and free, to choose among an indefinitely large number of alternatives." [8]

While Barnett and Morse's basic point is probably true and people are more able than ever before to escape the effects of scarcities by shifting to other raw materials or other kinds of products, we may legitimately question how free they really are to make these choices.    Flexibility is certainly desirable, but it probably is not as general and automatic a part of man's relationship to the physical universe as their statement might imply.    Another quotation from Clawson casts some doubt on this.    "[The] trend toward greater intensity of use, within each major land use, will in turn mean that each use gets more and more firmly established on the land it occupies.    As it gets more firmly established, it can be displaced only with more difficulty.    A greater rigidity in land use thus seems probable in the future." [9]    Since land is the basic forest resource, this implies that the flexibility Barnett and Morse talk about may exist in the form of the ability to substitute spectator sports such as professional football for wilderness camping or metal for wooden furniture, but for many people these may appear to be rather inferior substitutes.    The kind of flexibility that is relevant for forest policy would try to avoid the rigidities of land use foreseen by Clawson.

It appears that in view of how difficult it is to read the future far enough ahead to make significant changes in forest use, flexibility is an absolute essential in forest policies.    "Permanence and stability may create a false air of security while really leading to obsolescence and irrelevance in an expanding economy.    A process of continuous planning is needed to balance the use of forest resources.    This process should be predicated on the necessity of meeting relatively uncertain needs by the flexible combination of labor and capital with land in an expanding and open economy." [10]

[7] Marion Clawson, R. Burnell Held, and Charles H. Stoddard, Land for the Future, The Johns Hopkins Press, Baltimore, 1960, p. 476.
[8] Harold J. Barnett and Chandler Morse, Scarcity and Growth, The Johns Hopkins Press, Baltimore, 1963, p. 11.
[9] Marion Clawson, Land for Americans, Rand McNally & Company, Chicago, 1963, p. 133.
[10] Ernest M. Gould, Jr., Forestry and Recreation, Harvard Forest Paper No. 6, 1962, p. 16.

# MEANS

Up to this point, our discussion of forest policies has been rather general and abstract. We have talked about policy objectives, the general way in which a group of people decide on an acceptable policy, the criteria that might be useful in forming and judging policies, and the problems in anticipating future wants. But we have said little about how policies are made effective.

It is obvious that a society has not accomplished much by agreeing on a settled course of action unless it actually proceeds to follow that course. A policy does not really exist unless people act according to it. Only then do members of the society know how others are going to act and how the others expect them to act. The existence of a policy therefore necessarily implies the existence of means for making the policy effective.

The implementation of a policy involves three elements which are recognizably different but which still get confused in our thinking. Once some policy has been accepted as a proper course of action, there will be various "techniques" that can be used to implement it or to make it effective. For example, suppose it is accepted as a general policy that forest-type recreation is to be made available to the residents of a state. A number of techniques might be used to accomplish this. Among them are that the state might (1) buy land and manage it as state parks, (2) buy land and turn it over to the counties to operate as local parks, (3) buy land and contract with private individuals or companies to operate parks on a concession basis, and (4) contract with private landowners to operate private parks under some form of financial guarantee. Such possible techniques for implementing any policy are likely to vary in cost, effectiveness, and acceptability. Also it often may be possible to combine two or more techniques in implementing one policy.

The selection of a technique is a *policy* decision. So in order to implement one policy, it is necessary to choose and agree on some subpolicies. As we saw in Chapter 2, policies form hierarchies with each one serving as the means of achieving some "higher" policy but usually also serving as the end of some "lower" policy. Now let us suppose in our example that a policy of concessions or subsidized private parks is generally unacceptable to the citizens of this state. A number of people would prefer county-operated parks, but others oppose this idea. The only technique on which a sufficiently broad consensus can be obtained is that of state-owned and operated parks. It therefore becomes an accepted policy that the state should own and operate parks as a means of implementing the "higher" policy of making forest-type recreation available to state residents.

Despite the fact that there now is a policy as to the technique to be used in making recreation available, nothing concrete has yet been done to implement either policy. What is lacking is a "program" for applying the technique. Some new or existing agency in the state government must be given the responsibility for carrying out a program of acquisition, development, and operation of a system of parks. Arrangements must be made for providing this agency with a budget, administrative and other personnel, and the authority to develop a program and put it into effect. At this point, more policy decisions obviously become necessary. But these policies are only concerned with implementing the policy of state owned and operated parks and therefore occupy a lower place in the hierarchy of policies. They can take for granted that forest-type recreation is to be made available and that this is to be done through a system of state parks.

Again it becomes necessary to choose a technique or techniques for implementing the policy by means of a program. But here there appear to be two different kinds of techniques involved. One, which we might call *technical,* is concerned with questions such as: should there be a few large parks or many small ones; should they be restricted to day use, or should overnight camping be permitted; should there be elaborate facilities or only the bare necessities? The other kinds of techniques are *administrative:* should the agency be controlled by a commission; should it be independent or a department in a larger bureau; should authority be centered in the capitol or decentralized through regional offices; how should its programs be coordinated with those of other agencies? The line between technical and administrative problems and decisions is obviously a fuzzy one, and this is an important characteristic of the implementation of forest programs.

We will go into the administrative problems of executing forest programs in Chapters 10 and 11. But first we must take time to analyze the major types of techniques that are used in implementing forest policies at high levels. These fall into four major categories:

Public ownership and operation
Public regulation of the use of private forests
Public stimulation, guidance, and assistance to private forest management
Private implementation of forest policies

In general, policy decisions about these techniques precede the establish-ment of programs.   We therefore find that virtually all forest programs and most forest administrative organizations are set up to apply one or more of these techniques and not to question them or to choose between them. This does not mean that all the policy decisions about these techniques have already been made.   There are still many questions and much con-troversy over the choice between them and even more over how they should be applied.   It will be better to consider these before we get involved with the administrative problems and existing institutional arrangements for executing policies.   In the next four chapters, we will look closely at the advantages, disadvantages, and problems of these major means of imple-menting forest policies.

# Public Ownership and Operation

The forest resource is basically a land resource. Forest policies deal with the uses man makes of forest land. But use involves actions by people, and this means that decisions have to be made about who is to act and the actions they are to perform. People differ in their desires, and the actions they take in trying to realize their individual desires bring them into conflict with other individuals. The social group has therefore had to work out systems for giving certain people authority to make decisions and of compelling other people to accept and abide by these decisions. One result has been the institution of property.

## FOREST RESOURCES AS PROPERTY

In our society, an exclusive right to possess, enjoy, and dispose of a thing is called *property*. But Harris points out that "property is concerned with relations among men, and not physical objects. Property is *rights*, not *things*. The things are property objects, and tenure is concerned with rights in these things." [1] This distinction is sufficiently important to an understanding of forest policies to bear repeating. Wehrwein has expressed it clearly: "Property is not a material thing but consists of *rights* which

[1] Marshall Harris, *Origin of the Land Tenure System in the United States*, Iowa State College Press, Ames, 1953, p. 2.

extend over the property object, or rather over the activities which involve the use of things.    As legal writers have said, it is a 'bundle of rights'." [2]

The owner of a forest possesses exclusive rights to use that forest in the way he sees fit.    In the United States, we have a long tradition of permitting and recognizing private property rights in forest resources.    Such private ownership can only exist, however, where there is a sovereign power that sanctions and protects the property rights that are vested in individuals or groups.    No private owner in our society ever has absolute property rights in forest resources.    "The largest and most exclusive estate in land that a private party may hold consists of all of the sticks in the bundle of rights except those reserved by society.    This is spoken of as a fee simple estate. . . .    Society always reserves at least three specific sticks out of the bundle of rights in land—the rights to tax, to condemn, and to police." [3]

It is important in a society where private property rights are so universal to understand clearly the situation with regard to public ownership.    To begin with, "all land within the jurisdiction of a state or nation always has an owner.    If it is not owned privately, it automatically becomes public property." [4]    But it is not quite as simple as this might imply: that all land must be either publicly or privately owned.    "Society, represented by federal, state, and local government units, cannot transfer all of its rights in land . . . the right of escheat . . . cannot be transferred. . . .    A unit of government is free to grant its land to a private party . . . but always it must take back the rights which constitute ownership whenever the private party does not choose to maintain them.    That is, land escheats automatically to some unit of government when certain conditions develop." [5]    For example, if a landowner dies intestate and without any legal heirs, his land becomes the property of the public.    If an owner abandons his rights in a tract of land rather than pay the taxes assessed against it, the land is forfeited to the local unit of government which holds the tax claim.

This means, then, that public and private ownership of forest resources are not mutually exclusive.    The public always has some property rights in all such resources.    It may exercise its rights with regard to private property in three main ways:    (1) through its spending power, it may influence the actions of private landowners or buy their properties from them if they are willing to sell, (2) through its police and taxing powers, it may force private owners to handle their properties in the ways which are considered publicly desirable, and (3) through its power of eminent domain, it may take over the ownership of forest resources against the wishes of the private owner.    We will consider the ways that the public exercises its rights without abrogating private property rights in Chapters 7 and 8.    The remainder of this chapter will deal with the situation in which the public assumes full property rights in forest resources.

[2] Richard T. Ely and George S. Wehrwein, *Land Economics*, The University of Wisconsin Press, Madison, 1964, p. 76.
[3] Harris, *op. cit.*, p. 5.
[4] Ely and Wehrwein, *op. cit.*, p. 76.
[5] Harris, *op. cit.*, p. 7.

# HISTORICAL DEVELOPMENT OF FOREST OWNERSHIP

When the North American continent was settled by people from the various European countries, the sovereigns of those countries claimed ownership of the land and other resources in the areas controlled by their representatives. The indigenous Indians apparently had only a general concept of common property in these resources.   We might therefore say that at one point all the forests of the present-day United States were in some form of public ownership.   The European sovereigns, however, quickly made provision for disposing of their lands by granting charters for their settlement and development.   Parts of the area were granted to and operated by proprietors (such as Pennsylvania) or corporations (such as Connecticut), and the remainder were operated as royal colonies.   In all cases, steps were then taken to dispose of the lands to private owners, and this process continued up to the time of the American Revolution.

After the successful termination of the Revolution, the thirteen states claimed ownership of all lands within their original colonial boundaries which had not already passed into private ownership.   These included large areas of western lands whose boundaries were vague and sometimes overlapping.   Since only seven of the states claimed such western lands, an agreement was worked out that they would cede the publicly owned lands outside of their existing borders to the federal government to be used for the benefit of all the states.   The policy of both the state and federal governments continued to be one of disposing of these lands to private owners by sale and grant.   This policy was continued with the additional lands obtained by the federal government through the Louisiana Purchase and later acquisitions.

Situations did arise, however, in which this general policy was not followed.   The development and maintenance of a strong navy was an important policy objective in the early years of the United States.   This required adequate supplies of timber suitable for naval construction.   The existing supply appeared to be dwindling with dangerous rapidity under the unrestricted private exploitation of the lands bearing suitable timber.   So Congress appropriated money in 1799 to buy lands and preserve the timber for naval use and in 1817 authorized the Secretary of the Navy to reserve from sale public lands containing live oak and red cedar for the sole purpose of supplying the navy.   Such reservations were made and eventually totaled somewhat over a quarter of a million acres.   By the time of the Civil War, iron and steel had begun to replace wood in shipbuilding, and the preservation of a source of wood for the navy lost its urgency.   The bulk of the reservations were restored to the unreserved public domain in 1879.   Gradually the others were also freed and again made available for disposal to private owners.

In 1864, Congress granted the Yosemite Valley and the Mariposa Big Tree Grove to the State of California with the stipulation that they be held forever for public use and recreation.[6]   In 1872, Yellowstone National Park was reserved as a public park for the benefit and enjoyment of the people.   The New York State Legislature in 1885 constituted all the lands then owned or thereafter acquired by the state in 14 Adirondack and Catskill counties a forest preserve, and a section of the new constitution drafted at that time provided that all lands in this preserve shall forever be kept as wild land.   In 1890, three more national parks were established to join Yellowstone Park in a national park system.

The total area permanently dedicated to public ownership had been very small up to this time.   A vast area of forest lands still remained in public ownership, but this was considered to be a temporary situation pending their eventual transfer to private ownership.   Then in 1891, Congress empowered the President to set apart and reserve public lands covered with timber or undergrowth as public reservations.   During the following two years, President Harrison proclaimed fifteen reservations with a gross area of over 13 million acres.   President Cleveland added almost 26 million acres to the forest reserves during his term, which ended in 1897.   In that same year, Pennsylvania embarked on a program of acquiring land for state-forest reservations.   By 1900, a very sizable area of forest land was committed to some form of public ownership.

This trend continued into the twentieth century.   More land was set aside from the public domain and other lands previously considered as only temporarily in public ownership.   In 1911 Congress passed the Weeks Act, which provided for the purchase of privately owned forest lands located on the headwaters of navigable streams.   The Clarke-McNary Act of 1924 amended the Weeks Law to permit the purchase of forest land for the production of timber as well as the regulation of stream flow.   Many of the states began to buy land for state parks and forests.   In some states, owners forfeited sizable tracts of cutover land to the counties rather than pay taxes on them.   During the Great Depression, even virgin timberlands found their way into public ownership by the tax delinquency route.   Public-spirited individuals and groups gave forest lands to the counties, states, and federal government for permanent dedication, usually as parks but often as public forests.   Acting under the authority of the Taylor Grazing Act, President Roosevelt issued executive orders in 1934 and 1935 which withdrew from disposal the remaining unappropriated and unreserved public domain lands.   Although the purpose of withdrawal specified in the Act was for classification and the executive orders did not specify the permanence of the withdrawals, it appears that most of this land will stay in public ownership.

At the present time some 320 million acres of forest land are owned by the public.   This is about 40 percent of the total forested area of the United States.   People who have studied the situation are in general agreement that most of this land will stay in public ownership.   Clawson,

---

[6] California re-ceded these lands to the United States in 1906 and they were added to the Yosemite National Park which had been established in 1890.

for example, has estimated that not more than 10 million acres out of the total public holdings of 890 million acres (of all kinds of land, not just forest) might be disposed of in the future.   He feels that "popular sentiment will demand that most land now publicly owned remain that way." [7]

It is clear from the preceding history that public ownership has been used extensively as a means for implementing forest policies in the United States.   But it has not been applied as a universal tool, since 60 percent of the forest land is privately owned.   The interesting question, then, is why has public ownership been used where it has and to the extent it has?

## REASONS FOR PUBLIC OWNERSHIP

Scott presents six classes of arguments which might be used to support the socialization of natural resources: emotionalism, idealism, scale, simplicity, economy, and permanence.[8]   The emotional argument is that natural resources are an original endowment of the nation which should provide benefits for all the people.   These resources should not be allowed to become the property of a few persons who can thereby enrich themselves while depriving the others of their just shares.   But as Scott points out, this is not an argument for socialization of the resource, because what is actually desired is the socialization of the proceeds from the resource. This is a matter of income distribution and is not necessarily best achieved through public ownership of the means of production.

The idealist argument is that if all industry were socially owned and managed, it would be possible to operate according to some rule which would allocate all factors of production to where they would produce the things consumers want most and otherwise do the most good.   Whether things would actually work this way under a completely socialized economy may be questioned.   But in any event, it is difficult to argue that forest resources should be managed according to this rule unless the rest of the economy is also operating by the rule.   Such a rule would have to use market prices as a guide to the particular forest products to be produced. But if monopolistic elements in other parts of the economy are holding wood-product prices up or stumpage prices down, managing the forest resources according to these prices may not really result in producing the right quantities of the things consumers want most.   The public owners may merely respond to the same erroneous price signals as private owners would have, and the result may be no nearer to a social optimum.

The third argument—that publicly owned forests would obtain advantages from operating on a large scale—must be given serious consideration.   There are definite economies of scale in forest management. Essential fixed costs of technical and administrative overhead can be spread

[7] Marion Clawson, "What Is the Future of Public Lands?", *American Forests*, August, 1965, p. 59.
[8] Anthony Scott, *Natural Resources: The Economics of Conservation*, University of Toronto Press, Toronto, 1955, pp. 106–110.

over more units of output; larger and more efficient equipment can be used; practices such as aerial spraying for insect control become feasible on large areas; and so on.   However, a forest property does not have to be publicly owned in order to be large and to operate on a big scale.   In 1953, there were almost 300 private forest owners in the United States who each owned at least 50 thousand acres and 50 of these owned over 250 thousand acres apiece.   Probably all of these are large enough to achieve any feasible economies of scale in land management.

There are obvious objections to concentrating economic power in the hands of a few people or corporations, and on these grounds it might be argued that it is better to achieve the economies of scale through large public forests than through large private forests.   But this is a weak argument in the case of forest resources, where the field never has been dominated by a few giant corporations as it has in automobiles and steel.   It was estimated in 1959 that the seven largest private landowners—all of which are clearly large enough to achieve any possible economies of scale —together controlled only 3 percent of the commercial forest land in the United States.[9]   Mead estimates that in 1960, the four largest firms in the Douglas fir region held in fee ownership 13.7 percent of all the commercial forest land in the region.   As a result of mergers, they had increased their proportion from the 11.7 percent which they had held in 1953.   However, his figures also indicate that the four largest firms in 1953 held only 8.2 percent of all commercial forest land in the entire states of Oregon and Washington as compared to the 13.1 percent which had been held in 1910 by the owners who then were the four largest.[10]   Despite the continuing mergers and expanding landholdings of the larger forest owners, there does not at present seem to be a solid basis for fear of private monopoly.

There also is the opposite side of the coin.   Scott points out that "Just as it may be unwise to entrust economic power to giant firms, so there may be other objections to entrusting it to huge government corporations.   Run by civil servants, responsible to political masters, inflexible, bureaucratic, they may in practice be as anti-social as any industrial giant. . . . The final choice between the giants is perhaps merely a matter of personal economic philosophy." [11]

The argument of simplicity claims that by comparison with the other means that might be used to implement forest policies, it would be much simpler to have the public take over and manage the forest resources itself. It assumes that the public is going to have to adopt some positive measures to achieve its objectives.   Private landowners tend to be guided in their management by the prospect of short-run and tangible benefits.   The existing market structure does not impel them to produce things from which they cannot realize personal benefit, such as watershed protection and

---

[9] Albert C. Worrell, *Economics of American Forestry,* John Wiley & Sons, Inc., New York, 1959, p. 15.
[10] Walter J. Mead, *Competition and Oligopsony in the Douglas Fir Lumber Industry,* University of California Press, Berkeley, 1966, p. 85.
[11] Scott, *op cit.,* p. 108.

scenic beauty nor to conserve the forest for the distant future. If the public wants these things, it must influence the private landowners' actions through some of the means we will discuss in Chapters 7 and 8.

This argument is often coupled with the idea of multiple use and the tendency of the private owner to concentrate solely on the use or uses of greatest direct value to him. It is claimed that the public forest manager is in a position to recognize all uses regardless of their immediate monetary return. All that is necessary is to instruct him to manage his forest on a multiple-use basis, whereas the private forest owner may have to be forced or bribed to practice multiple-use management. However, a very strong case can be made for socialization in certain single-product situations, such as the preservation of wilderness or the protection of natural wonders. Ciriacy-Wantrup appears to use this argument most logically: "If the practices required are very detailed and stringent, or if a large compensation (large relative to other costs of the utilization plan) is necessary for a considerable period, public management is administratively more effective and cheaper in accomplishing objectives of conservation policy than regulation of private enterprise." [12]

The argument of economy appears to be a very weak one if it is restricted to actual operating costs of comparable public and private properties. However, if the comparison is between a publicly operated forest and a publicly controlled privately operated forest, the total cost may be less under public ownership. This would be especially true if it is a comparison between a large number of small private properties operating under government assistance or regulation and one large public forest of the same total acreage. A given annual appropriation spent to intensify the management of the national forests, for example, would certainly produce more forest benefits than the same amount spent on a program of assistance to small forest landowners. The effect here may be due largely to a more efficient scale of operation on the public forests, however.

It makes considerable difference whether the argument of economy is applied to lands now in private ownership or not. If the public has to buy the forests from their private owners and then manage them, the total cost will be much larger than if it is a case of forests which originated in the public domain or which were given to the government. Comparative operating costs are always deceptive if the investment in land and timber is ignored or not treated equally in the properties being compared.

Permanence appears to be a fairly strong argument for public ownership. The limited lifetimes of individual owners means that eventually a new owner inevitably succeeds to the property, and there is no assurance that he will continue the practices of the present owner. Corporations also are not as immortal as their charters might indicate. Recent corporate mergers and outright purchases have in some cases led to drastic changes in management of the forests involved. Corporations also do get into

[12] S. V. Ciriacy-Wantrup, *Resource Conservation Economics and Policies,* University of California Press, Berkeley, 1963, p. 301.

financial and other difficulties which may force them to liquidate their timber or sell part of their land holdings.   Private owners are typically reluctant to dedicate their lands permanently to any particular use.   Those who have wished their properties to be permanently dedicated to some forest use have in the past often deeded these lands to the federal, state, or local government as a means of achieving permanence.

However, permanence may be only relative even under public ownership. The Constitution gives Congress the "Power to dispose of and make all needful Rules and Regulations respecting the Territory or other Property belonging to the United States."   Congress has in various ways authorized the reservation of parts of the lands belonging to the United States for national parks, national forests, and other specified uses.   It has officially stated how these lands are to be used or has delegated certain responsibilities for such decisions to the administrative branch.   In some cases, it has added a degree of permanence by providing by law that something should be done which already was in effect under administrative regulations. An example of this is the Wilderness Act of 1964 which legally established as wilderness certain areas which the Forest Service had already designated and was administering as wilderness.   Part of the pressure for such a law resulted from uncertainty as to whether the Forest Service might in the future change the classification of some of these areas to permit logging or other uses.   The erection of such a structure of laws and regulations makes it difficult to change an established use of the public lands, but apparently Congress has the legal power to reverse any of its earlier actions. It cannot therefore be said that the National Wilderness Areas are absolutely permanent, but they are probably about as permanent as any use of forest land is likely to be.

With this analysis as background, it is interesting to look at some opinions as to why public ownership has been used in the United States.   William B. Greeley, a keen observer looking back over almost fifty years of public and private service, said:

> The reservation and purchase of land for Federal and state forest management . . . [has] . . . rested generally on two premises:
>
> 1.  That private ownership is unwilling or economically unable to give the land continuing, productive forest management.
> 2.  That private ownership particularly cannot conserve special public interests, like flood control, which are important on many forest areas.[13]

Writing in 1952, he felt that both of these premises needed realistic examination in the light of then current conditions.   In view of the progress made in private forest land management since 1952, he probably would feel even more strongly that way today.

Dana and his co-authors list five major advantages which they say are claimed for public forest ownership:

[13] William B. Greeley, *Forest Policy*, McGraw-Hill Book Company, New York, 1953, p. 250.

1. Governments are in a stronger position to apply the principle of multiple use because they are not under the necessity of showing a financial profit.
2. They can look further ahead than private owners. The first duty of a state is to assure its own prosperous perpetuity.
3. They can take into consideration the needs of a larger population—county, state, or national—than can most private owners.
4. By and large, although with notable exceptions, administration of public lands . . . has been more efficient than that of forest and related lands in private ownership.
5. Public ownership gives greater assurance that small timber producers will have continuous access to supplies of stumpage which will enable them to remain independent enterprises.[14]

These advantages fall into three categories: (1) the public owner has a longer-range view, has more widespread concern for all members of society, and has particular concern for the small operator; (2) public administration is more efficient; and (3) the public is better able to practice multiple use. The first category of advantages appears to be the strongest, although these are the advantages that seem to receive least emphasis.

The relative efficiency of public and private forest-land management is not so clear. The statement by Dana is hedged around with qualifications like "by and large" and "with notable exceptions." This is too broad a generalization to be really useful, since there is such a diversity of private owners. There is probably little question but that the most efficient forest management being practiced in the United States today is to be found on the lands of some of the large private corporations. By contrast, the average small forest property is very poorly managed. From the viewpoint of policy formation, Clawson describes the situation quite accurately. "The dominant reason for strong support for large-scale public ownership of forest, grazing, and other relatively 'wild' lands is the widespread conviction that these lands will be more efficiently managed, more conservatively managed, if publicly than if privately owned."[15] The conviction is not so strong, however, as to press for all forest lands in public ownership.

The multiple-use argument has been a strong one for years and still retains its validity. This is particularly true if multiple use is not defined as producing various forest goods and services simultaneously on one small area but rather as managing forest properties to produce the best combination of the various possible benefits. Satisfactory means have not yet been developed for compensating private owners fully for the costs of producing public benefits which they are not able to sell in the market. And yet there is widespread demand for such benefits as watershed protection, recreational opportunities, and scenic beauty. Clawson again seems

[14] Samuel T. Dana, John H. Allison, and Russell N. Cunningham, *Minnesota Lands*, The American Forestry Association, Washington, 1960, p. 218.
[15] Marion Clawson, "Public and Private Interest in Public Land," in Howard W. Ottoson (ed), *Land Use Policy and Problems in the United States*, University of Nebraska Press, Lincoln, 1963, p. 359.

to express the attitude of the public succinctly: "It is possible that all these values will be given reasonable consideration in private ownership, yet it is unlikely that they will." [16]

## THE NATURE OF PUBLIC OWNERSHIP

Public ownership has some characteristics which must be recognized in assessing it as a means of implementing forest policies. To begin with, it does not represent as much control over land use as might be assumed. "The nearest approach to absolute rights of ownership in our system is found in the land holdings of the state and federal governments. . . . The rights they hold, however, are definitely limited by public opinion and by various reservations of public economic and social policy." [17] The mere fact of proprietorship does not necessarily give complete control. Various pressure groups and interested people are constantly trying to influence the use of the public lands to their own advantage.

The nature and effects of these influences is rather peculiar and worth analyzing. Suppose a public forest has been set aside—as were the forest reserves—for the stated purposes of "securing favorable conditions of water flows, and to furnish a continuous supply of timber." Now suppose that pressure is brought to preserve this forest as a wilderness area, and in response to this pressure the legislature either designates it for exclusive wilderness use or refuses to allocate funds for roads and other developments within it. The legislature which presumably represents the public is thereby restricting the right of the public to manage its forest for those purposes it had in mind in setting the lands aside. The public thus appears to now be limiting its own right to do something it originally wanted to do.

The key to this situation lies in the fact that "modern states, even in the most democratic nations are separate entities—abstractions apart from the group of individuals within them. When the modern state acts, some official really does the acting. . . . there is a considerable margin of discretion within which the official or administrative agency acts to interpret and enforce the law; and within this margin, the official or agency *is* the state—at least for all practical purposes." [18] In effect, when we use public ownership as a device for implementing forest policies, we are delegating responsibility for managing certain lands to some public agency, and in reality even to some officials or employees of that agency. The history of the public forest lands in the United States emphasizes this fact. There have been periods of intense agitation for transfer of some of the federal forest lands to the states. The question was not whether they should be in public ownership but whether they should be administered by state or

[16] Clawson, *op. cit.*, p. 360.
[17] Raleigh Barlowe, *Land Resource Economics*, Prentice-Hall, Inc., Englewood Cliffs, N.J., © 1958, p. 340.
[18] Roland R. Renne, *Land Economics*, Harper & Brothers, New York, 1947, p. 129.

federal government.   There have been bitter struggles as to whether federal forest lands should be administered by the Department of Agriculture or the Department of the Interior.   Within the Department of Agriculture itself there have been jurisdictional disputes between the Forest Service and the Soil Conservation Service over who should control certain public lands.

In our consideration of the public interest in Chapter 4, we found that in most cases it is impossible to define *the* public interest.   The public itself is made up of many groups, and on most policy issues only part of these make up the relevant "public," unless the others are somehow indirectly involved in ways which are not apparent to them.   Public ownership presumably means that resources will be managed in the public interest. But when the public interest is not clear, the individual groups try to get it defined to conform to their own group interests.   Public agencies and administrators cannot be free of biases and preferences which may be so ingrained or deep seated that they are not even aware of having them. Even when they are acting in what they are firmly convinced is the public interest, some of them will be more favorably inclined to certain interest groups than others.   The Forest Service, for example, has been accused of being biased in favor of commercial timber growing and the Park Service of a bias toward mass, spectator-type recreation.

The outcome of this situation is that public forest management is a rather malleable tool for implementing forest policies.   Placing, or keeping, forest resources in public ownership does not by itself guarantee that they will be handled in any specific way.   All it means is that they will be in a situation where those who exercise the immediate control over them will probably be more susceptible to the varied interests that make up the public interest than would be true in most kinds of private ownership.   The actual outcomes of public ownership will depend on the policies which are formed for the management of these public forests.   And these policies will evolve through the political process which we will consider in Chapter 12.

## PROBLEMS OF PUBLIC FOREST OWNERSHIP

Public forest ownership produces problems, and many of these will appear in other sections of this chapter and book.   Two classes of problems are of sufficient importance, however, to raise questions as to how satisfactory public ownership is as a technique for implementing forest policies, and we will consider them in somewhat more detail here.

The first involves the use of property as a tax base for the support of government.   County and other local governmental units depend heavily on the property tax as a source of funds for their operation.   A problem arises when property owned by one unit of government lies within the taxing jurisdiction of another, because one unit of government is not allowed to levy taxes on property owned by another unit.   Public ownership of forest land in a county therefore prevents that land from being a part of the ordinary tax base of the county.    It clearly creates a serious problem for a rural county which depends heavily on real estate taxes if a substantial part of the land in the county is in nontaxpaying public ownership.    An objection to public ownership that is frequently heard in popular discussion is that "it takes the property off the tax roll."

This problem has been recognized for a long time, and various steps have been taken to meet it.    New York, for example, has by law declared that certain state lands (including the Forest Preserve) are subject to taxation for all purposes.    The local governmental units can therefore treat these lands the same as private lands for tax purposes.    There remain problems in assessing such public lands, however.    This is especially true in the case of the Forest Preserve which by Article XIV of the New York state constitution must "be forever kept as wild forest lands . . . shall not be leased, sold or exchanged . . . nor shall the timber thereon be sold."    Yet the law provides that state land is to be valued for tax purposes "as if privately owned."    The State Board of Equalization and Assessment has developed a workable procedure for approximating such a value, which was approved by a Joint Legislative Committee after an intensive study of its own.[19] The only federal forest lands on which the tax problem is handled in a similar manner are the Coos Bay Wagon Road Grant lands in western Oregon which were reconveyed to the government and are now administered by the Bureau of Land Management.    The government makes payments to the counties involved equivalent to the taxes that would be paid by private owners.

The more common way of handling this problem is through a voluntary contribution in lieu of taxes.    The usual procedure is to pay a specified percentage of the receipts from the land to the state or local governmental units.    Sometimes a limitation is placed on the purposes for which the contribution may be used.    The pattern is not the same on all public lands. The national forests and wildlife refuges pay 25 percent of their gross receipts to the counties to be used for schools and roads.    The O. & C. lands in western Oregon (railroad grant lands whose title was revested in the government because of failure of the company to comply with terms of the grant) which are administered by the Bureau of Land Management pay to the counties 50 percent of their revenues plus any part of an additional 25 percent which is not spent on an agreed-upon program of road building, reforestation, and recreation development.    There is no limitation on the ways in which the counties may use these funds.    The unreserved public lands administered by the Bureau of Land Management pay 5 percent of the net receipts from the sale of either land or the materials therefrom to the states (not the counties) for schools and roads.    The national parks, for all practical purposes, make no payments in lieu of taxes to the counties or states.

In addition to the diversity of these procedures (under which some

[19] *Report of the Joint Legislative Committee on Appraisal and Assessment of Publicly Owned Lands,* State of New York, Legislative Document No. 23, 1965.

counties can be receiving in lieu contributions based on several different procedures), there are other objections to this sharing of public land revenues. Clawson gives three major objections: "the level of shared revenues may be wrong, their timing may be bad, and revenue-sharing includes no allowance for services provided by the landowning agencies." [20] Under the usual ad valorem property tax procedure the tax rate is determined by dividing the proposed net budget of the taxing unit by the total assessed value of all property in the unit. This means that the amount of taxes a forested property pays depends on both the size of the budget of its local governmental unit and the amount of other tax-paying property in the unit. The in lieu payments, however, are based on a fixed percentage of the forest-land revenues. These payments may therefore be either greater or less than what the same property would have been charged if it had been privately owned. As a result if the local unit contains a relatively large proportion of publicly owned land, the in lieu contribution may be less than the local government absolutely needs or more than it can effectively use. (Two Oregon counties, for example, received almost 7 million dollars apiece in 1965.)

The timing of the in lieu payments is related to the management plans for the public lands and the state of the market for their products rather than the local government's need for funds. Unless the public forests within the taxing unit are on a sustained-yield basis, their revenues will fluctuate periodically. There could even be long periods with little current revenue while timber is in the growing stage.

Finally, some of the public land-managing agencies build roads and provide fire and other protection that would be the responsibility of the local government if the land were in private ownership. These are actually a contribution in kind to the local government. If the in leu payment in cash is calculated so as to be the equivalent of what a private owner would pay, the public owner who also makes these in-kind contributions is being overcharged and not treated equitably with the other tax payers.

Other objections have been raised about the types of in lieu payments and their possible effects on the management of the public forests. The critical point, however, is that decisions about the use of public ownership to implement major forest policies may be controlled or distorted by the relatively minor policy problem of not upsetting the fiscal situation of the local units of government. Dana says that in the common complaint about public ownership taking land off the tax rolls there is an implication that there is no satisfactory substitute for the payment of taxes by private owners.[21] This implication, even if true, would not by itself outweigh the advantages of public ownership as a policy tool, but it is desirable that satisfactory substitutes be found as promptly as possible.

The second major problem of public forest ownership has to do with the

[20] Marion Clawson, "Should Public Lands Pay Taxes?", *American Forests*, March, 1965, p. 13.
[21] Samuel T. Dana, *Forest and Range Policy*, McGraw-Hill Book Company, New York, 1956, p. 336.

disposition of the goods and services produced.   Two approaches are to be found in public operation in other fields.   The first is to provide the benefits without charge to any person who cares to avail himself of them, as is done with primary education, police protection, and city streets.   The second is to require some payment from the person who uses the benefits, as is done with postal service, ferries, and public hospitals.   In both cases the cost of providing the services is paid by the general public through taxes but in the second case the direct beneficiaries are required to reimburse the public for at least part of the cost.   The pattern of choice between these approaches is not very clear.   Public thoroughfares are normally free to all, but tolls are charged for the use of certain roads and bridges.   Education is free through high school, but tuition and other fees must be paid by students in colleges.   Where charges are made, the proportion of the actual cost that the user must pay varies widely.   Only nominal fees are usually charged for adult education programs, but the full cost of fire protection is assessed against forest landowners in some states.

The general logic behind this pattern appears to be threefold.   First, there may be benefits to the general public as well as to the direct user, and in these cases the user should pay only part or perhaps none of the cost beyond his contribution as a taxpayer to the total cost of government.   Second, there may be large differences in ability to pay between individual users, and charging for the service may make it unavailable to those members of society who are least able to pay.   Third, the service may be one which the recipient is able to use in some kind of commercial operation which results in profit to him, he is able to absorb or pass on the full cost of the service, and he should therefore have to pay the full cost to the government of providing it.

A rather clearcut example of the first case is the regulation of streamflow and amelioration of flood conditions through watershed management. Here the benefits are so widespread that the cost of their production is reasonably charged to the public as a whole.   A plain example of the third case is the growing of commerical timber.   Here the benefits flow directly to the timber buyers, manufacturers, and wood-product users, and the production cost is reasonably charged to them.

The second case is often advanced as an argument for free recreational use of public forests.   However, this case is not as clear as the others, because it involves an obvious but rather complex redistribution of income. It says that recreational opportunities should be provided at public expense for anyone who may wish to use them.   The cost will be borne by all the taxpayers, but not equally since the amounts of taxes that individuals pay vary with their income and wealth.   If every taxpayer used the recreation areas, this might be considered as a case of price discrimination, with each recreationist being charged through taxes more or less in relation to his ability to pay.   But only part of the taxpayers use these recreation areas, and these users are thus receiving a transfer of income from the nonusing taxpayers.   It has even been pointed out that the other costs of using areas that are remote or difficult of access (such as some wilderness areas) may be large enough to prevent any but the well-to-do recreationists from using them.    Free use in such a case would actually result in a transfer of income from poorer taxpayers to these more wealthy recreationists.

The redistribution of income described in the previous paragraph is somewhat exaggerated, because the activities of governments are so multifarious today that they involve countless income transfers in all directions among taxpayers.    The wealthy wilderness user who is benefiting in this way from the taxes paid by his poorer compatriots may, for example, be paying a larger share than they are of the cost of educating their children, providing them with police and fire protection, maintaining highways for their use, and so on.

The problem posed by the redistribution effect of free public services is that they decide for the recipients of the additional income the form in which they are to receive it.    Suppose, for example, that instead of providing free parks, the government charged an admission fee of exactly the amount necessary to cover the total cost of operating the parks.    And suppose that it was possible to identify in advance all of the people who would use the parks in the coming year and to give each one of them at the beginning of the year a sum of money sufficient to pay the admission fees to which they would be subjected during the coming year.    The situation would then be the same as if there were no admission charge to the parks, but with one important exception.    Unless there was a requirement that these people could use the bonus received from the government only to pay for admission to the parks, there is little doubt that some of them would spend it for other purposes.    Some would prefer to have other benefits instead of park use if they could make a choice.    So long as the parks are free they will use them, because abstaining from park use does not free any money to buy the other things they value higher.    But if the additional income were distributed in cash, they would not spend it on park admissions.

The significance of this is that the income redistribution effect of free public services tends to distort the apparent demand for those services. The fact that a large number of people patronize free public parks does not necessarily mean that they would not prefer to do something else if they could afford to.    It is therefore difficult to judge how badly people want parks and whether the park budget might not have been better spent on some other kind of public service.    If the parks were operated on a pay-as-you-go basis supported by admission fees and large numbers of people patronized them, there would be a clear indication of a large demand for park services.    The only real way to test whether the fees are keeping people from using the parks would be to give each one a sufficient sum to cover the cost of the entrance fee and see whether he then used the park.

This is not necessarily an argument against charging less than the total cost to recipients of benefits from public forests.    It does point out the necessity for being clear about the objectives of public ownership; that is, the policies which are being implemented by means of the public forests. Making recreation equally available to all citizens of the country is a different policy from simply making outdoor recreation facilities available. The first policy requires overcoming the existing inequalities of income in addition to developing the recreation facilities. If equality is part of the objective, then different areas will have to be handled in different ways. (Equality of income cannot in any case be achieved through public forest ownership; all that can be done is to offset part of the existing inequalities.) Forest recreation areas that otherwise are within reach of low-income groups should probably not make any charge. Those areas (such as most of the national parks) to which the low-income groups (such as those in the Eastern cities) cannot afford to travel anyway will not be made available to these groups by not charging for admission. People who can otherwise afford to visit these areas will not be deprived of using them by an admission fee. As Clawson says: "Can we argue with a straight face that an entrance fee equal to the cost of 1, 2, or 3 tankfuls of gasoline is really the margin which would keep many people out of a national park?" [22] Where a clear case cannot be made that charging for services from a public forest will discriminate against some group which it is felt must be served, or would interfere with the achievement of some other policy objective, there does not seem to be any reason why the recipients of the benefits should not pay their full cost to the public.

There actually may not be many situations in which the decision is this simple. Governments are trying to implement so many different policies at the same time that most publicly owned forests are probably involved with a number of policies. Even commercial timber presents problems in places. Some communities are absolutely dependent on a local wood-processing plant which gets its raw material from a public forest. If in order to repay the public for growing the timber it is sold to the highest bidder, the local firm may be outbid by some other buyer or in self defense may have to bid more than it can afford to pay for logs. The result may be that the local plant has to shut down for lack of logs or goes bankrupt by paying too much for them. In either event, the local community would face an economic crisis. Obviously this would run counter to other welfare policies (like community stability) that the government is trying to implement.

In general, the trend is away from free distribution of the services of public lands. In the Land and Water Conservation Fund Act of 1964, Congress provided that "Entrance and admission fees may be charged at areas administered primarily for scenic, scientific, historical, cultural, or recreational purposes. . . . All fees . . . shall be fair and equitable, taking into consideration direct and indirect cost to the Government, benefits to the recipient, public policy or interest served, and other pertinent factors." [23] The Congress has not required the public agencies to charge for

[22] Marion Clawson, "How Much Should Users of Public Lands Pay?", *American Forests,* April, 1965, p. 38.
[23] 16 U.S.C. 460L-5.

recreation services, as it has required them to charge for timber and grazing rights, but the policy clearly is that in most cases the users should pay for what they receive.

## OBJECTIONS TO PUBLIC OWNERSHIP

The last section discussed at considerable length two serious problems of public ownership, and some people use these as arguments against socialization of forests.    They claim that under private ownership forests pay taxes just like any other property, and the existing price-and-market system takes care of the distribution of their products.    The tax situation is annoying but by itself does not seem to be of sufficient magnitude to discredit public ownership.    The failure of the price-and-market system to do what its proponents claim for it—particularly with respect to the nonwood forest products—is a major reason why public ownershp is used as a policy tool.

Some other objections do need to be considered, however. Wehrwein makes the point that "public ownership, as such, is negative and is in itself no guarantee that resources will be conserved."[24]    Public ownership takes the initiative for forest use away from private entrepreneurs, but whether it actually implements desired policies depends on how the public forests are managed.    Many objections to public ownership are in reality objections to public management.

Dana reports that people claim as the major disadvantages of public ownership that:

1. Public owners lack the initiative and flexibility of private owners.
2. Bureaucracy inevitably becomes enmeshed in red tape and paper work, with consequent increase in cost and decrease in efficiency of management.
3. While public agencies may have greater financial resources than many private owners, there is no assurance of their willingness to use them for intensive forest management.
4. The large private owners are doing a good job and the small woodland problem cannot be solved by public ownership.[25]

The first three of these "disadvantages" concern management and not ownership, as such.    The fourth really contains two different ideas.    First it questions the feasibility of public ownership as a technique for implementing better forest management on the small forest properties.    Whereas the other objections rest on the ground of efficiency, this rests on feasibility. It does not question public ownership as such but says it is just not a good tool for the job at hand.

The objection that the large private owners are already doing a good job

[24] Ely and Wehrwein, *op. cit.,* p. 481.
[25] Dana, Allison, and Cunningham, *op. cit.,* p. 219.

involves something broader than just the question of whether public owners could manage the land better than private owners. That question can validly be asked, but also involved is the American tradition of private property and private enterprise. After the Revolution it was accepted as a basic policy that the states and nation should own only the small amount of land needed to carry on the functions of government and that all other land should be the property of private owners. This tradition has persisted despite a gradual increase in public ownership. For example, in North Carolina "all acquisitions of land for State purposes . . . require the approval of the Governor and Council of State. They authorize the acquisition of land only when there is a justified need for it, and approve of its disposal whenever there is not a foreseeable use for it. It is not the policy of State officials to take land out of circulation and hold it." [26]

This inherent prejudice in favor of private ownership is a real factor in American land policy. Given a choice in a situation in which some objective could be achieved equally well under either public or private ownership, many Americans would choose private ownership. Some would certainly favor public ownership and some would be indifferent, but the continuing stream of objection to increases in public ownership indicates that many feel strongly about the desirability of private ownership.

This has broader implications for our purposes than just its relation to public ownership. It indicates that people are not solely interested in the ends toward which policies are directed and indifferent to the means employed in attaining them. ". . . it is simply not true that only ends are the object of valuations and that means are valued only as instrumental to ends. . . . The value premise which has to be introduced in order to allow policy conclusions to be reached from factual analysis has therefore to be a valuation of means as well as ends." [27]

To make the point, let us take an extreme example. An accepted objective of our society is greater individual income of real economic goods and services. Suppose now that as a means of achieving this end it is proposed that there be complete government regimentation of the economy, including the compulsory assignment of individual citizens to the type and location of work in which the government feels they will be most productive. It is obvious that Americans place a very high value on individual freedom. As a consequence, regimentation of individual action is bound to have a very high negative value. There is little question but that in our present state of affluence the majority of the people would feel that the negative value of complete government regimentation is so high that it would outweigh any possible increases in economic benefits.

Myrdal also points out that "in reality . . . a desired end . . . is never attained in purity. The dynamic social process initiated by the means results in many other changes besides the positive achievement of the end.

[26] Kenneth B. Pomeroy and James G. Yoho, *North Carolina Lands*, The American Forestry Association, Washington, 1964, p. 130.
[27] Gunnar Myrdal, *Value in Social Theory*, Routledge & Kegan Paul, Ltd., London, 1958, p. 49.

These accessory effects of the means have also to be taken into account in the chosen value premise."[28]    This is particularly significant in cases where new public ownership is proposed as a means of implementing some policy.    Almost perfect examples are provided by the numerous conflicts around the country over the taking of land for the construction of new highways.    There is general agreement that more rapid and safer transportation is a desirable objective and that a policy of improving the public highway system is therefore also desirable.    The trouble arises when the highway departments attempt to implement this policy by modifying the existing highway system or designing and building new segments.    This requires taking land out of previous uses and displacing its occupants.    The tragic picture of the elderly lady with her shotgun and rocking chair trying to block the inexorable advance of the bulldozers on her old family homestead is familiar to all of us.    But the effects are not limited to the land actually occupied by the new highway.    A particularly bitter fight has been waged in the city of New Haven for a number of years in an attempt to block the construction of a connector to Interstate Highway 91 which would run through a portion of East Rock Park and within a few feet of a newly constructed high school.    The destruction of irreplaceable scenic and recreational areas in the park, the noise and other effects of a major traffic artery on enjoyment of the park and operation of the school, and other less obvious accessory effects have been advanced as arguments against the construction of the connector.

In this regard it is important to recognize that this conflict of values has been minimized by the way that most of the present publicly owned forest lands in the United States originated.    Gulick has pointed out that the national forest program did not require a large initial government investment or the dispossessing of numerous private owners or tenants.[29]    Of the some 186 million acres of land now administered by the Forest Service, only 26 million were acquired by purchase, donation, or in other transfers from private ownership.    The other 160 million acres—or 86 percent— were reserved from the public domain and therefore never were in private ownership.

Another characteristic of the publicly owned lands in the United States which has minimized conflict is brought out by Peffer.    "The truly vacant public domain as it stands today comprises the 37 million acres outside of grazing districts, of which some 12 million acres are covered by leases. The remaining 25 million almost worthless acres are the land that 'nobody wanted very much,' at least on the terms at which it was offered."[30]    It is estimated that only 28 percent of the commercial forest land—land which is capable of producing crops of industrial wood and is not withdrawn from timber utilization—in the United States is in public ownership.    By contrast, the public owns about two thirds of the noncommercial forest land.

[28] *Ibid.*
[29] Luther H. Gulick, *American Forest Policy*, Duell, Sloan & Pearce, New York, 1951, p. 69.
[30] E. Louise Peffer, *The Closing of the Public Domain*, Stanford University Press, Stanford, 1951, p. 312

"For a great deal of both federal and state lands, the chief reason they are now in public ownership is that in the past they were not in much demand for private ownership." [31]

## FUTURE USE OF PUBLIC OWNERSHIP

Public ownership has been and is being used as a major tool for implementing forest policies in the United States.   Current questions seem to be concerned more with how the public forest lands are to be used than with whether they should be in public ownership or not.   They question not its usefulness as a tool but rather the particular policies it should be used to implement.

There does not even seem to be much question as to the extent to which public ownership should be used.   Over a decade ago, Dana observed that "Neither the advocates of a marked expansion of public ownership nor the advocates of a marked reduction seem likely to convince the great body of voters that there is anything seriously wrong with the status quo; but it would be surprising indeed if some changes in ownership in both directions did not prove to be in the public interest." [32]   Such changes have indeed taken place since he wrote, and the great bulk of them have represented increases in public ownership.   Compared with the total area of forest land, these additions have not been large; but in actual area they have been substantial.   It is estimated, for example, that by the end of fiscal year 1967 a total of 400,000 acres had been acquired by state and local governments and the federal agencies with money allocated from the Land and Water Conservation Fund, which did not come into existence until 1965.

Clawson and Held noted this bias against decreasing the proportion of the forests that is publicly owned when they wrote:   "The vigor with which proposals interpreted as disposing of federal lands or weakening control in their management have been fought is a convincing expression of popular will.   The issue has been decided, and further discussion is fruitless so long as this attitude remains. . . .   Popular support for additional land is vastly less than for retention of the land now owned." [33]

An interesting example of this attitude is to be seen in Alaska today. Under provisions of the Statehood Act, Alaska was given the right to select approximately 104 million acres from the federal public domain within its borders.   As Cooley says:   "No other state has had quite the same opportunity to conceive and carry out a rational land program on such a gigantic scale." [34]   The Alaska state constitution provides that the state cannot sell, grant, or deed its rights to the renewable natural resources belonging

[31] Clawson, "What Is the Future of Public Lands?" *op. cit.,* p. 15.
[32] Dana, *Forest and Range Policy, op. cit.,* p. 338.
[33] Marion Clawson and Burnell Held, *The Federal Lands,* The Johns Hopkins Press, Baltimore, 1957, p. 7.
[34] Richard A. Cooley, *Alaska, a Challenge in Conservation,* University of Wisconsin Press, Madison, 1966, p. 3.

to the state but can only lease them with proper precautions for their conservation.  Lands selected by the state from the public domain are classified according to their highest and best use by the State Division of Lands before they can be disposed of.  The only lands that will be available for disposal through sale or lease are those classified as agricultural, commercial, industrial, private recreation, residential, and utility lands.  Those classified as timber, public recreation, and watershed lands (along with some other classes) will be retained permanently in state ownership.  It appears likely that virtually all forest land in Alaska—both state and federal—will remain in public ownership indefinitely.

# Public Regulation of
# Private Forest Use

In the previous chapter, we considered at some length the matter of property rights in land resources. We saw that ownership is a bundle of rights and that a private owner never has the entire bundle because some rights are always retained by society. Now a society could retain the entire bundle and not permit private individuals to own property at all. But our society has traditionally considered it desirable that exclusive rights to most property rest with private individuals and groups.

Cases have arisen, however, in which it was felt that the way some private owners exercised their property rights was detrimental to the interests of society as a whole. With the forest resources this has usually been a case of preventing some of society's objectives from being achieved rather than a case of the private forest owner's directly doing injury to the society. Some agreed-upon policy—such as that the forests of the country should provide an adequate future supply of wood—was not being satisfactorily implemented by unrestricted private ownership and management of the forest resources. The governments—acting for the public—therefore felt it was necessary to use some other means of implementing the policy. An obvious means is for the public to take over the ownership and management of the forests, as discussed in Chapter 6, but this runs counter to our general preference for private ownership and operation.

Another possible approach is to allow the private owners to retain their property rights in the forest resources but to compel them to manage their properties as the public desires. "Although it is clear that privately held rights cannot be adjusted . . . without due process of law, it is equally

100

clear that society may restrict the freedom with which the owner uses his land where necessary to protect and promote the public health, safety, morals, and general welfare."[1]  The states have traditionally had a "police power" to restrict the actions of private individuals and groups for these purposes.

Schulz says that the use of the police power to force wise use of resources "is not considered consonant with our accepted governmental philosophy except as a last resort because it impinges upon individual freedom, although properly drawn it seems such legislation is constitutional."[2] This is probably the basic reason why public regulation of private forest management has not been used more extensively in the United States. However, it seems to state the case too strongly since the states have used their police power to control forest fires for half a century with apparent widespread public approval.  Hannah and Krausz describe the situation more completely:  "The extent to which a state may control land use is dependent in part on what the public will accept, in part on constitutional authority, and in part on what the courts will uphold as a reasonable exercise of the police power."[3]

All this means that as things now stand in the United States, there are severe restrictions on how far the public can go in forcing a private forest owner to use his lands in any particular way.  Private persons (and corporations are legally considered persons) are protected by the due-process provisions of the constitution from arbitrary and unreasonable actions by the state and federal governments.  In a procedural sense, due process requires that any person brought to trial be notified of the nature, time, and place of the proceedings; that it be established that the tribunal has jurisdiction; and that the tribunal provide a fair trial.  More important from a forest-policy viewpoint, due process also requires, in a substantive sense, a determination of whether the statute in question represents a legitimate exercise of legislative power.  As Johnson points out:  "The social and economic philosophies of judges come into play here."[4]  A new effort to regulate the actions of private landowners will inevitably be questioned, will have to be tested in the courts, and will be a very uncertain instrument until its legitimacy has been established.

One further point is important to note here.  "In the United States the individual states are pre-eminent in matters of property and land law, simply because the federal constitution reserves to them all rights not expressly given the federal government; and expressly gives but few such powers to the federal government."[5]  Because of this, it would be difficult to implement a nationwide forest policy by regulating the actions of private forest owners.  Public regulation is therefore used to implement forest policies

[1] Marshall Harris, *Origin of the Land Tenure System in the United States,* Iowa State College Press, Ames, 1953, p. 6.
[2] William F. Schulz, Jr., *Conservation Law and Administration,* The Ronald Press Company, New York, 1953, p. 557.
[3] H. E. Hannah and N. G. P. Krausz, "The Role of Law in the Development of Land Resources," in Land Economics Institute, *Modern Land Policy,* The University of Illinois Press, Urbana, 1960, p. 326.
[4] Arthur M. Johnson, *Government-Business Relations,* Charles E. Merrill Publishing Co., Columbus, Ohio, 1965, p. 76.
[5] Hannah and Krausz, *op. cit.,* p. 325.

accepted by the people of the individual states.   Since the policies of all the states are not identical, there is considerable variation in the use of public regulation throughout the country.

## OBJECTIVES OF PUBLIC REGULATION

In commenting broadly on interference by government in the economy, Musolf has stated that regulation is economically and politically based on three kinds of motivation:

1.  The desire to curb the abuses of an economic group that has gained significant power over others
2.  The desire to shape the economy along lines considered compatible with the spirit of democracy
3.  The purpose of protecting an established occupation or profession through restrictions on entry and standards of performance [6]

The use of public regulation to implement forest policies in the United States has been based mainly on the second motivation.   No private individuals or corporations have as yet achieved a dominant enough position of forest ownership or control of the forest-product market to warrant governmental regulation.   The licensing of professional foresters in some states is the only example of regulation based on the third motivation.   Basically, public regulation—where it has been used—represents an attempt to guide the development of forest resources in the public interest in a democratic manner.

In Europe the use of private forests on mountain watersheds has been strictly controlled for centuries to provide protection against floods and avalanches.   At one time very severe regulation of all private forestry was practiced in most of Europe, and this was probably related to the local needs for wood for fuel and construction.   These regulations were relaxed following the French Revolution, and "most of the countries in western Europe fell back upon the legal thesis that forests must not be destroyed without consent of the state and otherwise left the owner relatively free in managing his land." [7]   Such regulation as exists in the United States also appears aimed at preventing the destruction of the forest or of its long-run productivity.   However, the specific preservation of scenic and aesthetic values is receiving much attention today as a possible reason for restricting what a private owner can do with his forest lands.

## FORMS OF PUBLIC REGULATION

Anderson classifies measures which prevent private owners from making free use of their forest properties in three major categories: compulsory

[6] Lloyd D. Musolf, *Government and the Economy,* Scott, Foresman and Company, Chicago, 1965, p. 35.
[7] William B. Greeley, *Forest Policy,* McGraw-Hill Book Company, New York, 1953, p. 21.

preservation, restrictions on management, and direct public participation in private forest management.[8]   Compulsory preservation may take the form of prohibiting diversion of forest land to other uses, breaking of forest properties up into smaller units, or felling trees without sanction.   Restrictions on management may require the use of specified silvicultural systems, managing forests on the principle of sustained yield, or limitations on the size of trees to be cut.   Direct public participation may see the government stepping in to do something that private owners cannot or will not do, such as controlling insect epidemics or reforesting unstocked lands.

Troup reported the chief regulatory measures in force in the European countries in the late 1930s to be:

1. Compulsory preservation of existing forest
2. Prevention of speculation in woodlands
3. Compulsory reafforestation or regeneration of felled areas
4. Prevention of forest devastation, and compulsory working on the principle of the sustained yield
5. Restrictions as to rotation or size of trees to be felled
6. Limitation of area or quantity of material to be felled
7. Requirements as to silvicultural practice and other operations
8. Measures to secure proper forest management [9]

These appear to be self-explanatory except for the eighth.   Under this heading Troup reported that some countries required all private forests above a certain size to be managed by a professionally trained forest manager.

Compulsory preservation has been used to only a limited extent in the United States thus far.   One example is the Allagash Wilderness Waterway established in 1966 by the state of Maine in which no timber-harvesting operations will be permitted on privately owned lands within 1 mile of the shoreline of the river.

Restrictions on management are the most common form of control applied in the United States.   Of the measures listed by Troup, the only one used to any extent in the United States is compulsory regeneration after logging.   Oregon, for example, requires that when timber is harvested in the Douglas-fir type, not less than 5 percent of the area must be left uncut as a source of seed and that this area must be well stocked with commercial coniferous tree species of seed-bearing size.   (The operator may substitute some other plan—such as planting seedlings—if it is approved in advance of cutting by the State Forester.)   Six other states have some form of regulation aimed at regenerating cutover lands.

Restrictions on the size of trees to be felled have been tried in some states.   The California Forest Practice Act divides the state into four districts, for each of which forest practice rules are established.   The rules in two of these districts require that all thrifty immature trees of certain

[8] M. L. Anderson, *State Control of Private Forestry under European Democracies*, Oxford University Press, London, 1950, p. 9.
[9] R. S. Troup, *Forestry and State Control*, Oxford University Press, London, 1938, pp. 19–22.

species which are not at least 20 inches in diameter at breast height must be left uncut. An Idaho law required the leaving of all western yellow pine trees 16 inches or less in diameter and all white pine trees 12 inches or less. For most forest types, minimum diameter limits have no silvicultural basis and therefore are not likely to be effective in perpetuating the forest.

While the other measures mentioned by Troup have never been used in the United States, some of them have been advanced at times during controversy over private forest use. In the days when current annual growth was constantly exceeded by the volume of timber harvested, someone seriously suggested that the number of years required to grow various species to merchantable size be determined and that the annual harvest be restricted to the volume of timber then standing divided by that number of years. An equally serious suggestion incorporated in a bill actually introduced in Congress would have required that no trees could be cut for commercial purposes unless they had been marked by a professional forester.

Other restrictions on forest management are more important in the United States. The most severe have to do with fire. Most states have laws under which the governor or some designated official can "close" the forests during periods of severe fire danger. Such a closure applies not only to loggers and forestry crews but also to hunters, fishermen, and other recreationists. Some states have laws prohibiting any fires in the woods at specified times or dates. Some require the felling of snags and burning of logging slash as fire-prevention measures. There are also a variety of restrictions on the aerial spraying of pesticides. Attempts are being made through regulation of logging to protect streams from damage by tractors and from blockage by logging debris. There is a beginning on restricting cutting or the conditions left after cutting along scenic and other tourist-traveled highways.

## PROBLEMS PECULIAR TO REGULATING PRIVATE FOREST USE

An attempt to implement a policy of managing the forest resources of the country to achieve certain social objectives by forcing private landowners to handle their forests in some specific way runs into serious problems. To begin with, the private owner must already be using his forest lands in some manner which is not considered socially desirable, or there would be no need to try to get him to change his practices. Now he may be doing some things that obviously are so damaging to other members of society as to leave little question but that the government should make him desist or change his actions. Such is the case of the owner who starts fires on his own land and lets them spread and do damage to other properties. All states have laws prohibiting the release of wildfire to the lands of others, and in addition the injured parties can resort to the courts to recover damages from the offender. The same reasoning applies to the pollution of air with smoke and of streams with logging debris.    It can be extended even to the despoiling of natural beauty.

However, some practices which are not considered desirable do not damage other members of society directly as wildfire does.    They have indirect effects, such as reducing the future supply of forest products or failing to contribute to the economy the full potential yield of water, game, wood, or other benefits.    Their problem is that they are not managing the forest in the way that will be most beneficial to society as a whole in the long run.    In this case, the purpose of public regulation is to make the owner do something that is considered desirable rather than to stop him from doing something undesirable.    Of course, in many cases the purpose may be to make him change from doing one thing to doing something else.    But the regulation is not purely preventive.

These private landowners will ordinarily have what they consider to be good reasons for not managing their forests the way society thinks they should.    They may feel that the risk is too great and therefore prefer to do something safer.    A landowner may be so worried about fires, for example, that he will just accept whatever regeneration occurs naturally on his cutover land rather than take the risk of losing the money required to plant trees.    They may know that the way they are operating is actually more profitable to them than the way society wants them to operate.    An owner may be making more money by concentrating exclusively on timber, for example, than he could by managing his land for multiple products.    Or they may lack the knowledge or ability to practice the kind of management that society would prefer.

These resistances have to be overcome before the landowner will change his practices, and there is some question as to how effective compulsion alone is for accomplishing this.    Scott feels that "In North America, it is doubtful whether compulsory measures which actually achieve a change of land-use practices can succeed without there being also some financial incentive (or at least the realization that to abandon the land in order to avoid the regulation would bring about a greater personal loss than to accept the regulation)." [10]    A compulsory change in forest use which reduced the owner's net returns from his property would probably be tolerated, though not without complaint.    A change which eliminated all net revenue from the property or which required a net outgo or a sizable investment which the owner felt he was almost certain to lose could well lead to attempts to dispose of the property and perhaps even to its abandonment. Regulation might then be little more than a device for forcing land into public ownership.

The alternative is to compensate the owner for his loss due to the required change.    If he is forced to produce a social benefit such as watershed protection or scenic beauty from which he can derive no direct revenue, it would seem reasonable that society should somehow pay him for

[10] Anthony Scott, *Natural Resources: The Economics of Conservation,* University of Toronto Press, Toronto, 1955, p. 112.

these benefits.    However, in some cases his previous practices will have been profitable to him because he did not have to bear certain social costs, such as those resulting from the aggravation of flood and erosion conditions or the destruction of scenic values.    The revenue he loses when forced to change practices in such a case has been realized by his exploiting of the society in general, and there may be no ethical argument against depriving him of it.    However, if he bought the forest and this revenue opportunity was capitalized into the price he paid for it, the previous and not the present owner is the one who benefited from exploiting society, and there may be a legitimate question as to whether the present owner should not be compensated for his loss due to regulation.

## Large Number of Owners

A major practical problem involved in any attempt to regulate private forest use is the very large number of people who own forest lands.    The Forest Service estimated that in 1953 there were at least 4.5 million private forest-land owners in the United States, and it is doubtful whether the number has decreased since then.    Fewer than 50 thousand of these owned more than 500 acres of land, and only 2,600 were believed to own over 5,000 acres apiece.[11]

For a variety of reasons, the quality of the management applied to private forest lands in the United States has varied inversely with the size of the property.    A sizable proportion of the largest landowners are corporations, and many of them are also manufacturers of wood-based products. They are acutely conscious of public opinion and of the threat of public control.    In general, their forest management is already quite satisfactory from the public's viewpoint, but where further modification has become desirable they have tended to respond voluntarily to public pressures. Thus, this small group of owners whose regulation by the government is entirely feasible is the one for whom compulsion appears unnecessary.

By contrast, there are some 3.8 million people who own less than 100 acres of forest land apiece.    Most of these are individuals.    In 1953 about three-fourths of them were farmers, but this proportion is undoubtedly less today.    The others are a great variety of people who own forest land for all kinds of personal reasons.    Most of them have little knowledge of forest management, and many do not even reside on their properties.    It is generally agreed that these small holdings are not contributing anything like their potential to the national wood supply.    They contribute little in the way of recreation facilities to anyone beyond the immediate families of their owners.    And in some cases of flagrant mismanagement, they have negative effects on soil and water control and scenic beauty.    Since these small holdings include at least one-third of the forest land of the country, many people feel that the public cannot remain indifferent to what is done with them.    They have shown little sign so far of responding to public

[11] U.S. Forest Service, *Timber Resources for America's Future*, U.S. Department of Agriculture, Forest Resource Report 14, 1958, p. 293.

opinion, and it appears that if they are to be better managed, some positive governmental action is necessary.

The problems of regulating the actions of some 4 million people are formidable in any case.    But these particular people are scattered over the entire extent of the country.    The actions it is desired to control are not obvious and performed in public places but rather take place largely on lands which are some distance from concentrations of population and often are remote and inaccessible.    The determination of whether the owner's actions are acceptable or not usually requires an actual inspection of the forest on the ground.    The only firm way of determining what the owner is doing with his forest is to make such inspections periodically.    It is doubtful whether an inspector could make even a cursory check on an average of six such properties every working day in the year.    But even if this were possible, it would still require about three thousand inspectors to check every one of these small landholdings once a year.    And this would not include locating the owners, notifying them of violations, and prosecuting those who refused to comply with the regulations.    The magnitude of the job might be reduced somewhat by a system of licensing, by spot checks rather than complete inspections, by deputizing local residents to report on their neighbors, and similar expedients; but it remains a formidable prospect.

## Specifying Forest Practices

A further problem in regulating private forest management lies in specifying exactly what the owner must do.    This may be relatively simple in some cases.    For instance, Oregon law says:    "It is unlawful for any person to build a campfire upon lands not his own, without first clearing the ground immediately around it free from material which will carry fire."    There is no question what the campfire builder is compelled to do.    However, sometimes even what appears to be a simple policy such as felling dead snags to reduce the fire hazard can be implemented effectively only through compulsion if the required actions are spelled out in considerable detail.    The relevant section of the Washington Code, for example, reads:    "On forest lands west of the summit of the Cascade mountains, all snags or standing dead trees over twenty-five feet in height and sixteen inches and over in diameter breast high, shall be felled currently with the felling of live timber or with the current logging operation."

When attempts are made to compel owners to carry out more complex forestry activities, the difficulties multiply.    There is such a large variation in the local conditions affecting the establishment, growth, and survival of forest trees that no one practice is likely to be effective over wide areas. If the regulation is left general like the Washington requirement that in the course of logging adequate precautions must be taken "to leave reserve trees of commercial species deemed adequate under normal conditions to maintain continuous forest growth, or provide adequate stocking to insure future forest production," the private owner is not sure what he must do to comply with the law.   If an attempt is made to remedy this, as in Washington, by adding a clause that the law will be satisfied in the area west of the summit of the Cascade mountains if "there have been reserved and uncut not less than five percent of each quarter section, or lesser subdivision, well stocked with commercial coniferous trees not less than sixteen inches in diameter breast high outside the bark until such time as the area is adequately stocked by natural means," the practice thus specified may be effective in some places but fail completely to produce the desired results in others.   Silviculture is still largely an art today, but even when our scientific knowledge is greater it will require the skill of an experienced forester to decide exactly what practices will be effective in each situation. It is generally agreed that regulation of silvicultural management is on treacherous ground if it tries to specify detailed practices that must be followed.   If instead it merely specifies that certain ends must be attained —such as adequate restocking after harvest cuttings—then the government probably will have to be prepared to help private owners find the means of complying with the regulations.

## PUBLIC REGULATION TECHNIQUES

There are two basic means for compelling a private owner to manage his forest lands in the way it is felt will contribute most to policy objectives. The public may prohibit him from doing certain things that are considered undesirable or require him to do things considered desirable.   These are not exactly two sides of the same coin, even though in many cases they are close to it.   The state may, for example, prohibit people from allowing fires to escape into the woods, or it may require anyone building a fire in the open to take certain specified steps which presumably will make it impossible for the fire to escape.   In a situation where practically all wildfires started from intentionally built fires, requiring a specific performance from all fire builders would get results.   However, if wildfires were also originating from cigarettes, railroad trains, logging equipment, and children playing with matches, a prohibition against allowing fire to escape into the woods would be more effective.   Both of these approaches are followed in regulating private forest practices, but some of the techniques that can be used work better with one approach than with the other.

### Policing and Prosecution

Probably the simplest technique—in concept, if not in application—for regulating private practices is the establishment of a law and its enforcement by policing and the prosecution of violators.   A clearcut example of such a law is Oregon Revised Statute 477.715:  "It is unlawful wilfully and maliciously to set fire to any forest land, or any place from which fire may be communicated to forest land."   This law is designed to implement a policy of protecting Oregon's forests from fire by prohibiting people from starting fires intentionally to destroy forests.    (The presumption is that there are people who do, or are likely to do, such malicious fire setting.)

Two things are necessary if such a law is to serve its purpose: there must be some penalty for violating the law, and there must be some means of apprehending violators.    In our example, the penalty is provided by Oregon Revised Statute 477.993:    "(4) Violation of ORS 477.715 is punishable, upon conviction, by imprisonment in the penitentiary for not more than two years."    Severe though it is, this law by itself will not stop anyone from setting fires.    Unless there is some machinery for catching those who break the law and prosecuting them for their violations, the law will be ignored. This is a general problem of law enforcement but an especially difficult one in attempts to regulate the actions of private landowners.    As was noted earlier, many of the forest actions which are to be policed take place in areas where they are not easily noticed or observed.    The malicious setting of fires is an extreme example of this because anyone engaged in such an activity would be taking considerable pains to avoid detection.    All states have laws similar to that in Oregon, but few incendiaries are ever brought to trial.

A second reason for the poor enforcement record against incendiaries lies in the words "upon conviction."    In the United States, a person cannot be "deprived of life, liberty, or property without due process of law."    This means the prosecutors of the presumed incendiary must present evidence that proves beyond any reasonable doubt that this person did indeed wilfully and maliciously set the fire in question.    Now in most courts this will require a witness who actually saw him start the fire.    And even then there will be questions as to whether he acted wilfully and maliciously in doing so. The law against incendiaries is especially difficult to enforce, but other laws about forest use have the same problems, though in lesser degree.    Obviously, it is easier to enforce ORS 477.695 which says:    "Every person operating a railroad . . . shall annually . . . destroy or remove all flammable material from the right of way of the railroad."

## Permits and Licenses

Since one serious problem in enforcing regulation of the actions of private landowners is that of knowing when and where they are carrying on these actions, control can be made more effective by requring the landowners to notify the enforcing agency in advance of their proposed activities.    Some states merely require that the local fire warden be notified when an owner is planning to do some burning.    This can be made more formal and effective by requiring the owner to obtain a permit to carry on the activity in question.    Section 76.04.150 of the Revised Code of Washington, for example, says:    "No one shall burn any inflammable material within any county . . . in which there is a warden or ranger . . . without first obtaining permission in writing from the supervisor, or a warden, or ranger, and afterwards complying with the terms of said permit."

From the enforcement viewpoint there are many obvious advantages to a permit system. To begin with, the enforcing officials know in advance about all private actions which might involve a violation of the law and that therefore should be checked for compliance. Any such action which they do not know about in advance is bound to be a violation, because the person involved has not obtained the required permission. Secondly, the individual involved knows that the enforcing officials are aware of what he is doing and that he may be checked. Of course, he may still try to avoid some of the requirements of the law in the hope that he will not be checked, but a permit system seems certain to improve overall compliance. Thirdly, the private operator is made fully aware of the specific requirements of the law by the procedure he has to go through to get the permit and by the instructions printed on the permit form or given to him by the person who issues it. Finally, the official issuing permits can control the action involved in much greater detail than could have possibly been incorporated in the written law. Burning permits, for example, are not issued on days when weather conditions make it hazardous to build fires in the open. The warden often is also empowered to refuse to issue a permit when he feels that conditions at the proposed location are unduly hazardous.

A permit system gives the public agency a great deal of power over the actions of private individuals. Loss of an existing permit may have serious economic consequences for an individual, and he must be protected against arbitrary public action. "If a statute merely confers power on an administrative agency to grant a license, there is no implied power in that agency to revoke a license already granted, since the grantee of the license becomes vested with an interest which cannot be lightly revoked. However, if the legislature expressly confers power to revoke licenses already issued, the grantee of the license is legally subject to the hazard of revocation. . . . If an administrative agency seeks to revoke a license, the courts usually require as a matter of due process, that the licensee be given notice of the intended revocation and an opportunity to be heard." [12]

The Washington law specifically says: "The supervisor, any of his assistants, any warden or ranger, may refuse, revoke, or postpone the use of permits to burn when such act is clearly necessary for the safety of adjacent property." The loss suffered by the holder of a revoked burning permit cannot be very large, and no protection beyond the last clause of this law is apparently considered necessary.

The Oregon Forest Conservation Act, by contrast, is quite explicit. It first says that "it shall be unlawful for any person to harvest or cause to be harvested any timber or other forest tree products for commercial purposes from lands within Oregon without first having obtained a written permit for that year from the State Forester." It then provides that any such permit shall require the operator and landowner to comply with the other provisions of the act. These specify that certain seed sources must be left when the rest of the timber is cut. (Many specified details will be omitted here for brevity.) The act then provides for an examination by the state forester

[12] Jesse S. Raphael, *Governmental Regulation of Business,* The Free Press, New York, 1966, p. 63.

following harvesting and the issuance of a release from further penalties and obligations if the operations have complied with the law.   If the state forester detects any violation, he must notify the operator and landowner and direct the steps he deems necessary for future compliance.   If the operator fails to comply, the state forester is to order the operation discontinued and may suspend all permits for it.   Should the violation still continue, he may revoke the permits.

The law also specifically provides that "Any person affected by any finding or order of the State Forester . . . may appeal to the State Board of Forestry. . . .   An appeal from any decision of the board . . . may be taken . . . to the circuit court of the county in which the land . . . is located."   This gives the state forester considerable power to require steps to regenerate cutover lands but also protects the owner from arbitrary actions by him in exercising this power.   The revocation—or even prolonged suspension—of a harvesting permit could obviously work serious economic hardship on both operator and owner.

## Direct Public Intervention

We have already seen that it is often easier to prevent a private-forest owner from doing something considered undesirable than it is to compel him to do something desirable.   But the implementation of some policies requires actions by private landowners which they, for one reason or another, are not willing to do voluntarily.   In some cases, the difficulties involved in compelling the private owner to act are so great that it is simpler for the state to step in and act for him at his expense.

The Oregon Forest Conservation Act, which we have been using as an example, provides that when there has been a violation, the offending operator must furnish a cash deposit or surety bond to ensure that he will artificially restock the area within five years of the completion of the harvesting operations before he is permitted to resume operations.   If at the end of this five-year period the owner has not restocked the area and it has not become restocked naturally, "the State Forester shall enter upon the lands and take such steps as are necessary to correct the conditions caused by the violation."   The owner and operator then forfeit however much of the cash deposit or bond is needed to pay for the restocking work done by the state.

This is a fairly common technique for implementing protection policies. In an attempt to control the white pine blister rust by eradicating the currants and gooseberries which are the essential alternate host for the rust organism, the New York Conservation Law provides that:   "Owners shall remove from their lands . . . the plants of the genus Ribes. . . .   If any owner upon not less than 30 days' notice in writing fails to destroy Ribes on his property as herein provided, the Commissioner may cause such plants to be destroyed and the expense of such work shall be a charge aganst the owner which shall constitute a lien upon the land."

In such cases of public action on private lands, the line is rather fuzzy between the situation in which the public is forcing the private owner to carry out a desired action by doing it for him at his expense and the situation in which the public is carrying out a desirable activity and charging the cost to the beneficiaries roughly in proportion to the benefits they receive.  The latter is the situation in some states where forest fires are controlled by the state, but the cost is assessed against the forest owners on an acreage basis.  This could probably still be considered a form of compulsion, since the landowners are given no option about paying the assessment.  However, we do not usually define public regulation broadly enough to consider that we are being compelled to provide police protection for our property when part of the property taxes we pay are used to support our local police department.

## Zoning Forest-land Use

Zoning is basically a process of dividing land into districts and prescribing the use that may be made of the land in each class of district.  It may place restrictions on the dimensions of buildings and structures, the size and coverage of individual building lots or tracts, the density of population, and the use of structures and land.  "Zoning is mainly negative; it prohibits nonconforming uses but does not require positive actions.  Direct public controls that regulate practices are generally not applied as zoning ordinances." [13]

This negative aspect of zoning is probably the reason it has not been used more in rural and especially forested areas.  It often serves as a means of protecting landowners from undesirable actions by their neighbors, and this type of conflict has been more acute in the urbanized areas.  However, the current trend of urban sprawl is producing undesirable and conflicting uses even at some distance from the cities, and rural zoning may well play a larger role in the future than it has in the past.

The only major example of forest-land zoning is to be found in Wisconsin.  The first such zoning ordinance was adopted by Oneida County in 1933.  The county's initial objectives were: "to separate forest land from farm land; to facilitate the blocking-up of forest holdings; to prevent prospective farmers from wasting labor and capital on barren acres; to decrease forest-fire hazards; and, of great urgency at the time, to reduce the need for and the cost of road, school, and other services of local government." [14]  The county was divided into zoning districts of two types:  Forest-recreation districts and unrestricted districts.  In the forest-recreation districts only the following uses were permitted:

Production of forest products
Forest industries

[13] S. V. Ciriacy-Wantrup, *Resource Conservation Economics and Policy*, University of California Press, Berkeley, 1963, p. 283.
[14] Erling D. Solberg, *New Laws for New Forests*, The University of Wisconsin Press, Madison, 1961, p. 349.

Public and private parks, playgrounds, camp grounds, and golf grounds
Recreational camps and resorts
Private summer cottages and service buildings
Hunting and fishing cabins
Trappers' cabins
Boat liveries
Mines, quarries, and gravel pits
Hydroelectric lines, power plants, flowage areas, transmission lines, and substations

Family dwellings were expressly prohibited, and all other uses not listed above were excluded by implication.    In the unrestricted districts, any lawful use, including farming, was permitted.

Similar zoning ordinances were later passed by the other northern Wisconsin counties.    This zoning has apparently been quite successful in meeting the original objectives.    However, many conditions have changed since the 1930s, and the counties realize that their zoning will also have to be modified to meet the new demands on the land.    It is important to recognize that "Zoning is a tool for carrying out a land-use plan, not a substitute for planning; and its worth-whileness and general effectiveness always depend on the character of the planning upon which it is based." [15]

In a leaflet prepared for popular distribution, Solberg points out that zoning in primarily agricultural areas may serve mainly to protect the farmer. Among other things, it may protect him against curtailment of his normal farming practices.    "Nonfarm residents may object to some normal farming operations and practices.    Their objections may result in prohibition or regulation of . . . smoke from smudgepots; dust from farming operations; noises made by farm animals and by tractors that operate at night and in the early hours of the morning; poisonous pesticide sprays and dusts used on tree and field crops." [16]    The relevance of this for commercial forestry is indicated by a recent case where land developers bought a tract surrounded by industrial forest property and subsequently protested against logging activity on the industry lands as being inimical to their rights. Zoning may serve a useful purpose in keeping incompatible minor uses out of areas which are primarily suitable only for some other forest use.    The exclusion of logging or permanent recreation facilities from a wilderness zone is a good example.

Because of its relative inflexibility, zoning is hedged around by many legal requirements for public hearings, elections, and appeals procedures. It is not a tool that can be used easily to regulate private-forest use.    But as the pressure on land resources grows in the future and the conflicts between demands become more intense, zoning may be the ultimate solution to many forest land-use problems.

[15] Raleigh Barlowe, *Land Resource Economics,* Prentice-Hall, Inc., Englewood Cliffs, N.J., © 1958, p. 495.
[16] Erling D. Solberg, *Zoning for Rural Areas,* U.S. Department of Agriculture, Leaflet 510, 1965.

## Punitive Taxation

Where land is being underutilized or allowed to lie idle, it is sometimes suggested that it be appraised and taxed on the basis of its potential productivity rather than its actual current use.   The idea is that the owner will be forced to use his land more intensively or more efficiently in order to be able to pay the taxes.   Since much forest land is producing much less than the yield it is capable of, such a tax might appear a good way to implement a policy of increasing the yield of forest goods and services.

There are, however, many problems involved in trying to use taxes in this way.   A very careful and realistic appraisal would have to be made of the *net* returns that might be realized from more-intensive managment, because this will require the use of more capital and labor which may be quite expensive to obtain.   If more intensive management should actually be uneconomic, higher taxes might serve only to drive the land into other uses or even lead to its abandonment.   The "highest and best use" for much forest land appears on the current market to be something other than timber growing.   Higher taxes on such land might impel the owner to convert to this other use or to sell out to someone who wants land for that use. (Of course, the high prices paid for some of this forest land result from a "scarcity value," and if all forest owners tried to escape taxes by converting their lands to these other uses the market would be glutted and prices would collapse.)

Higher taxes could hardly serve to compel owners to manage their lands more aesthetically or to provide better watershed protection or for any other purpose from which they could not realize a financial gain.   In fact, the exact opposite course would appear to be the logical one with the owner being compensated for providing these social benefits by reduced taxes. In general, taxation does not appear to be a feasible means of implementing forest policies.   Tax concessions or adjustments are really a form of subsidy or of public assistance, and we will consider them in that context in Chapter 8.


## CONCLUSIONS

We saw in the last chapter that complete public ownership of the forest resources was not a feasible means of implementing forest policies in the United States.   Since a large part of our forest resources seem destined to remain in private ownership, we have explored in this chapter the idea of compelling these private owners to use their lands in the public interest and have found it to be more complicated than it might at first seem.   As Ordway says: "there is a considerable degree of speciousness in the thinking of those who believe that the law, if 'properly enacted,' could assure wise resource management.   There is a vast difference between laws that seek to establish national or state policy and create administrative agencies to carry out the policy, and laws which seek to compel, or prohibit, or regulate the cutting of trees, or the number of trout that may be taken in a day, or the number of ducks of one kind or another that can be killed in a year." [17]

Still we have a considerable amount of public control over private forest use in the United States, and it appears to be quite effective in the protection of the resource. Dana concluded in 1956 that "Although no one believes that legislation can force unwilling owners to adopt intensive forest practices, there is widespread belief that it can force them to stop destructive practices." [18]    Public control is probably necessary for this purpose regardless of what other actions are taken to implement forest policies.

With regard to the use of public regulation, Troup seems to have summarized it neatly: "Experience in countries where control over private forestry is exercised has shown that too strict a measure of compulsion destroys personal interest and leads to evasion of regulations, while too rigid a control over forest technique may result in killing initiative and sense of responsibility. So long as public interests are safeguarded, and a policy which ensures this is followed, the ideal is to promote community of interest between the private owner and the State, to encourage initiative, and to apply compulsion only where other methods fail." [19]    In Chapter 8 we will see what some of these other methods are and how effective they appear to be.

[17] Samuel H. Ordway, Jr., "The Law and Progress in Conservation," *Journal of Forestry*, June, 1959, p. 403.
[18] Samuel T. Dana, *Forest and Range Policy*, McGraw-Hill Book Company, New York, 1956, p. 345.
[19] Troup, *op. cit.*, p. 26.

# Public Cooperation
# with Private Forest Owners

We saw in Chapter 6 that a significant part of the forest resources of the United States is owned and operated by the public.   But we also observed that such public ownership runs counter to our general policy of private property rights and that there is strong opposition to increasing materially the public's share of forest ownership.   If forest resources are to remain in private ownership, they must be used in ways that conform to desired policies.   In Chapter 7 we saw that it is possible to compel private owners to use their lands as the public desires but that the government's power to do this is restricted in many ways in order to protect the private owners. Besides, compulsion often involves otherwise undesirable actions and runs into other difficulties in application.   It would not be feasible for the public to completely control all forest use in the United States.

This leaves a situation in which either the private owners will be allowed to use their forest properties largely as they see fit, or else the public must find ways of influencing what they do.   Historically our governments have always engaged in many activities affecting private owners and en-trepreneurs.   "Although government in this century is often seen primarily as restricting or restraining business, it has in fact continued to play an important role in protecting and aiding private enterprise." [1]   There are many ways that the public can influence the actions of private forest owners by cooperating with them.   The choice among these will depend on what is actually keeping the owner from acting the way society wants him to.

[1] Arthur M. Johnson, *Government-Business Relations*, Charles E. Merrill Publishing Co., Columbus, Ohio, 1965, p. 128.

116

## PROBLEMS IN PRIVATE LAND USE

In the United States most decisions about the use of private property are left to the owners of the property or to the entrepreneurs who manage the property for its owners.   Most goods and services are exchanged through a relatively free market system, though some groups and firms do have enough concentrated economic power to enable them to exert some control over prices and distribution.   A number of legal and other institutions supplement the market system to form the environment within which private property rights are exercised.

The existing market system and the other institutional influences encourage the private owner to use his forest lands in certain ways.   In general he does the things that produce benefits for him and avoids those actions which impose costs or other unpleasant effects on him.   He does not respond exclusively to monetary benefits and costs, but these do exert a strong influence on him.   He is not usually interested in producing benefits for other people unless he can sell them.   Where he has an opportunity to make choices, he is likely to select the action which will yield him the largest net personal revenue.   His choices are always limited, of course, by the restraints imposed on him by the market and existing institutions.

Now the course of action which is best—or appears to him to be best—under the existing circumstances may not be the one that is best from society's viewpoint.   (He may be able to make a handsome profit, for example, by logging a stand of redwood that the public would like to have preserved for the future.)   So the government steps in to try to change some of the circumstances that cause him to behave as he does.   The government's hope is that circumstances can be changed enough to make it most beneficial to him to do what society desires and that he will therefore proceed to do it voluntarily.

Many different kinds of situations may cause an owner to use his forest lands in socially unsatisfactory ways.   Public cooperation must overcome the specific limiting factors of the situation in which the owner actually finds himself if it is to be effective in getting him to change his land use.

### The Conflicting Interest Situation

The most difficult situation is that in which it actually would not be best for the owner himself under the existing circumstances to use his forest in the way that society desires.   The reasons why an owner may be better off personally not to manage his property according to society's desires fall into four main categories.   First, he may not be able to obtain a satisfactory revenue—and perhaps none at all—from the goods or services society wants him to produce, as in the case of scenic beauty.   Second, he may not be able to obtain—or could do so only at exorbitant cost—some factor essential to the socially desired use.   For example, the public may wish him to reforest an old burn, but the area may be so remote that he cannot get men to work there or else has to pay them such high wages that any future timber crop that might result from the planting will cost more than it could possibly sell for.

Third, final returns from the use the public desires may be realizable only at some distant future time.   The owner, for example, may be in his sixties and better off to continue growing Christmas trees with current annual revenues than to start growing sawtimber which will take sixty years to mature.   Fourth, the risk of loss may be greater in the socially desirable use than in some other.   In an area where wildfires are frequent and damaging, the owner may be better off to grow a fire-resistant but low-valued species of tree rather than a higher-valued species that is especially susceptible to fire.

In this first kind of situation the owner is led to act as he does by circumstances outside of his own personal control.   He may understand completely all the different ways in which he might use his forests and the personal benefits he might realize from these alternative uses.   He may be completely competent—in technical knowledge and in financial and other resources—to do what the public wants him to do.   He may even be sympathetic to the public's viewpoint.   But it is clear to him that circumstances outside of his control are such that to do what the public desires will mean a personal sacrifice on his part.   In this situation, and except in the cases of public-spirited or philanthropic individuals, the government can bring about a change in private forest use only by altering or offsetting the external conditions which control what the landowners are doing.

## The Lack of Knowledge Situation

In contrast to this first kind of situation is that in which the private owner actually would be as well or better off to use his forest as the public desires rather than in the way it is being used.   But he fails to change because he lacks the information or knowledge required to use his lands in the publicly desired manner.   Most government efforts to cooperate with private forest owners have assumed that it was this kind of situation that caused owners to act as they were doing.

It is rather obvious that an owner will not manage his forests in ways that he does not know about even if he would be better off to do so.   Two kinds of knowledge may be involved here: knowledge of possible uses and potential benefits from them and knowledge of techniques for applying these uses to the forest.   The first is most important because so long as it is lacking the second has no significance.   However, it may also be the easiest to overcome by government action.

A substantial part of the extension effort in agriculture over the years has been aimed at bringing to farmers information about new crops, new strains and hybrids, and new market outlets.   The extension agents have found it necessary to demonstrate to the farmers that such new uses for their lands are possible and that the returns from them can be attractive.   Only after they are aware of these things and interested in them is it possible to help farmers learn to use them on their own farms.    The primary problem is one of motivation.

However, even when an owner is aware of a particular use for his forest, realizes that he could benefit materially from it, and is anxious to put it into effect, he may not be able to do so for lack of the necessary technical knowledge.    Very few landowners are personally knowledgeable about the technical aspects of managing forests to produce goods and services. Helping motivated owners close this information-gap appears to be one of the most fruitful areas for public cooperation.

## The Lack of Ability Situation

There remains a third situation in which a different type of forest use would benefit the owner; he is aware of this, motivated to make the change, and perhaps even has the technical knowledge of how to do it; but for some reason he is not able to embark on the new practice.    There undoubtedly are psychological blocks to change on the part of many individuals.    But an owner may also lack any or all of three kinds of real and essential ability: physical, technical, and economic.

Many owners of small woodlands are women, are advanced in years, or are physically handicapped in some way that prevents strenuous outdoor work.    They may be well informed about what they could and should do with their properties.    They may even be desirous of using their forests differently.    But they are not physically able to plant trees, control insects, or maintain picnic grounds.    They might not even be able to inspect and supervise such work if they could hire someone else to do it.    Many such properties are therefore virtually unmanaged except for sporadic timber sales initiated by the buyers and casual use by hunters and fishermen. What these people obviously need is some means of delegating the physical care of their forests to someone capable of managing them.    Unless the public desires these forests to remain in status quo, some kind of management service has to be provided for such owners.    (Of course this does not necessarily have to be provided as a public service.)

Even if the owner is physically capable of managing his forest property, he may not be technically competent to do so.    The practice of silviculture and wildlife management are complex undertakings.    They require an understanding of the basic sciences, the working of the forest ecosystem, and the results that may be obtained by manipulating the vegetation, animals, and environment.    The owner may know in general what should be done with his forest but not enough to actually mark trees for a thinning, prepare a site properly for natural regeneration, or control an introduced disease. He needs varying degrees of help depending on the extent of his own technical knowledge and skills.

Finally, even a professional forester will not be able to put some practices into effect on his forest lands if he cannot obtain the financial means of paying for them.    Many changes in forest use require substantial investments, particularly when a use is proposed that will not bring in any revenue for some time. In the meantime, the owner must be financially able to carry the original investment and the current operating costs. The situation may also exist where the owner depends on the income from his property, and this would be curtailed or postponed for some time if he changes to some socially desirable form of use.

Although the above situations have been described separately, it is probably most common that a number of them impinge on one owner at the same time. The order in which they have been presented is significant, however. It is first necessary to overcome factors that keep it from being in the owner's personal best interest to manage his forest as society desires. Suppose investigation shows that even though it is socially desirable to keep the forests growing as much wood as possible, individual landowners are not justified in planting to assure full stocking after harvest cutting because of the very high cost of planting stock. Somehow planting stock must be made available to the private owners at a reasonable cost before any other efforts to promote better regeneration will be effective.

However, even if the state started a program to provide planting stock free, nothing still may happen if the landowners are not aware of the potential benefits to be derived from reforesting their cutover lands. It will also be necessary to get this information to the owners and to convince them that they should plant. But even then they may know nothing about planting so that additional information may also have to be provided.

But even if free planting stock is available and the owners are aware of the potential benefits of reforestation and generally informed as to how it is done, still nothing may happen. For the owners may not be physically able to plant trees and may not have sons or others who can help them; or they may not know the specific techniques of handling seedlings, preparing the site, and assuring survival after planting; or they may not have the financial resources to pay the costs of site preparation and planting even though the seedlings themselves are free.

It is thus important to seek for the limiting factor in each case and not to waste time and money trying to overcome some other factor that at present is not really the limiting one. But it also is important to recognize that if the currently limiting factor is overcome, some other factor may then become limiting and prevent the desired change from taking place. Public cooperation is a complex undertaking and one in which there are many opportunities for misguided and fruitless efforts.

## KINDS OF PUBLIC COOPERATION

As we have seen in the previous section, there are a variety of problems that prevent private forest owners from managing their lands as the public desires. There also are many different actions that governments might take to overcome these problems and encourage voluntary changes in private forest use.    In this section we will see what the major kinds of actions might be.    Then in the next section we will look at the specific government actions now in use.

The first kind of action that a government may take in an effort to implement a forest policy is a general promotional campaign.  We have defined a policy as an agreed-upon course of action but have recognized that there will seldom be complete agreement by everyone in the society.    If the policy is acceptable, the extent of the agreement should increase as more people become informed about the policy and their original misconceptions or biases are overcome.    A government may therefore engage in propaganda for a particular forest policy in order to develop a favorable climate of opinion for changes by the private owners.

Governments may then engage in five kinds of actions which are aimed specifically at overcoming the problems that prevent individual landowners from changing their practices.    The first of these is the assembly and dissemination of information needed by the owners in making management decisions.    As far as the landowner is concerned this kind of information might just as well not exist if it is not in a form that is readily available to him.    All kinds of media may be used to get information about forest practices, markets, prices, sources of materials, laws, and many other relevant items to the owners.

A second form of action is education of the landowners.    This goes beyond the mere distribution of information to programs in which forest owners can learn to use the information.    They may run the gamut from illustrated lectures on television through field demonstrations and correspondence courses to quite formal short courses at colleges.    These are normally mass efforts aimed at groups of people rather than individuals.

A third form involves individual guidance of the owner.    The aim here is to come to grips with the specific problems of a particular owner through personal counseling.    It may be done by phone or correspondence, in the government agent's office, or at any place where the two get together.    The most effective work of this kind is done on the ground where the problems actually exist.

A fourth form of action may carry this a step farther and provide assistance to the landowner in performing certain operations.    The government forester may help the landowner mark trees for a thinning or locate a road or picnic ground.    The owner is still doing the work himself but with actual physical assistance.

The final form is a service program in which the government agency does the work for the landowner.    The public foresters conduct a spraying operation for insect control or mark timber for harvest.    Usually the landowner is billed for at least part of the cost of such service activities.

These five kinds of public action are not mutually exclusive, and many government agencies engage in a number of them at the same time.    However, they are not all equally effective for dealing with the same kinds of private-owner problems.    The amount of public effort and the cost per landowner affected increase in the order in which they have been listed. A public service program represents a much larger and more expensive undertaking than an information program.   There are many difficulties, therefore, in fitting the actions to the problems in order to accomplish objectives at the least cost.

There is still another kind of possible public action aimed directly at individual owners that differs from the five described above.   Those five are intended primarily to offset disadvantages that a private owner faces in managing his forest under existing market and institutional conditions. But the situation may exist where even with such public assistance the landowner will not find it attractive to manage his forest as the public desires.   However, it may still be possible to get him to change his practices by means of a subsidy.   The subsidy may take the form of a cost reduction such as the production and sale of planting stock at cost by state nurseries.   It may consist of a modification of taxes, or it may be an outright incentive payment for carrying out some practice.   Many private forest owners shy away from the idea of a public subsidy, but the fact is that private business and agriculture are both already heavily subsidized in many ways today.

Another type of public cooperation consists of activities beneficial to all of the forest economy.   The outstanding example is publicly supported forestry research.   The education at public expense of professional foresters and forestry technicians is another.   Without such public activities it would be very difficult for most private owners to manage their properties at all intensively.

There is still one other form of government action that is not strictly cooperation but does serve to affect the use of private forests.   This is the case where the government takes an easement on private property to permit certain public uses.   A similar situation would be the leasing of private land for public use.   In both cases the private owner retains title to the land, and in the case of an easement he continues to be able to use the land in any way that does not conflict with the rights granted to the public by the easement.   These are techniques that may serve to compensate private owners for social benefits—such as scenic beauty—from which they cannot obtain any ordinary revenue.

## GOVERNMENT PROGRAMS FOR PRIVATE FOREST OWNERS

The public is actively trying to influence private forest use through a variety of programs.   A detailed consideration of these many programs would fill a book by itself.   Here we will just try to see what kind of programs have been developed to deal with the problems we have been discussing and what they indicate about feasible approaches to public cooperation.

A useful way of grouping these programs appears to be in terms of the three broad classes of problem situations discussed at the beginning of this chapter.    It will be more effective, however, if we reverse the order in which they were presented earlier and start with the private owners' lack of ability.

## Overcoming a Lack of Ability

It is very difficult for a private owner to protect his forest against fire, insects, and epidemic diseases by himself.    For this reason among the earliest public actions were programs of fire prevention and control.    Fire prevention is mainly a public activity, although the "Keep Green" and other private programs have played an important role.    The detection of wildfires is also largely handled by public organizations.    Fire suppression is more truly cooperative, with the state agencies doing most of the preplanning and overall organization and the private owners cooperating in the actual fire fighting.    Organized fire protection now covers most of the forest land in the country.

Insects and diseases respect neither property lines nor political boundaries so that even the states cannot always cope effectively with them. The federal and state agencies handle the necessary occurrence surveys and operate the quarantines where these are used.    Suppression of outbreaks is a cooperative undertaking, but since it often involves large-scale operations such as aerial spraying, the activities of all but the largest forest owners are often limited to helping defray the cost.

Most owners of large forest properties employ foresters to handle the technical details of their management.    But the small-property owners have no such employees and most of them lack this technical ability themselves. To meet this need, the states provide service foresters (called farm foresters in some states) under the Cooperative Forest Management Program which is partly financed by the federal government.    The service foresters inspect private properties and give on-the-ground advice and planning assistance for tree planting, forest improvement, and the harvesting and sale of mature timber.    They do a limited amount of tree marking for cutting and in some states will mark entire tracts on a fee basis.    They also attempt to make follow-up inspections to be sure the work is done properly and to advise on future management of the forest.

Assistance in planning the use of their land is provided to farmers through the Soil Conservation Districts, which are legally separate units of state government.    The actual technical help is given by work unit conservationists employed by the federal Soil Conservation Service.    These conservationists draw up basic plans for the farms and include the woodlands as part of the whole.    The attention given to the woodlands is of a very general nature, and where more detailed help is necessary the owner is usually referred to the state service forester.    The greatest value of this service perhaps lies in the integration of the forest land as a part of the overall going farm operation.

Many owners lack adequate economic resources to manage their lands as the public might prefer.   An early and continuing effort to overcome this part is the operation of state nurseries and the sale of tree seedlings to landowners at cost.   Only the largest forest owners can afford to operate their own nurseries.   Although many independent private nurseries exist, most state nurseries are larger and more efficient and provide a cheaper source of planting stock.   An exception is the Nisqually Nursery in Washington, which is operated cooperatively by forest industries.

Financial aid is made available to landowners for some forestry practices through the Agricultural Conservation Program.   This is basically a farm program and covers a wide range of agricultural practices, but cost sharing for forestry practices is not limited to land on farms.   The particular practices which the available federal appropriation will be used to support in any year are selected locally and vary from one state to another.   Only two forestry practices have been supported: "planting trees or shrubs for forestry purposes" and "improvement of a stand of forest trees."   The landowner must request the ACP to share his cost and perform the work according to recognized standards.   The ACP payment he receives is based on fixed amounts per acre which have represented about three-fourths of the average actual total cost.   In 1967 the average per-acre payments were $16.19 for tree planting and $8.42 for stand improvement.   In that year, trees were planted with ACP assistance on 174,000 acres and stand improvement was done on 220,000 acres.[2]

Since most forest-management practices will eventually bring in a return, the owner's lack of capital might be met satisfactorily if he could borrow money to carry him over the intervening time between outlay and income. One attempt to make credit more readily available is provided by the Federal Land Banks which make loans through local Federal Land Bank Associations.   Although all stock in the Land Banks is now privately held, they were started with federal funds and are supervised by the federal Farm Credit Administration.   The Land Banks make loans for agricultural and forestry purposes at rates which cannot by law exceed 6 percent.   They require a first mortgage on the property and have fairly exacting requirements as to the condition of the collateral property and the use that is made of it.   In October, 1966, a total of 960 loans were outstanding with a value of 45 million dollars.[3]

This very sketchy summary of government programs aimed at overcoming the forest owner's lack of ability to change his practices indicates that considerable help is available to any owner who wishes to manage his forest lands.   The assumption has been that a lack of physical, technical, or economic ability was largely to blame for people not using their forests differently.   Public assistance in fire control dates back to the turn of the century.   State distribution of planting stock began in 1924.   Cost sharing of the ACP type dates from 1936, and management assistance to farm-

[2] *Agricultural Conservation Program, 1967, 1966, 1965 Summary*, Agricultural Stabilization and Conservation Service, Washington, 1968, pp. 61, 67.
[3] William C. Siegel, *Federal Land Bank Timber Loans in the United States*, U.S. Forest Service Research Paper SO-29, 1967.

woodland owners began in 1940.  These programs have had a decided effect.  But since many private forest lands are still not being managed to the satisfaction of the public, it is obvious that they do not provide the entire answer.

## Overcoming a Lack of Information

Part of the reason that private forest owners have not taken more advantage of the forms of public cooperation described above may be that they have not understood the potential of their forest holdings nor known what they could do with them.  The governments have long tried to provide this sort of information for private owners starting with the Division of Forestry in the Department of Agriculture in the late 1800s.

Cooperative agricultural extension work between the Department of Agriculture and the land-grant colleges began in 1914.  Forestry became a part of the cooperative extension program in 1924.  This program functions through a system of county agents backed up by a staff of specialists in the state headquarters.  The extension foresters work largely through the county agents but also do a considerable amount of direct educational work with landowners through demonstrations, meetings, correspondence, and some on-the-ground advice.  They prepare bulletins and other forms of printed material for distribution to forest owners.  In some states the extension foresters collect and distribute information on markets and current prices.

The federal Forest Service and most state forestry departments carry on programs of information and education, at least part of which is aimed at forest owners.  These programs use the mass media—radio, television, newspapers, magazines, advertising posters—as well as bulletins, leaflets, and moving-picture films which are distributed or made available to interested groups.  They have been most effective, perhaps, in fire prevention but have also carried forestry information of all kinds to a wide public.

Various departments in a number of states regularly publish information on markets for forest products and the prices currently being paid.  Some include specifications and other information helpful to an owner who wants to sell his own timber.  Vocational agricultural programs in some rural high schools include a limited amount of forestry in their subject-matter coverage.  The cooperative forest-management and soil-conservation programs also do a good bit of general educational work in addition to their specific services.

As in the case of overcoming a lack of ability, we see that the governments have been striving for many years to overcome forest owners' lack of information.  It is therefore rather surprising that so many of these owners are still quite ignorant about forest-land use and the many sources of public assistance available to them.

## Overcoming a Lack of Incentive

We find ourselves back at the situation, then, where it may not be in the forest owner's personal interest to use his lands as the public desires. If satisfactory land use is to be obtained voluntarily, the government must provide an incentive for the landowner. Such an incentive may take various forms but it is rather generally assumed that the strongest incentive is a financial one. A landowner will be reluctant to change to a use that will make him worse off financially and will have little incentive to change to a use that will not make him better off.

Many of the progams described in the preceding two sections function to reduce the cost to the landowner of managing his forest. For example, in most cases the full cost of fire protection and insect control are not charged to the private owners who benefit from them. In many states the private owner makes no direct contribution to the financing of the state and county forest-fire control organization. (Of course he contributes through the taxes he pays but so do the other taxpayers who own no forest land.) Such programs usually not only help the forest owner by doing something that would be very difficult—or perhaps impossible—for him to do himself but they also do it at little or no direct cost to him. Where the full cost of protection activities is not charged to the private-forest owners, they are at least partly a form of subsidy to him.

Similar partial subsidies also exist in the state-forest tree-nursery programs, the cooperative forest-management tree-marking programs, and the soil-conservation land-planning programs. In all of these cases, the same service could be obtained from private sources but usually only at a higher cost. Objections are occasionally raised by private business to this kind of public competition. State-grown tree-planting stock is ordinarily restricted to use in actual forest planting or on farms and cannot be resold with roots attached. In order to avoid competition with private nurserymen, the Oregon Forest Nursery, for example, requires buyers to sign a certification that "the trees included in this order will be used in compliance with the above limitations and are to be planted on farm or forest land owned or leased by me, which is outside of incorporated city limits."

Marking of trees for cutting under the cooperative forest-management program is often limited to demonstrations involving only a few days' work. The state service foresters generally profess to the practice of referring marking jobs of any size to the nearest private forestry consultants. Even where such private services exist, however, the fees they necessarily must charge may be high enough to eliminate any incentive for some owners to have their harvest cuttings properly handled. Any subsidy program is likely to involve some conflict with private business, because there would be no need for the subsidy if the landowners did not consider the cost of the available private services to be relatively too high. An effort by the government to overcome some of the existing market or institutional factors that lead private owners to behave as they do will almost inevitably work to the disadvantage of some existing private interests.

A government action aimed at part of the problem of waiting a long time for the returns from some kinds of forest use is the substitution of a yield tax for the ordinary annual property tax.   Under most yield tax laws the owner pays only a nominal annual tax on the land until he finally harvests his timber.   At that time he pays a yield tax based on the actual value of the timber sold.   The objective in most yield tax laws is to impose about the same amount of tax but to collect it at a time when the landowner has income from which to pay.   The yield tax also eliminates some of the risk from growing timber in that if anything should happen to reduce the value of the final crop, the tax will also be reduced, which would not generally be true of taxes paid annually in advance of harvest.   Not all states have instituted a yield tax, and where they do exist they usually give the forest owner the option of continuing under the regular ad valorem tax arrangement.

A more widely applied government action of a subsidy nature is the capital gains treatment of income from timber allowed in the computation of a forest owner's federal income tax.   The actual application of the capital-gains provision for timber income involves many complexities that are not significant for our present discussion.   In simplest terms, this provision allows an owner to report the increase in value of his timber between the date when he obtained it and the date when he sells it as a capital gain rather than as ordinary income.   For example, if a man buys a tract of timber for $10,000, holds it for five years, and then sells it for $12,000, the $2,000 difference is considered to be a capital gain.

The significance of this is that capital gains are taxed at one-half the ordinary income tax rate, and the maximum capital-gains tax cannot exceed 25 percent.   Since after-tax income is what a person can use for consumers goods or other purposes, this provision of the income tax law has the same effect as an increase in revenue from the property.   Suppose an individual who is in the 50 percent income tax bracket has a net revenue from a timber sale of $1,000 (after deducting what he paid originally for the timber).   His capital gains tax will be $250 and his after-tax income $750.   If he received his income from ordinary sources he would have to get $1,500 to be as well off after taxes as he is with the timber.

The size of the effect of the capital-gains provision depends on the income tax bracket in which the owner falls.   If the man above with the $1,000 from the timber sale were in the 20 percent bracket, he would have an after-tax income of $900.   To be equally well off after taxes he would have to receive $1,125 of ordinary income.   In any case, when the government allowed owners to treat timber income as a capital gain the effect was the same as if it had increased their revenue from timber by a substantial amount.

A government might offset some of the risk of price changes by supporting prices as has been done with some agricultural crops.   The only current example is the Naval Stores Price Support Program.   (Naval stores are products made from pine resin and consist mainly of turpentine and rosin.)   This program applies only to gum collected from living trees and not to products distilled from stumps or extracted in the process of making paper pulp.   The price of crude pine gum is supported through loans on gum rosin.   Under the loan program, if the price of rosin falls below the support level, the producer can deposit his rosin as collateral and borrow its value at the support price.   Depending on what the market price does, he may later retrieve his rosin and sell it in the market or let the government assume its ownership.   For 1967 the support price was set at 74 percent of parity (parity being the price which is assumed to give an exchange value for things a farmer buys equivalent to that existing in the period 1910–1914).   While this is not exactly an example of government action to encourage a particular type of forest use, it does show how price supports might be applied to forests; in this case with an objective of stabilizing a domestic industry and local economy.

We see that although the governments have taken some actions to overcome a lack of incentive, these have been neither as numerous nor extensive as the actions aimed at information and ability.   They also have been concerned almost exclusively with timber growing.   There have so far been no real attempts to use subsidies as a means of encouraging recreation development or the maintenance of natural beauty.

## PUBLIC COOPERATION IN PERSPECTIVE

It is difficult to find in the literature any real assessment of public cooperation as a means of implementing forest policies.   Dana has commented, for example, that "The steady growth of public cooperation with private owners during the last fifty years has been one of the most striking and most promising developments in the field of forest policy." [4]   Beyond this, however, he talks mainly about the successful development of legislative support for programs and of the establishment of these programs at the state and federal level. There is little discussion of what these programs have accomplished.

McMahon has noted a "seeming tendency to confuse program participation with program success" and points out that "total number of acres treated annually under a program, dollars expended per year in various programs, or number of owners assisted per year by service foresters do not show increases in intensification nor do they disclose permanency of results." [5]   Part of the reason for this is no doubt historical.   Forestry is only about 70 years old in this country.   In its early days, it was obvious that nothing was being done to perpetuate the forests, and there was serious talk of an impending timber "famine."   The problem seemed so large and urgent that any activity aimed at forest conservation appeared justified.   But forestry efforts seldom show immediate results.   The Nationwide Forest

[4] Samuel T. Dana, *Forest and Range Policy*, McGraw-Hill Book Company, New York, 1956, p. 339.
[5] Robert O. McMahon, *Private Nonindustrial Ownership of Forest Land*, Yale University, School of Forestry, Bull. No. 68, 1964, p. 91.

Survey continued to show timber drain far in excess of growth up to the early 1950s.  Most forest land was still virtually unmanaged, and the public programs had made only a slight dent in this huge problem.  It seemed clear that the programs must be expanded to reach more forest owners.

Another reason for confusion about the effectiveness of these programs is uncertainty as to their prime objectives.  In discussing four of these programs—Cooperative Forest Management, the Agricultural Conservation Program, Soil Conservation Districts, and the Forestry Extension Program— Muench emphasizes that "the objectives of these programs are far from clear and hence must be determined by inference—a task made even more difficult due to the complexity of the objectives." [6]  He shows that the objectives of these four programs are partly income redistribution and partly resource allocation.  They are aimed at least as much at increasing the incomes of the landowners as they are at producing more timber or other forestry objectives.

This brings us to another important fact—that a significant share of the public cooperation with private forest owners has been part of larger and broader programs of public cooperation with farmers.  Of the four programs discussed by Muench, only Cooperative Forest Management has been independent of an agricultural program, and it started out as the Cooperative Farm Forestry Program in 1936, being broadened to include all private forest owners only in 1950.  There is no objection to agricultural programs as such.  The unfortunate thing is that forestry has so often been added on as a sort of rider to agricultural programs mainly because they offered an opportunity to get financial and other support for forest activities.  Many of the objectives of agricultural policy—such as the achievement of parity incomes for farmers and the maintenance and improvement of the family farm—are only distantly related to most objectives of forest policy.  But the forestry parts of these programs have had to be developed with these other objectives in mind.

Public cooperation with private forest owners carries a heavy connotation in the United States of aid to small-forest owners.  In the early days of forestry in this country much was heard about the "timber barons" and the ruthless way in which they were exploiting their large holdings.  But as intensive forest management expanded rapidly on the industrial properties in the years following World War II, such talk rapidly disappeared and today little criticism is heard of the large private owners.  The small-forest owner has come to the fore as the nation's "number one forestry problem." Not much attention has been given, however, to the tremendous variability among these small-forest owners and the effect this is bound to have on their response to public cooperation.

Little real attention has been paid to the relation between the size of the small private holding and the cost of public cooperation with its owner.

[6] John Muench, Jr., *Private Forests and Public Programs in North Carolina*, The American Forestry Association, Washington, no date (circa 1965), p. 79.

It is true that Stoddard did note that "Public assistance programs have never given priority to ownerships with the greatest possibility for returns" and recommend that "Any acceleration of public or private forestry assistance should give priority to tracts of sufficient acreage to warrant the owner's attention and continued interest in forestry." [7] Many years ago, I pointed out that forestry education and advice to landowners in the South might cost over 20 times as much per acre on farms averaging less than 100 acres as it would on farms averaging over 500 acres in size.[8] Public foresters in the field are aware of this, but it has not entered much into program planning.

Public cooperation is not limited to the small-forest owners, however. Some forms like the capital-gains treatment of timber income are probably more significant for the large owner than for the small. Musolf has noted that "Promotionalism tends to produce great reticence among its beneficiaries." [9] The large private owners have had little to say about the cooperation they were receiving from the government except when some program is threatened. Very few people outside of the Deep South are even aware of the existence of a Naval Stores Price Support Program, for example. There is some justification for such reticence since the forest industry knows that because of its somewhat unsavory history it is a ready-made whipping boy for the press and politicians. Every attempt by the industry to promote a modification of tax or other policies—no matter how well-intentioned—is met with suspicion by the general public. Cooperation of the public with the larger owners therefore tends to receive much less publicity than do the efforts aimed at smaller owners.

One final point needs to be made and can perhaps be best approached through an example. In 1955, Resources for the Future asked a number of outstanding specialists in forestry and related fields to study the effect of credit on the ways in which forest lands were being used. The findings of this committee were published in 1958 as a 168-page book. Tucked away in the second paragraph of the "Summary and conclusions" is a key sentence: "Credit alone will not solve the problem of low production and poor returns on these small holdings." [10] But this is followed by 22 pages of conclusions about what is "adequate" credit for forestry, the institutional situation with regard to credit, ways of making credit more adequate, etc. The study itself was thorough and complete—on credit. But it did not come to grips with what would really implement the desired policy, which apparently was more intensive timber management on small properties.

Much of the public cooperation effort has been based on what people thought would implement desired policies. Experience has shown that many of these earlier ideas were incorrect. Perhaps even more important,

[7] Charles H. Stoddard, *The Small Private Forest in the United States,* Resources for the Future, Washington, 1961, p. 152.
[8] Albert C. Worrell, "Optimum Intensity of Forest Land Use on a Regional Basis," *Forest Science,* September, 1956, p. 218.
[9] Lloyd D. Musolf, *Government and the Economy,* Scott, Foresman and Company, Chicago, 1965, p. 26.
[10] *Forest Credit in the United States,* Resources for the Future, Washington, 1958, p. 72.

the world and forestry's place in it have changed since many of the existing programs were started.   The following general comment by Musolf appears to apply with considerable force to the forestry situation: "Just as generals are sometimes said to prepare for the last war, so some promotional policies appear to be designed to preserve outdated economic arrangements rather than to facilitate an adjustment to new trends." [11]

[11] Musolf, *op. cit.*, p. 33.

# Nongovernmental Implementation of Forest Policies

The three preceding chapters have been concerned entirely with ways in which governments act to implement forest policies.  But policies do not necessarily have to be implemented by governments.  We are basically a private enterprise society and historically have placed a high value on private initiative and freedom from governmental interference.  It is true that the scope of government activity in the United States has increased greatly and that today we accept without question government actions that would have been considered unreasonable fifty years ago.  But we still rely heavily on private actions to achieve many of our policy objectives.

This nongovernmental implementation takes two major forms.  Individuals, business firms, and associations of various kinds engage in a variety of overt actions with the intention of making certain forest policies effective. We will devote a large part of this chapter to a consideration of these kinds of private actions.  The social group also exerts many kinds of controls over the actions of its individual members that are not always obvious and some of which are not even recognized by the individual being controlled. We will consider how such social control may function to implement forest policies first and then proceed to the more specific private actions.

## SOCIAL CONTROL OF FOREST USE

Modern man spends all of his life as a member of various social groups. From his very beginning he is influenced in many ways by the groups with which he lives.    During the course of history, man has learned to live an orderly group existence, and the ways of doing this are passed on to new members as they are born into the group.    As Landis says, "The individual lives in society not with a consciousness that he is being beaten into subjection by some visible or invisible authority.    Instead he has a live consciousness of the presence of others in the world he inhabits, he is alert to the teachings that social experience brings, and he almost inevitably develops a sense of responsibility to others because of certain lessons that experience teaches." [1]

People adjust to the various pressures and influences that their society exerts on them and in most respects develop the feeling that this is the right way to live.    Part of this social control takes the form of governmental actions of the kinds described in Chapters 7 and 8.    However, "social control embraces not only such agencies as law, authority, punishment, codes, and creeds, mores, customs, traditions, and the subtle influence of group expectancy, but also the educational process, formal and informal, by which the individual is made a part of the social system." [2]    It is clear that there are many factors working to control not only what an individual does in certain situations but also how he thinks about most things.

This has had much to do with how forests have been used in the United States.    For centuries the forests were an obstacle to settlement.    The proper thing for a man to do was destroy the forest and clear the land so it could be cultivated and pastured.    There was no tradition or custom of managing forests permanently in this country, and rural people did not grow up thinking of forests in the same way that they thought of agricultural crops and livestock.    Even immigrants from European countries where forestry was practiced did not find a climate of opinion here that encouraged them to protect and manage their farm woodlands.

As we have noted in earlier chapters, the American attitude toward the forest resources began to change in the late nineteenth century and is now considerably different from what it was a hundred years ago.    The forest landowner today feels many new kinds of social control than those to which even his father was exposed.    The idea that property ownership carries public responsibilities is relatively new.    So is the idea that recreation deserves a prominent place in forest management.    Newest of all is the emphasis on natural beauty and the idea that a forest owner does not have the right to destroy it.

Aldo Leopold was proposing further changes in the direction of stronger social controls when he called for a land ethic.    "An ethic may be regarded as a mode of guidance for meeting ecological situations so new or intricate, or involving such deferred reactions, that the path of social expediency is not discernible to the average individual.    Animal instincts are modes of guidance for the individual in meeting such situations.    Ethics are pos-

[1] Paul H. Landis, Social Control, J. B. Lippincott Company, Philadelphia, 1956, p. 25.
[2] Ibid., p. 12.

sibly a kind of community instinct in-the-making." [3]    There appears to have been considerable progress in this direction since Leopold wrote this. By a variety of means people have become aware of the effects of man's actions on his environment and of the potential reactions of the environment on man.

The educational process is a potent force for changing land use in socially desirable directions.    The average forest-industry executive today has a much different attitude toward the resources on which his industry is based than did even the generation of executives that preceded him. Many forest owners are aware today that their fellowmen expect certain actions from them and are responding to this group expectancy in many ways, like voluntarily providing for public recreation on their lands.    Public opinion is widely respected in the business world, and great efforts are made to develop a favorable public image.    It is extremely difficult to measure the extent to which such forms of public control are actively serving to implement forest policies but there is no doubt that their total impact is large.


## EXPLICIT ACTIONS TO IMPLEMENT POLICIES

For purposes of discussion it will help to separate the private actors and actions into broad classes.    Those who implement policies divide into independent operators (individuals, firms, corporations) and organized groups (associations, societies, clubs).    The types of actions divide into those carried out by the actor himself and those which he tries to get someone else to do.

### Self-implementing Actions

The most direct and effective way to implement a forest policy is for the owner of the forest resource to decide and proceed to do whatever is necessary on his own property to make the policy effective.    Suppose it were an accepted policy that all commercial timberland should be kept in production by reforesting it immediately after harvesting or destruction of the stand by fire or other catastrophe.    If every landowner agreed that this was a good policy and voluntarily proceeded to reforest his own lands, there would be complete implementation of the policy.    Obviously, the reason that we have devoted so many pages to other means of implementing policies lies in the fact that this kind of self-implementation is not sufficiently common to satisfactorily implement most forest policies.

However, it is important to recognize that in many cases this is a feasible alternative to government regulation or public ownership.    And it is being used.    The large private landowners have for many years been implementing on their own properties the policy of adequate supplies of wood for the future.    They are moving toward implementation of a policy of out-

[3] Aldo Leopold, A Sand County Almanac, Oxford University Press, New York, 1949, p. 203.

door recreation for our people.    Now it may be argued that what they are really doing is responding to the kinds of social controls we discussed at the beginning of this chapter.    Or, less kindly, it might be said that they are merely reacting to the threat of government regulation or expropriation of their forest lands.    There are so many influences of these kinds operating that it would be hard to prove what actually moves the private owner to take the actions he does.    But there certainly are indications that in many cases these owners are acting voluntarily because they are convinced it is the right thing to do.

We saw in Chapter 8 that the price-and-market system does not function perfectly to guide the private forest owner into using his lands as the rest of society desires.    Sometimes it is because the signals from the potential consumers do not reach him.    Sometimes there are imperfections in the market or monopolistic controls which prevent him from moving as he would desire.    When the private forest owner recognizes these problems, he may take various kinds of private actions—by himself or jointly with other private owners—to overcome them.    The solution to these market imperfections does not necessarily lie in governmental actions, as may have been implied in Chapter 8.

A few examples will indicate the possibilities of private action.    We have seen that there are economies of scale in forest management so that large properties are more efficient to operate than small ones.    A forest landowner might therefore overcome some of the obstacles to certain kinds of use by increasing the size of his operation.    This process has been going on for some time as the wood-using-industry owners in particular have tried to put together properties of efficient size.    The Committee on Forest Credit concluded that "One of the most pressing problems with respect to the small non-farm holding is that of devising and encouraging steps that will lead to consolidation or joint management arrangements whereby such units can be brought under effective management." [4]    The general trend has been for such small properties to be absorbed by larger ownerships rather than to go together to form a larger operating unit.

Close to three hundred individuals and firms advertise their services as forestry consultants in the United States.    There is a great deal of variation among these consultants in the kinds of services they are capable of providing.    But the fact that so many of them are in business indicates that many private landowners are availing themselves of this means of overcoming some of the problems they face.    Particularly through assistance in marketing, a consultant may increase the economic opportunity for more intensive forest-land use.

## Self-implementing Group Actions

There are serious limitations to what a single landowner can do to overcome obstacles to better land use, especially if he does not control much land or has only limited financial resources.    But a group of such land-

[4] *Forest Credit in the United States*, Resources for the Future, Washington, 1958, p. 85.

owners working together often find it possible to accomplish things that none of them could do alone.   Over the years a number of groups have been organized to deal with various forest problems.   They fall into three general categories: cooperatives, management-service associations, and general forest-landowner associations.

**Cooperatives**   In theory, the cooperative appears to provide an answer to many small-forest-property problems; in practice, no forestry cooperative in the United States has ever enjoyed more than temporary success, and all have eventually failed.   Most of these have been cooperative-marketing associations, based on the assumption that the primary problem of the small-forest owner lay in obtaining a satisfactory revenue from his forest products.   Since timber and even logs are relatively low-value products, an attempt was sometimes made to extract more of the value added by expanding into the manufacturing stages.   Some of the more successful cooperatives—such as the Otsego Forest Products Cooperative Association—were actually integrated-processing organizations.   For a variety of reasons they have not proved capable of competing successfully with other private forest-product firms.   Experience seems to demonstrate rather conclusively that the cooperative is not an effective device for implementing forest policies in the United States.

**Management-service associations**   Associations of this type are organized primarily to perform management and operating services but may also arrange to market the products of their members or clients.   They do not usually go into the manufacturing stages as most of the cooperatives have done.   The function of a management-service association is to provide actual planning and supervision of going forest operations rather than advice or plans for an owner to carry out himself.   By combining enough small operations, it may build up enough total activity to achieve many of the economies of scale which could not be attained on a single small operation.

No true management-service associations exist in the United States today.   The nearest approximations are the New England Forestry Foundation and Connwood, Inc.   The New England Forestry Foundation is organized as a nonprofit service corporation.   Its capital has originated in the form of gifts and contributions.   The Foundation performs various management services for landowners in its operating territory.   The fees charged cover most of the cost of these services.   It is not a membership organization, and there is no permanent contractual arrangement with the owners serviced by it.   Rather it is a service organization which is available to any forest owner who wishes to take advantage of its superior ability to handle a particular management problem for him.

Connwood, Inc. is organized as a cooperative corporation, and its capital was obtained through the sale of stock.   It provides a variety of management and marketing services for landowners in southern New England.

These are not restricted to the stockholders, who actually are quite few in number.   It does not presently operate on the basis of providing services to its own members or a permanent set of clients, although it does have some continuing management agreements.   Instead Connwood functions much like any other private forestry-consulting firm.

Like the cooperative, the management-service association looks good on paper but does not seem to work out in the United States.   It is worthwhile to analyze the reasons for this in some detail for it probably provides important hints about future forest-policy development.   In describing the successful operation of the Forest Owners' Association in Sweden, Stoddard makes the following significant observations:   "The existence of compulsory public forestry regulations, which prevent liquidation cuttings and provide close technical guidance, appears to leave no alternative other than intensive forest management at a high-yield level.   Thus the combination of regulations and organized marketing constitutes a 'stick and carrot' approach which brings the economies of large-scale, efficient forestry to small holdings while preserving the institution of individual ownership." [5]   This raises the question of whether an economic motivation alone is sufficient to bring forest owners together in a cooperative or management-service association.

More important, however, is probably the fact that in order to operate economically a cooperative or a management-service association has to do a sizable volume of business.   This means that it has to control a substantial area of forest land.   And since these devices are intended to benefit small properties, this in turn means that such an organization has to have a large number of members or clients.   Attracting and holding together a large group of landowners is a serious problem.   But it is compounded by the fact that those owners who have properties with real productive potential often find other means of solving their problems.   (An historical difficulty of forest cooperatives in this country has been the fact that as soon as economic conditions picked up or new markets developed, many of their members withdrew, preferring to make their own arrangements with timber buyers.)   The group organization is therefore left with the properties which primarily need long-time rehabilitation of growing stock or which contain the poorest sites and least-productive forest types.   Such a low per-acre output and high average-cost situation has proved a fatal handicap in the very competitive market for timber products.

Stoddard's review of the group-management programs operating in northern Europe is perhaps even more revealing than he realized:   "Two important factors must be recognized in reviewing the relative success of these European efforts:   (1) forestry and forest products are, and have been for some time, a sector of major importance in the economies of these nations; and (2) their national philosophy, while firmly grounded in private ownership of property, does not hesitate to use governmental power or to engage in

[5] Charles H. Stoddard, *The Small Private Forest in the United States*, Resources for the Future, Washington, 1961, p. 115.

co-operative effort to solve problems the individual cannot handle alone. This situation does not prevail in the same way here in the United States." [6] The logical clients for a management-service association are likely to lack the necessary motivation for committing their lands to its care.

**General forest-owner associations**    This third type of self-implementing group does exist and appears to operate successfully.    Trade associations are found in the forest-products industries as in other branches of the economy.    They provide many services for their members but usually are concerned with the manufacture and marketing of products rather than with the raw material.    An exception is the American Pulpwood Association.    Its primary interest is in the supply of wood to pulpmills, but since harvesting is an essential part of timber management this association does service landowners as well as manufacturers.

A number of other associations exist which are not typical trade associations but have some of the same characteristics.    These associations usually do not concern themselves with the manufacture and marketing of products but are concerned with the maintenance of forests as a source of industrial raw material.    They always have many other purposes besides the provision of direct services to their members.    We will therefore encounter these same groups again when we discuss their educational and other programs for nonmembers and their efforts to influence the formation of forest policies.    They vary in the amount of effort they devote to direct services for member landowners, but none of them limits its activities entirely to providing such services.

(A particular kind of association which played an important role in the early days of forestry in the West is the timber-protection association.    The private forest owners banded together in these associations for mutual protection from fire.    As government fire organizations increased in size and effectiveness they gradually took over the protection responsibility from the private associations, but they are still significant in some of the western states.)

An important characteristic of these associations is that their membership is made up mainly of larger-forest owners.    Small-property owners are eligible for membership in most, but their main financial support and much of their guidance comes from the large members, most of whom are corporations.    Although these larger owners already enjoy many advantages over the smaller ones, they still have problems which they can meet best through group action.

The Industrial Forestry Association, for example, operates two nurseries to provide planting stock for its members and conducts a program of tree improvement aimed at better future stock.    The American Turpentine Farmers Association represents its members in dealings with the Naval Stores Price Support Program and assists them in improving their chipping and other practices.    The Western Forestry and Conservation Association

[6] *Ibid.*, p. 120.

acts as a coordinator of efforts in fire protection and pest control.    Most important, perhaps, these associations provide a means through which their members can work together on any problem which affects a large number of them and which would be difficult for one owner by himself to do anything about.

## Implementing Actions by Others

In addition to trying to make it possible to use their own forests according to accepted policies, private individuals and groups may also try to influence the actions of other owners.    In doing this they may use almost any of the same means as are used by governments.

This is not the kind of action that can be undertaken very effectively by individuals.    Usually such interested people will contribute to or join in the activities of some organized group.    Of course, as with all groups, the leadership and sustained drive of any forest-oriented group is provided by a few individual people.    In this sense, a dedicated individual can have a large personal role in implementing forest policies.

Many individual companies do have programs designed to encourage other forest owners to manage their lands in desirable ways.    These usually are aimed at small-property owners within the territory from which the company draws wood.    Some companies have foresters who assist landowners with the technical aspects of tree planting, timber stand improvement, and harvesting.    Some have made machines available for tree planting and others have even furnished planting stock.    Virtually everywhere, wood-using industry crews fight forest fires regardless of whose land they may be on.

The Tree Farm Family idea has been developed by companies in some areas to establish a continuing relationship with landowners in their wood-procurement territories.    Under these programs the company assists cooperating owners with technical problems of management and has at least an implicit understanding that when timber is ready for harvest, the company will get a chance to buy it.    Many landowners have viewed company programs with distrust, feeling that they might be just another way in which the industry was trying to take advantage of the timber seller.    This feeling does not seem to have been widespread enough to keep such activities from continuing and expanding.

**Association activities**    There are a variety of associations which have among their objectives the influencing of forest use.    Some, as we have already seen, provide services for their own members.    But the great majority of the forest and conservation associations exist to provide a mechanism through which their members can take group action to influence forest owners who in their majority are not members of the association.

Not many of these associations try to assist nonmembers directly.    Trees for Tomorrow, Inc., has prepared management plans, distributed planting stock, and provided planting machines for forest owners in Wisconsin. The Southern Pulpwood Conservation Association has provided technical forest-management assistance to landowners throughout the South. But most associations apparently have taken the attitude that such direct services are better provided by private forestry consultants or the government.

Many associations carry on programs of general education aimed at landowners. The American Forest Institute (formerly American Forest Products Industries, Inc.), which is supported by the forest-product companies, is the national sponsor of the Tree Farm programs and engages in many other educational activities. The American Forestry Association, Forest Farmers Association, National Wildlife Federation, and a number of state associations are among those engaged in landowner education.

A still larger number of associations try to influence the actions of private forest owners through programs aimed at making the general public aware of the situation and problems involved and thus developing public pressure for changed land management. All of the associations mentioned previously engage in this type of activity. Among other outstanding ones are the Izaak Walton League, National Audubon Society, National Forest Products Association (which is a national grouping of regional forest-industry associations), Sierra Club, and Wilderness Society. The public pressure efforts of this latter group are aimed at influencing the management of public lands as well as private.

A different type of approach is provided by the Save-the-Redwoods League and Nature Conservancy. Both of them follow a preservationist philosophy. Their procedure has been to bring about a transfer of forest areas from private to public ownership in order to make sure they would not be damaged or destroyed. However, since they have done this privately and have obtained the necessary funds through voluntary private subscription, they certainly fall in the category of nongovernmental implementation.

It is difficult to get an accurate count of the number of private associations which are engaged in one way or another in influencing the use of forest land. A list of organizations compiled by Kauffman in 1962 includes some 30 operating at the national and regional levels and an additional 50 independent state groups which apparently fall in this category.[7] Many others—such as the sportsmen's groups, garden clubs, and professional societies—have an influence which is hard to assess. The total number is so large, however, that it is apparent these private groups must exert considerable influence on how forest land is used.

## SUMMARY

The implementation of forest policies in the United States is clearly not exclusively a government activity. Private actions are very important and quite commonly have preceded government actions of a similar nature.

[7] Erle Kauffman, *The Conservation Yearbook 1961–62,* The Conservation Yearbook, Washington, 1962.

One of the problems of forest policy in the United States today is how best to combine private- and public-implementation efforts.    Since policy implementation is not always distinct from and independent of policy formation, the problem is not simply one of relative efficiency in carrying out prescribed policies.    We will see some aspects of this in the next two chapters and return to this question at greater length in Chapter 12 when we discuss the politics of forest resources.

# PROCESS

We have now laid a necessary foundation of knowledge about the ends of forest policies and the technical means of implementing policies aimed at those ends.   But we have not yet come to grips with the day-to-day realities of how forest policies are formed, changed, and made effective.   The final section of this book will try to analyze this real world situation.

First we will consider how forest policies are put into effect once agreement has been reached that they would be desirable.   Then we will look at the rather elaborate institutional structure that has developed in the United States to carry out this execution of forest policies.   With a clearer picture of these institutions in mind, we will then try to understand the major workings of the complex political process through which our forest policies are actually formed.

Up to that point we will be mainly concerned with finding out what is happening in the policy-formation process and with trying to understand why things develop as they do.   But finally we must face the problem that current situations and processes are not necessarily satisfactory, or perhaps even desirable, just because they exist.   We must ask how people can and do assess and make judgments about the policies which determine the use of our forest resources.   Although evaluation is a difficult and controversial process, it is absolutely essential that our forest policies and programs be continuously scrutinized if they are to accomplish the ends that society desires.   We will do our best to see how this can be done but will not try to pass any judgments ourselves on the current forest-policy situation.

# The Execution of
# Forest Policies

The last four chapters considered in some detail the major classes of techniques that are used to implement forest policies.   Executing a forest policy involves the application of such techniques in an effort to make the policy effective.   Without successful execution, a policy is merely a "good idea," and the proposed techniques are only theories of how that idea might be brought to reality.

We have defined a policy as a settled course of action adopted and followed by a society.   This means that for a policy to be effective it must first of all be accepted by the members of society as a desirable course of action, and then some provision must be made for getting people to follow this course.   The execution of a policy is largely concerned with the second step—making sure that the course of action is followed.   But since most forest policies involve many people, have fairly complicated effects, and practically never are concurred in originally by everyone, part of the job of executing a policy is one of increasing its general acceptance by the people it affects.   Execution is therefore the vital stage in policy development. If it cannot be carried out successfully, the policy never really comes into existence as far as the society as a whole is concerned.   Or a policy that has at one time enjoyed acceptance may slip from favor and eventually be abandoned altogether if it no longer can be successfully executed.

Gulick lists the processes involved in administering the development and enforcement of forest policies and programs as: the determination of major policy; the development and adoption of specific programs; the creation of the organization; the provision of personnel; the authorization of finances; the administrative supervision, coordination, and control of activities; and the audit and review of results.[1]   This provides a useful breakdown of the problems of executing policies, and we will follow it in a general way in the rest of this chapter.

"The determination of major policy" appears to be out of place in Gulick's list if it is to be taken as a list of the processes involved in the execution of policies.   It would appear that the determination of policies should precede their execution and that the executing processes should take the policies as a given.   Vieg, for example, says flatly:   "Whether the sphere of interest be public or private, administration is always the servant of policy.   Management—the largest part of administration—denotes means, and means have no significance except in terms of ends."[2]   He goes on to say:   "As a general proposition, policy and politics (in the sense of the political process of policy determination) are primary to administration, both logically and chronologically.   Policy defines the aims and ends of governmental action.   On the highest level, public policy is whatever the politically chosen representatives make it.   They set the goals and lay out the main lines for attaining these goals through administrative action. Once this is done, those responsible for administrative action must bend every effort to accomplish the program.   It is not their business to try to substitute any greater wisdom they may think they have for the wisdom of the people's chosen representatives.   The time to record their doubts is at the stage of policy consideration or reconsideration.   Here they will usually be heard with full appreciation of their judgment."[3]

However, other political scientists have pointed out that things do not always actually work out this way.   Simon noted, for example, that "In the first place the legislative body will often wish, for political reasons, to avoid making clear-cut policy decisions, and to pass these on to an administrative agency.   In the second place the administrator . . . may (and usually will) have his own very definite set of personal values that he would like to see implemented by his administrative organization, and he may resist attempts by the legislature to assume completely the function of policy determination, or he may sabotage their decisions by his manner of executing them."[4]   It is clear that forest-policy formation is influenced in various ways by those who execute it.   The situation is perhaps most clearly described by Jacob, who says: "administrators give shape to the policy process in two ways.   As advisors, they influence policy determinations, and, as implementors, they become decision makers in routine but, nevertheless, extremely important matters."[5]

We will return to a consideration of the influence of those who execute forest policies on their formation in Chapter 12 when we discuss the politics

[1] Luther H. Gulick, *American Forest Policy,* Duell, Sloan & Pearce, New York, 1951, p. 57.
[2] John A. Vieg, "The Growth of Public Administration," in Fritz Morstein Marx (ed.), *Elements of Public Administration,* Prentice-Hall, Inc., Englewood Cliffs, N.J., © 1959, p. 7.
[3] *Ibid.,* p. 8.
[4] Herbert A. Simon, *Administrative Behavior,* The Macmillan Company, New York, 1958, p. 58.
[5] Charles E. Jacob, *Policy and Bureaucracy,* D. Van Nostrand Company, Inc., Princeton, N.J., 1966, p. 134.

of forest-resource use.    But we should perhaps make one more point here. Millett says: "There is a great difference . . . between influencing the conduct of government and wielding governmental and political power. There is a difference between the power to advise and the power to decide. Bureaucracies must be expected to advise.    It is when they possess also the power to decide that bureaucracies become a factor in the system of political power." [6]    We may expect those charged with executing forest policies to have policy opinions and to try to influence policy formation. But they should not be in a position where they might try to impose their ideas on society as a whole.

## FORESTRY PROGRAMS

The execution of a forest policy generally involves an organized and sustained program which applies one or more of the implementation techniques discussed in previous chapters.    A program consists of definite and planned action intended to make some policy effective.    There is not necessarily a one-to-one relationship between policies and programs, however.    A broad policy such as providing adequate timber supplies for the future may be executed through a combination of programs of public-forest management, technical assistance to private landowners, fire prevention and control, tax incentives to timber growers, and many others.    By contrast, a program of management for publicly owned forests may help execute policies of flood control, maintenance of scenic beauty, and increased employment in depressed areas besides the more obvious ones of adequate timber supplies and outdoor recreation opportunities.

It is obvious that programs depend on the existence of groups of people who are especially organized to carry them out.    A typical hen-and-egg question can therefore arise as to whether organizations are established to conduct preconceived programs or programs are developed to provide effective activities for existing organizations.    Apparently both situations can occur, but the type of situation is related to the stage which has been reached in policy development.

An example of the first situation is to be found in the field of outdoor recreation.    Recognizing the growing importance of outdoor recreation, Congress in 1958 created an Outdoor Recreation Resources Review Commission and charged it with the job of studying this problem and recommending policies for dealing with it.    In January 1962, the Commission issued its report.    There were many specific recommendations, but basically the Commission proposed a program to consist of the development of an outdoor-recreation policy; the development of guidelines for the management of outdoor-recreation resources; the expansion, modification, and intensification of present programs to meet increasing needs; and a federal

[6] John D. Millett, *Government and Public Administration*, McGraw-Hill Book Company, New York, 1959, p. 12.

grants-in-aid program to the states.   It also recommended the establishment of a Bureau of Outdoor Recreation in the federal government.

In March of 1962, President Kennedy announced that a Bureau of Outdoor Recreation would be established within the Department of the Interior. Secretary Udall actually established this bureau by secretarial order on April 2.   Since the President had for all practical purposes accepted the program recommended by the Commission, the new bureau was established quite definitely to carry out that program.   This assignment was made more specific by the Bureau of Outdoor Recreation Organic Act—Public Law 88-29—which Congress passed in May of 1963.   Although this Act does not mention the Bureau by name, it authorizes the Secretary of the Interior to engage in eight specific activities related to outdoor recreation which are in effect those recommended by the Outdoor Recreation Resources Review Commission.

We thus have a case in which the development of a program clearly preceded the establishment of an organization to carry it out.   But, as the Director of the new bureau said:   "It is not often that the federal government initiates a wholly new organization in the conservation field. . . . How many federal career officials are given the opportunity to start a wholly new organization, to make their own mistakes, to select their own staffs from scratch, to build their own policies and create their own traditions?" [7] It is much more common for a new program to be assigned to an existing organization.   For example, when the Maine Legislature created the Allagash Wilderness Waterway in 1966 to protect and develop the wilderness potential of the Allagash River, the responsibility for carrying out this program was given to the already existing State Park and Recreation Commission.

Although the Allagash program is apparently not a case of this, it has become rather common for existing conservation organizations to promote the development of new programs for them to administer.   Gulick noted a trend in this direction a number of years ago:   "In the earliest days, the conservationists and political leaders not only pressed for major policy decisions, but had no hesitation in deciding exactly how any policy was to be carried out.   But . . . an important transition took place.   Since the development of federal and state administrative organizations concerned with forestry, and the rise of a recognized profession of foresters, it appears that every plan for undertaking new activities or for enlarging the sphere of governmental action has emerged from the experts, particularly from those in the public service." [8]   This was an overstatement even when Gulick wrote it because the impetus for the development of state forest-practice acts on the West Coast had come largely from the forest industry rather than the states.   No one group can really be credited with having promoted the new programs of recent years.

It appears that as lines of conservation activity are developed and organi-

---

[7] Edward C. Crafts, "Birth of a Bureau; The Recreation Challenge," *American Forests,* July, 1962, p. 26.
[8] Gulick, *op. cit.,* p. 58.

zations to deal with them are formed and become well established, new programs are more likely to be executed by one of these existing organizations than by a new organization created specifically to carry out that program.    Significant new lines of activity, by contrast, are likely to be assigned to new organizations as illustrated by the successive establishment of the Forest Service, National Park Service, Soil Conservation Service, and Bureau of Outdoor Recreation in the federal government.

## FORESTRY ORGANIZATIONS

As we saw in Chapter 9, the means of implementing forest policies are not restricted to government actions.    There can be private programs as well as government programs, and consequently we find private as well as government forestry organizations.    Much of the private activity to execute forest policies is conducted by individuals and corporations and the balance by various associations and other organized groups.    We have considered some of their organizational problems in Chapter 9.    In general they are simpler than the problems of government organizations, because the private goal is largely one of efficiency whereas the government must also try to operate under conditions of democracy.    The following discussion will be mainly restricted to government organizations, but part of the problems considered will also be relevant for the larger private organizations.

### The Basis for Organization

One of the first problems in developing organizations to execute policies is that of selecting an organizing idea to serve as the basis for establishing or separating individual agencies.    Fesler points out that "organization is rational only as it relates to problems expressible in nonadministrative terms." [9]    In forestry this opens up a number of possibilities.    To begin with, organizations might be separated on the basis of the resources which they administer.    This would call for a forest agency distinct from others dealing with range, cultivated crops, beaches, and other kinds of natural lands.    But this could be too broad an organizing idea, and it might be desirable to consider separate organizations to deal with public forests, industrial forests, farm woodlands, etc.    Or the organizing idea might be one of land use so that there would be agencies concerned with parks, wilderness areas, multiple-use forests, etc.    And the forest resource could be separated into component parts so that there would be departments responsible for land, timber, wildlife, water, etc.    In one form or another, all of these are found in existing organizations or in departments within them.

Another kind of organizing idea is that of the functions performed by the

[9] James W. Fesler, "National Water Resources Administration," in S. C. Smith and E. N. Castle (eds.), *Economics and Public Policy in Water Resource Development,* Iowa State University Press, Ames, 1964, p. 369.

agencies.   In forestry this could mean separate units for timber growing, recreation, wildlife management.   There might be one organization charged with forest protection or separate groups to deal with fire, insects, and diseases.   Logging is commonly separated from silvicultural management, and an engineering division often handles road and other construction.   Information and education, personnel relations, timber sales, and accounting are typically assigned to distinct groups or units.   Function is a common basis for departmentalizing larger organizations but may also serve as the main organizing idea as in the case of the Extension Service and the Soil Conservation Service.

Still another organizing idea may be the area served by the organization. Separate organizations may be based on geographic or other natural regions, river basins, watersheds, timber-sheds, or political subdivisions.   Examples are the regional forest-experiment stations, the Tennessee Valley Authority, the wood-procurement organizations of the forest industries, and the state forestry departments.

With so many possible—and apparently rational—bases for separating organizations to execute forest policies it is clear that there could be a very large number of such organizations.   But as Fesler has said of the federal government:   "Because so many problems clamor for governmental attention, only a few can be recognized as 'organizing ideas' at the higher levels of organization.   We cannot indefinitely multiply executive departments or even 'independent establishments.' " [10]   It has therefore been most common in forestry to use some broad organizing idea for the separation of the major organizations and then frequently different ideas for the subdivision or departmentalization of these into operating units.   This has even been carried a step or two backward so that in many states forestry is a division in a department of conservation, and the federal Forest Service is a bureau in the Department of Agriculture.

The question as to the proper organizing idea to follow in separating organizations dealing with forest problems has been the subject of much heated controversy over the years.   This has been pointed up by apparently irrational situations, such as that in which the Forest Service and Bureau of Land Management—both federal agencies—were attempting to manage alternate sections of land in western Oregon or the CFM service foresters and the state extension foresters—both partly supported by federal funds—were giving advice to the same landowners.   Clawson appears to have put this situation in the proper perspective in his statement that "The most serious issues which seem to arise between bureaus are not really organizational issues, but policy issues that would arise no matter what the administrative organization. . . .   The policy conflicts . . . arise out of competing demands for the same resource.   Such conflicts may indeed be worse when divided among two or more agencies, but the strictly organizational problem is likely to be of secondary importance." [11]

[10] Fesler, *op cit.*, p. 369.
[11] Marion Clawson, "Is Reorganization of Federal Resource Agencies a Mirage?" *American Forests*, July, 1965, p. 62.

## The Effect of Area on Organization

An important characteristic of forest resources is their wide areal distribution. Forests are by nature an extensive type of land resource. The word *forest* itself carries a connotation of a large tract of land. Although there has been much talk about the forty-acre farm woodlot, most organizations actually managing forest resources are involved with very large areas. Individual private corporate holdings range from a few thousand acres to several million. The National Park Service manages 22 million acres; the Forest Service, 186 million; and the Bureau of Land Management, 480 million. These are not all forest lands, but the larger organizations have to manage their forests along with their other lands.

Perhaps more significant than the size of the individual forest tracts is the broad geographical distribution of the forests. Only three of the united states contain less than one million acres of forest land and the smallest forest area in any state is the 392 thousand acres in Delaware. The federal Forest Service administers lands in 44 states, and the National Park Service in 42. The Georgia Forestry Commission provides fire protection and management assistance for landowners in all of the 169 counties in the state. The execution of forest policies cannot be done in state or federal capitals —it must go where the forests are; and in the United States that is almost everywhere.

This raises some questions as to how best to organize the administration of forest programs. Fesler points out that four factors have to be considered in working out the best adjustment between functional and areal responsibility: the natural distribution of phenomena, administrative efficiency, fiscal adequacy, and popular control. "No one of these four factors should be the sole touchstone in determining the size and functions of governmental areas." [12] Despite the wide areal distribution of the forests, the other factors play an important role in determining the kinds of organizations that are developed to execute forest policies.

Administrative efficiency is certainly affected in many ways by the relative concentration or dispersion of the activities and personnel which are being administered. Communication, supervision, and inspection all become more difficult as the activities of an organization are spread more widely and at greater distances from its headquarters. A highly centralized form of organization—with most of the decisions made in the headquarters office—has not proved very efficient in executing forest policies. It is difficult for administrators in a central office to understand all the complexities of local situations, which vary tremendously from one place to another. Decisions may therefore be based on erroneous objectives. It has been even more difficult to keep abreast of changes in local conditions and to make decisions fast enough to be effective. The administration of fire suppression presents an obvious example. As a result, the tendency has been to decentralize the administration of forest programs. This has been

[12] James W. Fesler, *Area and Administration*, University of Alabama Press, University, 1949, p. 27.

accomplished partly through independent local organizations (such as state forestry departments) and partly through a decentralized structure in larger organizations.

The historical reasons for decentralized administration may be losing some of their force, however, with rapid improvements in the means of communication and in the speed and ease of travel. The rapidity with which information can now be processed on computers and the development of simulation and other models to help the decision maker deal with complex situations are reducing the need for on-the-ground supervision and subjective evaluations. It is not yet clear to what extent this will permit more highly centralized organization of forest programs.

Fiscal adequacy is a factor which works against the fractionation of forest-policy execution among many small local organizations. The financial resources of both public and private forest-related organizations vary directly with their size. The other advantages of local administration may therefore be more than offset by inadequate financing. This disadvantage may be overcome in some cases through grants-in-aid or other forms of assistance which we will discuss in Chapter 11.

The factor of popular control may exert pressures toward both centralized and decentralized execution of forest policies. Wengert says that "one of the really difficult interests to deal with in a democracy is the geographic or spatial interest. Because so many resources are found at particular locations and can be economically developed only at particular locations, the politics of space is an important element of resource administration." [13] Local organizations are likely to be provincial in their outlook, may give little weight to the interests and desires of people in other parts of the country, and may be unduly susceptible to the pressures of local interest groups. An organization with broader geographical responsibilities and subject to pressures from a wider segment of the population may act more nearly in terms of the interests of the people as a whole.

On the other hand, a large regional or national organization might be callous to the problems of an affected local population and respond primarily to the wishes of some more numerous or more influential group which has little at stake in the local situation. It can be very difficult for local people to influence the decisions and actions of a large bureaucratic organization except in the case of some injustice or offense which is sufficiently flagrant to arouse the interest of the press and the indignation of the general public.

### The Form of Organization

It is clear from the preceding discussion that the administrative organization for executing forest policies can take a variety of forms. It might consist of one monolithic organization or of a number of separate agencies dealing with various aspects of the problem, individual functions, or specific geographic areas. Any one organization might be highly centralized, highly

[13] Norman Wengert, *The Administration of Natural Resources,* Asia Publishing House, New York, 1961, p. 62.

decentralized, or somewhere in between.   The forestry agency might be autonomous, or it might be an integral part of a larger organization with broader responsibilities.   Practically all of these forms except the single monolithic agency are to be found in the United States today.   We will consider these existing institutions in some detail in Chapter 11.

There has been a great deal of criticism of the present form of organization for executing forest policies in the United States and many suggestions for improving it.   Much of the criticism has revolved around the fragmentation of policy execution among many agencies and levels of government.   Durisch and Macon state flatly, for example, that "Program activities cannot be effectively planned when approached independently by the states and the federal government and carried out on each level by a multiplicity of agencies whose activities are largely uncoordinated." [14] This carries an implication that there is some "program" which is generally agreed to be desirable and that the only problem is organizing efficiently to carry it out.   In actual fact, as we have seen in previous chapters and will explore at much greater length in Chapter 12, there is considerable disagreement about policies, many conflicts between them, and an almost continuous evolution and modification of forest policies.   Any form of organization which would freeze policies in their present state or prevent innovation and experimentation is very questionable.

Some of the criticism appears to be overstated.   Hall, for example, has recently said: "although economic and technical factors complicate resource policy, the most serious constraint on obtaining policy and managerial improvements is the organization of the federal government's natural resource functions."   Although he presents a number of suggestions for doing something about this, his strongest recommendation is that "Ideally, there should be a Department of Natural Resources where the Secretary has authority to make decisions for the entire resource area." [15]   This has been proposed a number of times before but never seriously considered by Congress or the Executive Branch of the federal government.   The idea of concentrating power over the entire resource area in the hands of one secretary or department raises objections which appear to far outweigh the advantages claimed for such an organization by its proponents.

As we have noted earlier, forest policies have many different objectives. In Chapter 4 we saw that there are no foolproof criteria which can be used to determine the "right" or "best" objectives or policies for achieving them. As a result, we accept a considerable amount of flexibility in policies as one way of living with the conflicts between objectives.   This inevitably carries over into the structure of the organizations which try to execute these policies.   As Nigro points out: "policy disputes may arise over the *formation* of the structure itself; one form may promote one purpose, whereas another might hinder the achievement of this purpose.   These disputes originate in differences of opinion as to *which purpose* or purposes the organization

[14] Lawrence L. Durisch and Hershal L. Macon, *Upon Its Own Resources,* University of Alabama Press, University, 1951, p. 105.
[15] George R. Hall, "Strategy and Organization in Public Land Policy," *Natural Resources Journal,* April, 1967, pp. 172 and 181.

is supposed to serve.   One group may stand to gain from one set of goals; another group may have quite different objectives in mind." [16]   Under these conditions, it appears that fractionation of the policy-executing organization may be a highly desirable thing.

The best form of organization within a forestry agency has also been the subject of some disagreement.   Many different forestry agencies have apparently performed their functions quite successfully despite substantial differences in their internal organization.   Because the forest resources are so varied and the conditions under which they are used are so different, it seems only reasonable that the executing agencies would also organize differently in their efforts to deal most effectively with their particular problems or programs.   Durisch and Macon appear to support this view when they say: "No special type of agency organization can ensure good administration.   A sound legislative foundation, competent personnel, adequate financing, the interest and support of the public, and program planning are among the many essentials of good resource administration which cannot be assured through any one form of agency organization." [17]

## PERSONNEL

The execution of a forest policy depends ultimately on the actions of a number of people who assume or are assigned the responsibilities for developing and carrying out the programs needed to make the policy effective.   "Administration implies the existence of policies to be carried out and requires people, organized in offices, calculating means of implementation that are, again, conditioned by values.   The people (administrators) may be intelligent and competent or ineffective.   The organization may be structurally efficient and satisfying or conflict-producing and dysfunctional.   The calculation of means may be rational or nonrational.   The values may be the same as those of the policy maker or *different*." [18]   The outcome, in terms of executing the policies, depends absolutely on what these essential people do.

As we saw at the beginning of this chapter, they do more than just passively execute policies that have been selected by others.   Policies are modified and developed in the course of their execution, and the personnel of the executing agencies have much to do with the nature of the policies which actually become effective.   It is therefore not sufficient that these persons be able to carry out a given job expeditiously and accurately.   Efficiency can really be assessed only in terms of the objectives of the policies being implemented.   Otherwise efficiency may merely indicate facility in carrying out stereotyped activities which are unresponsive to changing conditions and needs.   The quality of the personnel involved is

[16] Felix A. Nigro, *Modern Public Administration*, Harper & Row, Publishers, Incorporated, New York, 1965, p. 129.
[17] Durisch and Macon, *op. cit.*, p. 110.
[18] Jacob, *op. cit.*, p. 4.

a vital factor in determining the real nature of the policies which control the use of our forest resources.

The personnel of importance are more inclusive than those ordinarily implied by the word *administrators*.  The execution of any forest policy involves numerous contacts with the public by almost everyone in the organization.  The local warden may be more effective in promoting a policy of fire prevention through his direct contacts with those responsible for starting fires than any of the higher level administrators can be.  The forestry technician who marks a stand for cutting may have a greater impact on future timber yields than any of his supervisors whose decisions are necessarily at least one stage removed from the actual forest situation. Much of the controversy in the West over national forest-timber sales has revolved around the work of scalers, timber cruisers, and road inspectors. Competent personnel are needed in all the jobs involved in executing forest policies.

Professional foresters have played a very important role among the personnel who have sought to execute forest policies in the United States.  In the early days, when the accepted policies consisted almost entirely of liquidating the virgin timber and converting the land to agricultural or other uses, the execution rested with loggers, farmers, stockmen, and miners. But when these policies began to change in the direction of protection, conservation, and continuous management of the forests, professional foresters appeared upon the scene.  The first were Europeans or European-educated, but they were followed in a few years by graduates of new American forestry schools.  The New York State College of Forestry at Cornell University and the Biltmore Forest School opened their doors in 1898, and the Yale Forest School started in 1900.  Professional forestry education expanded rapidly thereafter.

Because there were so few professional foresters available, the forestry organizations which grew up around the turn of the century were largely staffed with nonforesters.  However, as forestry-school graduates became available, the forestry organizations began to recruit professional foresters for their administrative positions.  This was carried to the point where in some organizations virtually all upper-echelon positions were filled with professional foresters, including such staff specialties as personnel administration, fiscal control, and information and education.  Some of the nonforesters who entered these organizations in the early days were competent men and rose to positions of responsibility despite their lack of a forestry education.  But the entering positions became restricted almost exclusively to professional foresters.

The large conservation programs carried out under the WPA and CCC in the 1930s were more than the existing supply of professional foresters could handle, and nonforesters had to be recruited for many administrative positions.  Many of these stayed on with the forestry organizations and diluted somewhat the heavy concentration of professional foresters.  In recent years there has been a growing recognition that professional foresters are not necessarily the best qualified people to hold many positions in forestry organizations, and most agencies have been hiring engineers, accountants, business administrators, and even social scientists for positions requiring their specialized competence.   This trend appears certain to continue.

In 1951, Gulick wrote: "Students of personnel administration cannot fail to recognize that the problem of meeting personnel requirements as an aspect of developing a national forest policy and program has been approached with great vigor and originality, and that the result of these efforts has been an extraordinary success." [19]   This vigor and originality are still evident today as the heavy reliance on professional foresters is being modified and new personnel concepts are being developed.   Not only are the forestry organizations turning to people with other skills, but the professional forestry schools themselves are in a state of ferment as they try to develop a type of education which will better fit their graduates for the kinds of positions they might fill in the policy-executing agencies.

In Europe, there traditionally have been two classes of technical forestry personnel: foresters, or forest managers, and forestry technicians.   In the United States, by contrast, although there have been technician schools (the New York State Ranger School, for example, has been in continuous operation since 1912), most of the technical forestry personnel have been educated in four-year professional curricula.   The graduates have found their natural aptitude levels in the course of their subsequent employment, and for some of them it has been in work which in Europe would be done by forestry technicians.   For all practical purposes, the United States has been educating technicians and forest managers in one common curriculum, but this situation seems unlikely to persist much longer.

There has been a rapid expansion in the number of one- and two-year technician programs in the United States and Canada, and their graduates are being accepted by both private and public employers.   At the same time there has been a gradual stiffening of the educational requirements for the professional-forester degree.   The trend is toward preparation of the professional forester for broad administrative responsibilities rather than as a technical specialist.   The high-level technical specialists are being educated in graduate programs and more and more at the doctoral level. This splitting up of technical forestry workers into scientific specialists, managers or administrators, and technicians appears to be one way of providing better qualified personnel to deal with the increasingly complex problems of executing forest policies.


## FINANCING THE OPERATION

As we noted earlier, the execution of forest policies generally involves organized programs for applying the implementation techniques.   To carry out such programs, there must be personnel, and these must be provided with facilities, equipment, transportation, and supplies.   Some programs will

---

[19] Gulick, *op. cit.,* p. 68.

require investments in land, growing stock, roads, and other forms of capital. Others will need funds for loans, subsidies, or other kinds of financial assistance.    Any forestry program that will be at all effective in implementing policies will require the expenditure of large sums of money.

The financing of the programs is therefore a critical phase in the execution of forest policies.    This is so obvious that it may not appear to be worth saying.    But the fact is that the approval of the idea of an organization or of a particular program and the provision of the financial wherewithal to set up that organization or carry out that program are not always one and the same thing.    For example, in 1935 Congress passed the Fulmer Act which authorized an appropriation of 5 million dollars for the purchase by the federal government of lands to be administered as state forests.    However, Congress never actually made an appropriation for this purpose, and the proposed program never became a reality.

Numerous other examples of this discrepancy between word and deed are to be found in the history of forestry.    In commenting on the nation's forest program Gulick noted: "During the early stages Congress was never enthusiastic about the program, and so gave authority to proceed with one hand, while withdrawing the power to act with the other by holding back the required appropriation." [20]    This indicates that the formation of most forest policies has to proceed through two major steps.    First is the development of a general agreement that a given policy would be desirable.    Second is the development of a general agreement to devote resources to the implementation of that policy.    In most cases, we cannot say that some particular course of action is the policy of a social group unless that society has actually proceeded through both of these steps.    Regardless of what Congress said in the Fulmer Act, it never really was the policy of the United States that the federal government should purchase forest lands to be administered by the states.    (Since the Land and Water Conservation Fund Act of 1964 provides federal funds for land purchases by state and local governments, we have finally come close to making this a real, rather than a paper, policy.)

The situation exemplified by the Fulmer Act is an extreme one.    In most cases the difference between the stated and effectuated policy has been a matter of degree.    Financial resources have been provided but not in amounts which were adequate to completely implement the avowed policy. In the first three decades of this century, for example, one state after another proclaimed a policy of protecting and developing the forest resources. State forestry departments were set up and forestry programs undertaken. But the financial backing of these programs was limited.    Referring to the period from 1911 to 1933, Dana says: "Fairly large percentage increases in appropriations, particularly for fire protection, were not uncommon, but these started from so low a figure that the amounts involved were far from impressive." [21]    Forest policies existed, but they were much more limited

[20] Gulick, *op. cit.*, p. 68.
[21] Samuel T. Dana, *Forest and Range Policy*, McGraw-Hill Book Company, New York, 1956, p. 238.

in their scope than one might have assumed from reading the laws or hearing about the programs. The policy was not really one of protecting all forests from fire, for example, but rather of protecting some forests to some extent. Society was not willing at that time to provide the financial resources necessary to do more than that.

We thus come up against the cold facts of economics. Resources are scarce in comparison with our desires for the things that might be produced with them. Choices are therefore necessary. The funds which would be required to implement a forest policy always have an opportunity cost in terms of the alternative uses to which they might be put. Legislatures and boards of directors are not necessarily being "tight fisted" when they refuse to make available the total amount of money requested for the implementation of some policy. Instead, they are probably demonstrating their conviction that the limited funds available to them can be better spent for other purposes. For those who control public appropriations this presumably means that they feel it is more in the public interest to appropriate funds for other purposes than for the proposed forest program.

As we have noted earlier, there are many desirable objectives which a society might seek and many desirable policies for attaining those objectives. There are conflicts between objectives and between policies, and many of these conflicts result from situations in which the use of the available resources to achieve one objective will preclude their use to attain another objective. When the resources available to a social group are not adequate to achieve all of its objectives, it must work out some compromise as to which of these objectives it will seek and the extent to which it will try to attain them. The result is that many policies are designed to achieve their objectives only to some limited extent, because it would cost too much to try to achieve them completely.

This is further evidence for the lack of separation between policy making and policy administration. The kind of policy which eventually becomes effective depends on the amount of financial support that can be developed for it in the execution phase. It is here that the people have to decide to "put their money where their mouth is." Much of what one reads and hears sounds as though there are conservation policies which everyone agrees are desirable, but "they" will not provide the necessary funds for making them effective. The real situation in most cases is that they are not convinced that the policy is sufficiently desirable to justify sacrificing other desirable policies or programs in order to have this one. And the they in question is usually the general public, taxpayers, or private forest users and owners rather than some mysterious "interests" or political powers.

Now obviously people can be just as wrong in deciding not to support a policy financially as they can be in deciding that a policy is not desirable when in reality it would be very beneficial to them. So part of the process of executing a policy is to provide those who are in a position to make the final decisions about financing it with the information they will need in order to make a wise decision. It is in this situation that benefit-cost analysis has been used so much in the development of water resource policies and programs.   Financial analyses of various kinds are used by private decision makers in determining whether to support particular programs.   Length of payback period, rate of return on investment, contribution to present worth, and other criteria are in use.   But in Chapter 4 we found that there are many questions about the proper criteria to be used in forest policy decisions and many weaknesses in all of those mentioned above.

The importance of the financing stage in policy execution lies in the fact that at this point value judgments must be made explicitly.   It may be very difficult to express these value judgments clearly in advance, but when it comes down to the actual decision to support or not support a program or to choose one alternative instead of others, value judgments obviously are made.   The more clearly the outcomes—both favorable and unfavorable—and the costs—both direct and indirect—of a proposed program are spelled out, the easier it is to make a decision and the wiser that decision is likely to be.

Davis and Bentley propose that this be done in the form of a "social account."   This social account would present as completely as possible the outcomes and costs involved in a proposed action, and preferably for various alternative actions.   Items that can be quantified would be presented in figures and others in the most satisfactory descriptive form. Monetary figures would be presented where firm market values could be used.   "The analyst avoids value judgments and provides only explicit, expert interpretations of possible consequences.   He presents a complete tabular accounting of all factual policy consequences as the objective basis of decision to the policy maker and public." [22]   Many people do not agree that the expert analyst should try to disassociate himself so completely from the decision process.

The federal government of the United States is presently involved in an attempt to apply a Planning-Programming-Budgeting System to the operation of most government agencies.   PPBS was first introduced in the Department of Defense, and, as a result of its apparent successes there, was then extended to all other departments.   The exact form which it eventually can take will probably vary with the kinds of situations and policies which individual agencies must handle.   The basic idea is one of performance budgeting in which an attempt is made to identify national goals, relate these to specific programs, determine the resource requirements of such programs, and finally translate these into the form of budgets on which the President and Congress can act.   PPBS involves planning ahead for some period into the future and should enable decisions about appropriations to be more firmly related to agency objectives than has been possible in the past.   Some of the states are also exploring the use of systems similar to PPBS in an effort to improve their policy-making processes.

[22] Lawrence S. Davis and William R. Bentley, "The Separation of Facts and Values— in Resource Policy Analysis," *Journal of Forestry*, September 1967, p. 616.

## SUPERVISION, COORDINATION, AND CONTROL

In discussing the execution of forest policies we have dealt successively in this chapter with the development of programs designed to make a policy effective, the establishment of organizations to carry out those programs, the provision of personnel to staff the organizations, and the authorization of finances to pay the costs of the program.   We have noted that execution does not necessarily proceed in this logical order and that policies are modified—and perhaps even given additional substantive content—by what takes place in these various stages of the execution process.

There are two more essential parts of this execution process: administration and review of results.   These too become involved in the formation of forest policies as well as in their execution, though perhaps not to the same extent as do the preceding steps.   The matter of review is sufficiently important that we will consider it at length in Chapter 13 on Evaluation of Forest Policies and Programs.   Administration will also be considered more thoroughly in Chapter 11 when we look at the existing administrative institutions in the United States.   In this section and the next we will just consider briefly some aspects of administration and review which seem appropriate to round out this discussion of forest-policy execution.

Administration is a large and complex field whose major emphasis is on ways of achieving effectiveness and efficiency in conducting organized human activities.   It obviously is of great importance to forest policy but represents a whole field of study by itself.   All we can do here is point out some aspects of administration that appear to have an impact on forest-policy formation.

### Supervision

Because of the nature of forestry and the forest resources, most agencies set up to execute forest policies are large and have activities which are geographically widespread.   The administrator in charge of the agency cannot personally supervise all of the people or individual activities for which he is responsible.   In most cases he cannot even be technically competent to personally supervise programs involving such diverse skills and knowledge as most forestry programs do.   He therefore has to depend on other people who can be present on the scene of activity or who have the necessary technical knowledge to act for him.   With the exception of the small forest properties and some of the smaller forestry organizations, extensive delegation of responsibility and authority are necessary in the administration of forestry programs.

The administrative structure that is developed to handle this delegation of responsibility usually combines two kinds of organization.   The first is a line organization in which each of the people involved is directly responsible to his immediate superior, who in turn is directly responsible to his immediate superior, and so on up to the top administrator.   This type of organization deals effectively with the geographic-distribution problem.   In a hypothetical organization, the national director would delegate part of his responsibility to a few regional directors.    Each regional director, in turn, would delegate part of his responsibility to a few district directors.    And each district director would delegate part of his responsibility to the individual forest managers in his district.    Each administrator would have better knowledge of local conditions than his superior but at the same time could draw on the even better local knowledge of those who report to him.

A line type of organization may also serve the need for specialized knowledge.    A state administrator might, for example, delegate parts of his responsibility to three assistants: one in charge of parks, one in charge of nurseries, and one in charge of forests.    The line of responsibility might flow through these assistants to the individual park, nursery, and forest superintendents.

The second type is the staff organization which is specifically intended to handle the need for specialized knowledge.    For geographic reasons, responsibility might most effectively flow from the national administrator through regions and districts to the individual forest administrator.    But the responsibilities of the agency might be so diverse that none of these line administrators would be technically competent to deal with all of them. Each might therefore have attached to him a staff of specialists whose responsibilities would be to advise him in the area of their individual specialties.    The line administrator could thus delegate part of his responsibility to his staff specialists.

Large forestry agencies usually combine the line and staff forms of organization.    With the help of his staff, the administrator is able to supervise more effectively the people and activities under his jurisdiction. In most large agencies, the staff specialists attached to the higher-level administrators exert a considerable influence over the lower-level staff specialists.    Although they ordinarily have no direct-line authority, they act in effect as an arm of their administrator in helping him supervise the specialized activities for which he is responsible.

The important point that this superficial discussion of the line and staff organization reveals is that there is an effective means for bringing specialized local and technical knowledge to bear on the diversity of problems which arise in the execution of forest policies.    This means has been employed extensively in the administration of forest programs in the United States.

## Coordination

It must be obvious by now that the only forest policies that can be executed by single individuals are rather trivial ones.    Individuals certainly do play significant roles in executing important forest policies, but many other people must also be involved if the execution is to be really effective. An individual can help to control the white pine blister rust by eradicating currants and gooseberries on his own property.    But unless the Ribes plants are also eradicated on most other properties, his efforts will do little to make a policy of blister-rust control effective.    In fact, he may not even be able to protect his own pines unless his neighbors take coordinated action with him.

The problem of coordination shows up in two main forms: coordination of efforts to make specific forestry programs effective and coordination of efforts to achieve common policy objectives.    The first of these is clearly the more limited in scope, but its total impact on policy execution is probably just as important as that of the second.

Most significant forestry programs cover such large areas and involve so many people that serious problems of coordination arise in carrying them out.    Protection of the forests provides an excellent example.    In the more heavily forested sections of the country, organized fire-suppression units are maintained at the same time by state forestry departments, the Forest Service and other federal agencies, large private landowners, and often suburban fire departments.    It is obviously essential that the efforts of these units be coordinated so that they do not all show up at every small blaze or all fail to respond to other outbreaks.    A great deal of thought and effort has gone into coordinating fire-control programs, and the results are evident in the forest-fire damage statistics.

Coordination is also clearly necessary within individual agencies.    All except the smallest agency will be involved in more than one activity and usually in more than one place.    The natural tendency for the employees is to concentrate their attention on the activity or location with which they are most directly concerned.    But the agency as a whole will be most effective if its resources are concentrated on certain things at critical times.    Thus we find that in hazardous periods, fire suppression is given highest priority by many forestry agencies, and coordinated arrangements are made to bring the full resources of the agency to bear in an emergency.

Within a large and scattered agency there are many opportunities for conflicting actions to develop.    Many years ago a district forester in one of the southern states was horrified to hear over the radio an announcement by his neighboring district forester that because of the low fire danger it would be an ideal time for the farmers to get their brush burning done. His own district had been without rain for many weeks and he was momentarily expecting fires to break out everywhere.    The other district forester's advice happened to be right for his own district, but he had failed to allow for the broadcast range of the radio station and the fact that his program would be heard outside his district.

The coordination of efforts to achieve common objectives is more complicated because it usually involves not only different groups and agencies but also different programs.    Even though these have certain broad objectives in common, they often may conflict seriously in the kinds of programs they carry on or even in the kinds of policies which they feel would be most effective for achieving the objectives.    We have already seen that there is considerable disagreement among people who all consider themselves to be "conservationists."    Everyone agrees that "conservation" is a good thing, but to one it means locking up and preserving the forest and to another developing the forest for its maximum sustained yield of material benefits.

Despite this, it is clear that actions to achieve forest-policy objectives have not been completely uncoordinated in the past.   As one result of his study of American forest policy, Gulick concluded that "the major co-ordinating force in the American forest policy and program . . . is not found in strong executive leadership by the President, or by the secretaries of the departments involved, or in the Cabinet, or in Congress and its diverse committees, or in similar state structures.   It is found rather (a) in the woods, and (b) in the forestry profession and its unified philosophy."  He went on to say that "there are few major differences of opinion as to what has to be done, or how to do it, among men who have been trained in the same schools, brought up on the same philosophy, and are working for the same great purposes." [23]

This sounds rather oversimplified and romantic to us who are reading it many years later.   Foresters are being turned out by 48 different forestry schools in the United States in 1969, and their education lacks the uni-formity it once had.   We no longer are in such complete agreement as to what has to be done and how to do it.   And yet there is something to what he said, for we still find the professional foresters in general agreement on many aspects of forest use that are questioned by other people.   The major change which has occurred is that the professional foresters no longer occupy as dominant a role in the development of forest policies as they once did.

However, the forest—or at least the natural outdoors—still provides a unifying force which draws together the diverse groups concerned with natural resources.   Violently though they may disagree among themselves on many things, the Sierra Club, National Parks Association, professional foresters, and sportsmen readily join forces against the highway and dam builders and the mining interests.   The Natural Resources Council of America, whose membership consists of individual resource associations, provides a somewhat limited means of coordination for these groups.   As things now stand, the differences among them are great enough that they probably would not favor any more formal type of coordinating organization.

## Control

It is not a very long step from coordination to control.   If an effort is to be made to carry on a coordinated program or even a program involving many people there must be some means of controlling the individual actions which make up the program.   In describing the procedures of the Forest Service, Hendee says: "Basically, the control measures needed in such a decentralized organization include assignment of program and work respon-sibilities; delegation of authorities commensurate with these responsibilities; and a system of checking to determine whether responsibilities are met

[23] Gulick, *op. cit.*, p. 74.

within the authority delegated." [24]    Control thus consists of clearly establishing what each part of the organization is to do and then making sure that it does it.

Probably the most elaborate system of organization anywhere in the whole field of forest resource use is that which has been developed by the U.S. Forest Service.   The basis for this system lies in the Forest Service Manual and Forest Service Handbooks, which spell out in great detail the program and work responsibilities and the accepted procedures for carrying out those responsibilities.   The manual and handbooks are under almost continual revision to keep them abreast of current thinking and practice. Every Forest Service employee thus has readily at hand a guide telling him how the Forest Service carries out its activities and what he as a member of the organization is, therefore, expected to do.   This is enforced by periodic inspections to assure that proper procedures are being followed.

The Forest Service system of organization has obviously been a success. Despite the wide geographic scatter and diverse nature of its activities, it has been able to resist the centrifugal forces which these characteristics generate and to maintain a closely unified program direction.   But this very success may bring problems with it.   As Kaufman points out, "An individual imbued with the spirit of an organization, indoctrinated with its values, committed to its established goals and customary ways, and dedicated to its traditions, is not likely to experiment a great deal, nor even to see the possibilities suggested by unplanned developments, . . . Directing a large organization is a delicate business of steering between the Scylla of policy disintegration and the Charybdis of torpor.   The avoidance of one often brings the agency closer to the other." [25]

While the Forest Service appears to have done a good job of steering between policy disintegration and torpor, Kaufman's observation is certainly relevant to policy execution in general.   In our present imperfect state of knowledge about the forest-resource potentialities themselves and the future directions of people's tastes and preferences, flexibility is to be desired in the execution of forest policies.   It appears better to take a chance on ineffective execution of desirable policies than to run the risk of being stuck with effectively executed but misguided policies.

## REVIEW OF RESULTS

The controversies over what policies we should follow are so stimulating and the problems of implementing and executing them so challenging that once a choice has been made and feasible means developed for effectuating it, we are inclined to feel that this problem has been "solved" and we can now look for fresh "issues" to conquer.   But in cold fact, our task may

[24] Clare Hendee, *Organization and Management Systems in the Forest Service,* Government Printing Office, Washington, 1967, p. 31.
[25] Herbert Kaufman, *The Forest Ranger,* The Johns Hopkins Press, Baltimore, 1960, pp. 235, 238.

have just begun.    For a policy is only an accepted course of action for achieving some objective.    And this policy, no matter how good it looks today, may prove with time and increased knowledge to be a poor means of attaining that objective.    Or it may have unforeseen side effects which will ultimately lead us to conclude that it is a "bad" policy.    In the same way, the implementing techniques and executing arrangements that now appear so promising may with use prove to be ineffective or at least inefficient.    Because of this it is very important that both policies and programs be subject to rather continuous review.    We know that changes in policies and programs are inevitable.    They will be dealt with much more effectively if provision is made for anticipating and meeting them rather than waiting for crises to develop.    Chapter 13 will consider this important matter of evaluation in detail.

# The Institutional Structure for Executing Policies

# 11.

In Chapter 10 we discussed a number of aspects and problems of executing forest policies but made only casual reference to the agencies engaged in this activity.  However, we are not really interested in some abstract or hypothetical situation, but in the way that forest policies actually are executed in the United States.  So it is important that we take a closer look at the agencies which administer forest programs and try to understand how they function and fit together into an institutional structure.

This structure has developed over a long period of time.  Certain ways of doing things have become "institutionalized," and they are not now readily changed.  This does not mean that they cannot be changed; in fact, most of these institutions do change gradually with time.  But because they have been accepted and have become firmly entrenched, it is difficult to make major or drastic changes in them.  This is important for an understanding of policy because, for all practical purposes, the only way that policies can be executed is through these existing institutions.

## OWNERSHIP OF THE FOREST RESOURCES

Property is one of the basic institutions of our United States society.  We agree that all property within the territorial limits of our country must belong to someone; if not to private persons, then to the public through the medium of some branch of government.  As we saw in Chapters 6 and 7, what can be owned are rights to the use of property, and some of these rights are always retained by the social group so that no private person can ever own all of the rights to a piece of property.

With the passage of time, the ownership of property rights in the United States has assumed a firmly established pattern.   These rights can be transferred voluntarily from one owner to another at any time.   Society can also take them away from private owners under its right of eminent domain but only after establishing conclusively that they are essential to some public purpose and fully compensating the former owner for his loss.   Property is constantly passing from one owner to another—both public and private—but the proportion that changes hands is small, and the overall pattern of ownership is rather constant.

This is important for the execution of forest policies because these accepted courses of action always ultimately involve some physical actions in the forests or on forest land.   And at this point they come into contact (and perhaps conflict) with the property rights of the forest or land owner. Ownership of land basically is the right to control most of what takes place on that land.   The courses of action which are followed in using forest land are therefore largely under the control of its owners.   And since one of our fundamental national policies is that private owners should have the maximum freedom to control the use of their property that is consonant with the general welfare, the ways in which our forest lands are handled depend very heavily on the attitudes of their owners.

This is also true of the publicly owned lands.   Public ownership may be federal, state, or local.   The attitudes of the particular "publics" involved will depend on their own circumstances and may differ from those of other publics.   In addition, the public cannot personally manage its lands but must delegate this to some agencies of its governments.   Individual agencies and their administrators always have attitudes toward and ideas about the use of forest resources, and these are usually about as firm as those of the private owners.

Ownership is thus an important factor which must be dealt with in executing forest policies.   One way of doing this is to change it, and as we have seen this is one technique that can be used in forest policy implementation. But regardless of which techniques are used, it is clear that execution of forest policies always takes place within some framework of land ownership.

## The Existing Ownership Pattern

The total land area of the United States is estimated to be slightly under 2.3 billion acres.   The ownership of this land is divided about as follows: [1]

[1] These and the other ownership estimates which follow were derived by combining figures from the Bureau of Land Management, *Public Land Statistics,* 1967; U.S. Department of Agriculture, *Agricultural Statistics 1967;* U.S. Forest Service, *Timber Trends in the United States;* and Marion Clawson, R. Burnell Held, and Charles H. Stoddard, *Land for the Future,* The Johns Hopkins Press, Baltimore, 1960.

| | |
|---|---|
| Privately owned | 59% |
| In some form of public ownership | 39% |
| Held in trust for the Indians by the federal government | 2% |

The large proportion of private ownership is significant.   Almost half of the land in the United States is on farms, and this has had an important influence on the development of land-use policy.

According to the Forest Service, one-third of the land area of the United States is occupied by forests.   About 532 million acres of this forest land is estimated to be producing or capable of producing crops of industrial wood and has not been withdrawn from timber utilization.   The other 228 million acres of noncommercial forest land is not capable of yielding crops of industrial wood because of adverse site conditions or else has been withdrawn from commercial timber use.   However, much of this noncommercial forest land is very valuable for recreation, water, grazing, wildlife habitat, and scenery.

The Nationwide Forest Survey has concentrated on the commercial forest land and ownership statistics for it are reasonably reliable.   The major classes of commercial forest-land ownership are:

| | |
|---|---|
| Private ownership | 69% |
| Public ownership | 30% |
| In trust for Indians | 1% |

This heavy concentration in private hands is a result of the historical development of land ownership in the United States.   About 81 percent of the present land area has been at one time a part of the public domain.   This federal domain was mostly obtained through cession by the original states; cessions by Spain and Mexico; the Louisiana, Gadsden, Texas, and Alaska purchases; and the Oregon Compromise.   It was disposed of mostly through sales or grants to private persons and through grants to the states.

Those who bought or obtained grants of land from the public domain sought those lands which were potentially most productive for agriculture, timber growing, or other commercial purposes.   No one wanted the "worthless" lands, and these were left in federal ownership.   By the time the federal policy changed in the late nineteenth century, much of the good land had already been taken by private owners, and the public was able to reserve or buy back only about a quarter of the commercial forest land.

Information about the ownership of the noncommercial forest lands is much less reliable.   A rough estimate of the major holdings is:

| | |
|---|---|
| Private ownership | 25% |
| Public ownership | 71% |
| In trust for Indians | 4% |

This pattern is not too surprising since it resulted from the same public domain distribution process. Some 36 percent of this noncommercial forest land is in Alaska, where almost all land is still in public ownership. As transportation facilities develop, it is possible that some of the Alaska forest will move into the commercial category. Probably most of the 16 million acres of the otherwise commercial forest land in the United States which have been withdrawn from timber utilization are also in public ownership in the form of parks, wilderness areas, watershed forests, and military reservations.

The overall picture of forest ownership which emerges from this analysis is as follows:

| | |
|---|---|
| In private ownership | 56% |
| In public ownership | 42% |
| In trust for Indians | 2% |

The institutional setting of forest land use in the United States today is an almost equally divided private and public control of the basic resources. We now need to look at these two sectors more closely.

## THE PRIVATE SECTOR

The United States has always relied predominantly on private enterprise to produce most of the material goods and services desired by its people. The manufacture, distribution, and sale of timber products is virtually a 100 percent private undertaking. Traditionally logging has also been an almost exclusively private activity. Thus, regardless of who owns the land and grows the trees, their harvest and conversion into useful products is largely controlled by the characteristics of the private logging and forest-product manufacturing industries.

The raising of domestic livestock for meat, hides, and wool on forest ranges has also always been a private business. The private grazing industry is the only existing mechanism for converting the forage resources of the nation's forests into benefits for the people.

By contrast, the management of forests for the yield of water is almost everywhere a public enterprise, although there are a few private water companies in the East. Forest recreation also is largely provided by public agencies. Private enterprise has concentrated mostly on the intensive forms of recreation, such as skiing, and on the provision of meals, lodging, and other services. Scenic beauty is rarely developed intentionally by private enterprise since there usually is no way of obtaining payment for it except perhaps indirectly through an increase in the prices that can be charged for the use of hotels, restaurants, and other resort facilities.

These basic economic situations lead the private forestry sector to be heavily oriented toward timber and livestock. The privately owned lands are managed almost exclusively for these products, and those private entrepreneurs who use the public lands are primarily interested in them as sources of these two products. Most of the private institutional setup is therefore likely to be favorable to the execution of policies aimed at producing wood or livestock but not much better than neutral concerning policies aimed at the other forest benefits.

## The Private Forest Owners

The Forest Service estimates the proportion of the total commercial forest-land area held by the major classes of private owners to be:

| | |
|---|---|
| Farmers | 28% |
| Miscellaneous private owners | 28% |
| Forest industries | 13% |

There has been a gradual transfer of forest land from farmers to industrial and other private owners. However, in terms of the total area involved these transfers have not been very large. The amount of noncommercial forest land in private ownership is relatively small, and its addition would hardly alter the above relationships.

The number of private forest owners in the United States is not known with any accuracy, but their magnitudes are such that we can get a reliable impression of the institutional situation even though the statistics we have may be off by a sizable amount. Based on estimates which the Forest Service made for 1953, there are about 4 million private forest owners in this country.[2] The numbers in the three major classes mentioned above are probably about as follows:

3 million farmers
1 million miscellaneous owners
20 thousand forest industry companies

It is obvious that the ownership of our private forest lands is fragmented among a very large number of individuals and companies.

**Nonindustrial owners**    A great deal of study has been devoted to the private nonindustrial forest owners because their control of almost 60 percent of the commercial forest area means that what they do with their lands is bound to have a major impact on the forest economy of the country. About all that has come out of these studies is a realization that many different kinds of people own forest land for many different reasons and that what they do with it is influenced by a great variety of individual circumstances.

Two characteristics of these nonindustrial ownerships are of great significance for policy execution: individually they are very small, and they rarely represent a major interest and source of income for their owners.

[2] U.S. Forest Service, *Timber Resources for America's Future,* U.S. Department of Agriculture, Forest Resource Report 14, 1958, p. 295.

In 1953, the Forest Service estimated, 86 percent of the nonindustrial owners had forest properties less than 100 acres in size.   Only one percent of all private owners controlled more than 500 acres apiece.[3]   (These proportions have probably not changed much in the meantime.)   Since the size of the average farm in the United States was reported to have been 350 acres in 1964, these private forest holdings are very small indeed.   This is further emphasized by estimates that three-fourths of the nonindustrial owners held less than 75 acres apiece, half had less than 30 acres, and one-third did not even own 20 acres in 1953.[4]   We not only have a very large number of private forest owners, but most of them individually control only an infinitesimal part of the forest area.   What any one of these nonindustrial owners does is obviously of little significance, but what they do as a group may be very important.

The number of owners gives a somewhat distorted impression of the situation of this nonindustrial group.   Although 40 percent of the nonindustrial area is estimated to be in properties of less than 100 acres, about one-fourth is in holdings of over 500 acres and 12 percent in properties of over 5,000 acres.   This means that one percent of the owners control 25 percent of the nonindustrial land, and only a handful control 12 percent of it.   There obviously are a few large owners along with the many small ones in this nonindustrial group.

It is only for these largest owners that the forests can be a major interest and source of income.   Even with good quality land and intensive management, forests do not produce high returns per acre.   In addition, there are definite economies of scale in forest management, since most necessary forestry operations can only be done efficiently with large equipment, skilled workers, and seasonal concentrations of activity.   Practically every forestry operation is much more expensive per acre on 10 acres than it is on 1,000.   The combination of a low gross revenue per acre and high operating costs means that a small forest property cannot produce much net revenue per year.   These small forests are therefore owned, almost without exception, by people whose real source of income—and consequent primary interest —lies elsewhere.

Some of the nonindustrial owners do have properties large enough to be a major source of interest and income for them.   These are usually corporations who hold forest lands as an investment.   The number of these larger nonindustrial owners is rather indefinite, but there cannot be very many of them.   The Forest Service estimated that there were only 2,600 private owners in 1953 who held over 5,000 acres apiece, and most of these undoubtedly were forest-industry companies.

We thus have an institutionalized ownership situation in which some 60 percent of the forest land of the country is held in about 4 million separate private properties.   On the average, these ownerships are much too small to be economic as independent timber growing ventures.   But the owners are independent.   In general they are concerned only for their own self-

[3] Ibid., p. 293.
[4] U.S. Forest Service, Timber Resource Review (preliminary draft), Chap. IVD, Forest Service, Washington, 1955, pp. 35, 37.

interest and do not give much thought to the effect of their forest-management practices on the rest of society.   There are no really effective private institutions for bringing these many owners together and getting them to use their forest lands in an integrated manner.   The various farm organizations do not seem to function in this area, and cooperatives have been a notorious failure in United States forestry.   The execution of forest policies on these nonindustrial properties depends ultimately on the individual owners and therefore on the institutions which are developed for influencing or controlling what these owners do with their lands.

**Industrial owners**   The industrial forest owners on the average control much larger properties than the nonindustrial owners.   At least 20 of these owners have more than half a million acres apiece.   In 1953, the Forest Service estimated, only 10 percent of the industrially owned land was in properties less than 5,000 acres in size.   The proportion of such smaller properties is probably less than that today.   Most of these owners are therefore in a position to enjoy the economies of scale in forest management.   A majority of these industrial owners—and certainly almost all of the larger ones—are managing their forests rather intensively today.   Since they depend at least partially on their own timberlands as a source of raw material for their plants, they have a definite economic incentive to manage their lands.   This incentive, of course, comes almost entirely from the demand for wood, and their interests are therefore very heavily concentrated on timber as their forest crop.

These industrial owners are of themselves much more responsive to the desires of society than the nonindustrial owners.   This is partly a response to the demand expressed through the market for wood products.   Because they are primarily engaged in manufacturing final products for the market, these owners relate their forest management much more directly to the ultimate consumer than do the nonindustrial owners who care very little to whom they sell their timber.   The attitude of the industrial owners is also partly defensive in nature.   They recognize the potential threat of public control and prefer to voluntarily anticipate the desires of society.   As a result, the industrial ownership forms a somewhat self-motivating institution for executing forest policies.

This self-motivating characteristic is strengthened by the fact that most of these industrial owners are members of organizations through which they can work together in executing policies that affect their own lands.   Organizations like the Industrial Forestry Association and The Southern Forest Institute provide certain services for their members but probably are more important as mechanisms through which groups of industrial owners can influence what individual companies do.   These private associations provide existing institutionalized means for working together in emergencies, such as the 1965 blowdown in the Douglas-fir Region.   They also are effective media for executing programs which originate elsewhere, since the associations already have organized channels of communication with their members.

## Other Private Institutions

The most important of the other private institutions are the various associations, clubs, and other organized groups.  We have already seen how associations provide a means by which individual forest owners can work together in executing policies on their own properties.  Most of these private groups also devote considerable effort to trying to influence policy formation.  We will consider this aspect of their activity in Chapter 12 when we discuss the politics of forestry.  At this point we will be concerned just with their role in the execution of forest policies.

The number of private associations, clubs, and other organized groups in the United States is very large.  The National Wildlife Federation listed 155 national and international and 33 regional organizations concerned with natural resource use and management in 1968.[5]  In addition it listed many which operate only within their own states.  This listing includes many groups of questionable significance but at least 25 of them appear to be important to forest policy.

The most common type of activity engaged in by these organizations is educational.  As we have seen earlier, policies cannot become effective until people are informed about them and learn how to conform to them.  This educational function is performed effectively by organizations such as the American Forest Institute, Forest Farmers Association Cooperative, and the National Wildlife Federation.  Most of the private organizations consider education to be a part of their programs.

Some of the organizations provide services for their members and others.  The American Forestry Association and the Sierra Club conduct organized trips into wilderness areas.  The Southern Forest Institute and the Industrial Forestry Association provide management advice and assistance to forest owners.  The Appalachian Mountain Club maintains trails for hikers.  In many other ways such private organizations facilitate desired uses of the forests.

Some of these organizations appear to perform primarily a watchdog function.  The National Parks Association and the Wilderness Society make it their business to see that the areas of their concern are managed according to accepted policies.  An example of this function—though not involving forests—is the recently formed Public Resources Association which is primarily concerned with oil-shale resources.[6]

A few private organizations work directly to execute the generally accepted policy of developing new knowledge about the forest resources.  The Conservation Foundation, Resources for the Future, Inc., and the Forest History Society promote research on various aspects of forestry and the forests.

Finally, a group of professional societies provide a means for stimulating and improving professional practice.  The Society of American For-

[5] *Conservation Directory 1968*, The National Wildlife Federation, Washington, 1968, pp. 28–54.
[6] James B. Craig, "The Watchdogs," *American Forests*, March, 1968, pp. 11, 51–52.

esters, American Society of Range Management, and the Wildlife Society play a big role in the lives of these professional conservationists and exert a considerable influence on how they perform their duties.

It is clear that an elaborate institutional structure of private organizations concerned with forestry and conservation plays an important role in the execution of forest policies in the United States. Through these organizations it is possible to reach the millions of individuals affected by forest policies and to get feedback from them on how the policies are being executed. These organizations are such an important part of the institutional scene in the United States today that they inevitably become involved in the execution of practically every forest policy.

One other institution of significance in the execution of many forest policies is the private forestry consultant. Almost 300 individuals and firms advertise their services as consultants on a variety of aspects of forest-land use. An unknown number of other foresters act as consultants but do not advertise in the journals. These are usually members of university faculties or foresters who have retired from public or private service. Much of the work of the consultants is with landowners who lack technical forestry knowledge themselves and cannot employ a forester on a full-time basis. The consultants keep abreast of both the latest technical knowledge and of public and private programs which might affect their clients. They are almost always involved in planning or action programs and thus have an immediate impact on forest-land use. Their number increases from year to year, and because of their expertise and experience they probably play an even more important role in forest-policy execution than their numbers alone would indicate.

## THE PUBLIC SECTOR

Traditionally, government in the United States has undertaken directly only those economic activities which private enterprise could not or would not carry out. The rest of the government's activities in the economic area has largely consisted of facilitating, guiding, and controlling what was being done by private enterprise. The original idea in the early days of the United States was clearly that the forests and rangelands should be operated by private enterprise the same as lands which were suitable for agriculture. This seemed to work reasonably well with the agricultural land but not with lands that are unsuitable for agriculture and must be maintained in grass or forest. The abuse of some of this permanent forest and grassland was so flagrant that it appeared imperative that the governments operate part of these lands as public enterprises in order to ensure future supplies of forest and range benefits. The public therefore came into the permanent land owning and managing business by reserving parts of the public domain and by acquiring other lands from private owners through purchase and gift.

At the same time it was clearly necessary for the public to take some actions regarding what was done with the substantial part of the forest lands that remained in private ownership.   This dichotomy of public activities in the forest-resource sector has existed for almost a century and has produced its own institutions, which have developed largely through modification of existing governmental institutions.   The two aspects of public action intermingle and overlap in many places, and consequently some of the institutions serve both functions.

## The General Pattern of Government Institutions

The institutional structure of government in the United States has a number of characteristics which are important in the execution of forest policies.   Probably the most important is the simultaneous existence and operation of federal, state, and local governments.   These three levels of government are related in a definite pattern of responsibilities and authority.

The Constitution and laws of the United States are supreme regardless of any contrary things in the constitution or laws of any state.   However, the federal government enjoys only those powers which are delegated to it by the Constitution or implied by the delegated power "To make all laws which shall be necessary and proper for carrying into execution the foregoing powers, and all other powers vested by this Constitution in the government of the United States, or in any department or officer thereof."   Some powers are specifically denied to the federal government by the Constitution, such as the right to take private property for public use without just compensation.

"The powers not delegated to the United States by the Constitution, nor prohibited by it to the States, are reserved to the States respectively, or to the people."   Some state constitutions prohibit other powers to their states. But in general the states retain broad powers over the lives of their citizens, and these include some of special importance to forest policy.   Barlowe notes that "in actual practice, . . . the federal government lacks many of the sovereign powers involved in familiar day-to-day cases of land-resource control. . . .   Most of our public powers over the ownership and use of land resources are vested in the several states." [7]

Local governments are legally creatures of the states and have only those powers which the states give them.   Counties are legal subdivisions of the states and were originally established for administrative and judicial convenience.   Municipalities and townships (called "towns" in New England) are chartered by the states and given only specified duties and powers.   The local governments have been of least significance for forest policy.   However, they do own 2 percent of the commercial forest land, are generally the only governments which levy property taxes on private forest owners, and probably will be the ones most directly involved in any future extension of rural-land zoning.

The distribution of powers among federal, state, and local governments

[7] Raleigh Barlowe, *Land Resource Economics*, Prentice-Hall, Inc., Englewood Cliffs, N.J., © 1958, pp. 323–324.

is important to an understanding of the execution of forest policies because forestry programs are operating at all three levels. But it would be wrong to place too much stress on this separation of power, for as Nigro points out: "administrative activities in the United States are not compartmentalized by levels of government. National, state, and local governments do not occupy separate administrative bailiwicks. Our federal system, in which state and local governments play a strong role, continues to show great vigor, but many of the most important governmental activities today are the joint responsibility of all levels of government. The term *cooperative federalism* is now familiar in American government." [8] A clear example is forest-fire control, which usually is a joint federal, state, and local undertaking. We will need to look in some detail at the institutional arrangements which have developed for joint execution of forest policies.

Another important characteristic of governmental structure in the United States is the division of powers among the executive, legislative, and judicial branches. All three are involved in the execution of forest policies. In a much oversimplified version of government operation, the legislative branch creates the statutory laws intended to execute a policy and appropriates the funds required to put those laws into effect. The executive branch develops programs to execute the statutory laws, creates administrative laws (rules and regulations) needed to administer the programs, and organizes and operates an administration to carry out the programs. The judiciary branch determines whether the administrative laws conform to the statutory and constitutional laws and whether the statutory laws in question are within the powers granted by the constitutions.

In practice there is no such neat division of activities. Both the legislative and executive branches in creating statutory and administrative laws guide themselves by the previous actions of the judicial branch in dealing with similar laws. The executive branch normally originates most new proposals for policy execution and presents them to the legislative branch for action. Frequently the legislative branch creates statutory laws in very broad or vague terms and passes the responsibility on to the executive branch to create administrative laws specific enough to enable it to actually carry on programs. At this point the judicial branch may be brought in by complaints that the executive branch is doing things which were not really authorized by the statutory laws under which it is operating. The legislative branch frequently investigates—or at least looks at—programs conducted by the executive branch and sometimes tries to influence their nature or administration (usually in the interests of individual legislators' constituents). This multifold interaction in no way reduces the significance of the three-way set of checks and balances for policy execution.

Suppose, to take a hypothetical example, that it is agreed it would be desirable to restock all forest lands in a particular state as soon as possible after the mature timber is harvested. And suppose that the state forestry department is convinced that a good way to implement this policy in the

[8] Felix A. Nigro, *Modern Public Administration,* Harper & Row, Publishers, Incorporated, New York, 1965, p. 121.

case of one forest type would be to require all landowners to leave a specified number of seed trees standing on each acre at the time of harvest. Now the state forester does not have the power to require landowners to do this.    So he prepares a bill, and one of the representatives introduces it in the legislature.    After thorough study, the legislature passes an act requiring all landowners in the state who harvest timber of this particular type to leave five seed trees of specified characteristics on each acre.    In order to make the act enforceable, they add the provision that any landowner who violates it may be fined a certain amount for each acre on which he does not comply with the law.

The state forester now issues a regulation that any state-forest warden who finds a landowner in violation of this law is to proceed to bring legal action against him.    But the state warden cannot fine a landowner.    Under our legal philosophy a person is presumed to be innocent until he is proved guilty.    So the warden must have the landowner summoned into court and there must present evidence intended to prove that he did violate the law. The decision will rest with the judge (and in some cases a jury).    The landowner may claim that the legislature exceeded its constitutional powers in establishing such a law.    Or he may claim that the law should not apply in his particular case or that he had in fact complied with the law and the warden was in error.    It is the responsibility of the court to determine the true facts of the case and accordingly to find him guilty or not.

In this simple example we find all three branches of the government actively involved in the execution of the policy of regenerating forest land. Often their involvement is not this obvious, but it usually is there nevertheless.

Still another important characteristic of government structure in the United States is the existence of relatively permanent bureaucracies.    In the federal government, for example, the President, members of his Cabinet, assistant secretaries, and a few other top administrative people come and go with changes in political control of the government.    But the career employees of the bureaus, under protection of the civil-service system, remain in their jobs and gradually advance with time and experience. Most of the actual execution of policies is carried on by the bureaucracy. And it has an important characteristic noted by Millett:    "Administrative agencies in our scheme of government are not part and parcel of the executive branch but constitute a distinct echelon of government subject to the separate direction of the executive, legislature, and judiciary.    Administrative agencies are politically responsible to all three.    And this responsibility is not channeled through any one branch; it is exercised directly." [9]

The administrative agencies (bureaus and departments) which make up the continuing bureaucracy at all levels of government are the key to an understanding of public execution of forest policies.    All public policy execution must in the last analysis proceed through them, and they therefore are in a strategic position to influence not only the execution but also

---

[9] John D. Millett, *Government and Public Administration*, McGraw-Hill Book Company, New York, 1959, p. viii.

the formation of forest policies.   The executive, legislative, and judicial branches of the government exert many controls over these administrative agencies, but often they are able to display considerable power of their own.

We will now pause to consider briefly the main outlines of the pattern of public forest-land ownership in the United States.   Then we will return to the institutional structure presented by the individual administrative agencies at the different levels of government.

## The Public Forest Owners

We saw earlier in this chapter that about 42 percent of all the forest land in the United States is in public ownership.   Of this, only 5 percent is in state, county, and municipal ownership and the remaining 37 percent in federal ownership.   Although the states, counties, and municipalities own some 38 million acres of forest land, they control only a very small proportion of the total forest resources of the country.

The ownership distribution of the commercial forest land is especially significant.   The combined public holdings amount to only 30 percent of the total, and this is divided as follows:

| | |
|---|---|
| National forests | 18% |
| States | 4% |
| Counties and municipalities | 2% |
| Other federal agencies | 6% |

Clearly the national forests have an overwhelming responsibility in any public timber-production effort.

The importance of the various federal agencies is indicated to some extent by the land areas they administer.   The federal government as a whole controls 765 million acres of land and this is distributed among the major agencies as follows:

| | |
|---|---|
| Bureau of Land Management | 63% |
| Forest Service | 24% |
| Fish and Wildlife Service | 4% |
| National Park Service | 3% |
| Army, Navy, and Air Force | 3% |

These are not all forest lands, of course.   The Bureau of Land Management's holdings include over 200 millions acres of tundra and well over 100 million acres of grasslands.   However, all of these agencies do control substantial areas of forest.

The public forest-owning agency which stands out above the others—as might be expected—is the U.S. Forest Service.   Of all the forest land in the United States, 19 percent is in the national forests.   Since this includes almost one-fifth of the commercial forest land in the country, it is clear that the Forest Service is an institution of tremendous importance to forest policy.

## FOREST–RELATED INSTITUTIONS IN THE FEDERAL GOVERNMENT

Actions which promote or affect the execution of forest policies are taken in a number of different parts of the federal government.   Forest problems appear rather minor among the many large ones burdening the President today, and he is not likely to have time to take a personal part in the execution of forest policies.   Members of his Cabinet in their roles as department heads do get involved in forest policies, though not on a continuous basis.   They are drawn in when some new policy is being launched, at a time of controversy, or when some existing program comes under fire.   The day-to-day administration of forestry programs is handled almost entirely by the bureaus.   The following sections will describe briefly the parts of the federal government that are actively involved in forest-policy execution.

### The Congress

Congress becomes directly involved with forest programs and policy execution through its committees.   The responsibilities of Congress are so broad that individual senators and representatives have neither the time nor the specialized knowledge to study and pass judgment on everything that comes before them.   Through the committee system, members of Congress can work intensively in the areas of their own committee assignments and depend to a large extent on the other committees to study the remaining issues for them.

Three committees each in the Senate and House of Representatives are directly concerned with forest policies.   The Committee on Appropriations in each house plays an obvious role in policy execution.   Here, the various forestry programs are scrutinized and decisions made as to whether they should be financed in full or, if not, which ones should receive financing and to what extent.

The Committees on Interior and Insular Affairs in the two houses are, among other things, responsible for the public lands generally, grazing on and mineral resources of the public lands, the forest reserves and national parks created from the public domain, and relations of the United States with the Indians and Indian tribes.   Since 86 percent of the national-forest area and 80 percent of the national-park area were originally in the public domain, this committee has responsibility for most of the federally owned forest lands.

The Senate Committee on Agriculture and Forestry and the House Committee on Agriculture are, among other things, responsible for protection of birds and animals in forest reserves, forestry in general, forest reserves

other than those created from the public domain, agricultural economics
and research, agricultural educational extension services, and soil conservation.   Much of the forestry research and extension work is done as parts
of the agricultural programs and thus comes under this committee.   The
splitting of responsibility for the national forests between these committees
and those on Interior and Insular Affairs on the basis of whether the forests
were set aside from the public domain or purchased is a peculiar arrangement.   As Clawson and Held note,   "The fact that two committees, of
completely different membership in the House and of largely different membership in the Senate, consider legislation relating to different types of
federal land introduces a measure of divergence at the legislative level.
A single committee would have a measure of co-ordinating power which is
now absent." [10]

## The Department of Agriculture

Because nearly one-fourth of the forest land in the United States is on
farms, there has always been a close relationship between forestry and
agriculture.   Forestry programs have sometimes proved suitable media for
helping to implement certain agricultural policies.   For example, programs
aimed at increasing the productivity of farm woodlands have been used as
one means of working toward a policy of higher farm incomes.   Perhaps
more important from the forest viewpoint, programs designed to implement
agricultural policies have often provided convenient media for simultaneously implementing forest policies.   Forestry programs have therefore been
attached to agricultural programs which could have operated perfectly well
without the forestry aspect.   The extension program, for example, was
devised originally to transmit knowledge about crops and livestock to
farmers but has proved to be an effective vehicle for also transmitting
knowledge about tree planting and forest management to them.   As a result of this situation, a number of agencies in the Department of Agriculture
play roles of one kind or another in the execution of forest policies.

**Agricultural Research Service**   The Plant Pest Control Division administers cooperative plant pest control and domestic quarantine programs which
include some pests of importance for the forest resources.

**Agricultural Stabilization and Conservation Service**   Among other programs, this agency administers the Agricultural Conservation Program.
The ACP program is intended to promote soil and water conservation by
sharing with landowners the costs of installing conservation practices.
Among the practices subsidized by ACP are planting trees and improving
stands of trees.

[10] Marion Clawson and Burnell Held, *The Federal Lands; Their Use and Management,* The
Johns Hopkins Press, Baltimore, 1957, p. 148.

**Cooperative State Research Service**   This agency administers federal-grant funds for research in agriculture, forestry, resource conservation, and rural life.   The funds are made available to the state agricultural-experiment stations and cooperating forestry schools, which actually carry on the research.

**Federal Extension Service**   This is the federal part of the Cooperative Extension Service which includes the land-grant colleges in the 50 states and Puerto Rico.   It serves as a liaison between the research and action agencies of the Department of Agriculture and the extension staffs in the land-grant colleges.   The actual extension programs are conducted at the state level.   Forestry is one of the technical fields included in these programs.

**Soil Conservation Service**   This agency provides technical assistance in the land-use and rural-areas development programs of the Department of Agriculture.   It works through the Soil Conservation Districts at the local level to assist landowners in planning the management of their lands to conserve soil and water.   Woodland conservation is included in the planning.

## The Forest Service

The Forest Service is such an important agency in the execution of forest policies that we need to consider it in more detail than we have the other agencies above.   The Forest Service carries the main federal responsibility for protecting and developing the forest resources of the country.   The scope of its activities is therefore much broader than that of any other federal agency concerned with forestry, and its organization is more complex.   It is organized along the lines of its three major areas of responsibility: national forest administration, state and private forestry cooperation, and research.   We will consider each of these in turn.

**National forest administration**   The Forest Service administers 154 national forests which are scattered over 39 states and Puerto Rico.   In order to deal with this geographic spread of its land-management operations, the Forest Service has divided the country into nine administrative regions. Each is headed by a regional forester who is directly responsible to the Chief of the Forest Service.   Part of the chief's responsibility for the national forests is delegated to the Deputy Chief for the National Forest System, who to this extent functions as a line officer between the chief and the regional foresters.

Each of the 154 national forests is administered by a forest supervisor who is directly responsible to the regional forester in whose region his forest is located.   Each forest in turn is divided into ranger districts which are the basic units of national forest administration.   The ranger district carries out practically all of the recurrent resource and protection programs and activities.   The line of authority for administering the national forests thus runs from the chief to the regional forester to the forest supervisor to the district ranger.

The Washington office is organized into specialized functional divisions such as timber management and fire control.   These divisions serve in a staff capacity to provide knowledge and advice to the chief.   The regional offices are organized into similar functional divisions although the grouping of functions varies somewhat from region to region.   The functional divisions have no line authority, but they do give technical direction and guidance to subordinate line officers.   The line officers obviously cannot personally supervise all the technical details of their responsibility, and consequently much of the technical program is worked out between functional specialists at the various administrative levels.

This administrative structure is continuously involved in the execution of forest policies on the national forests.   As policies change and new programs develop, the administrative organization absorbs them and finds ways of putting them into effect.   Since 85 percent of the national forest area is in the West, the institutional structure of national forest administration is much larger in that part of the country than in the East.   The national forests in California form one whole region by themselves, and Region 6 includes only the national forests in Oregon and part of Washington.   By contrast, the Eastern Region covers 20 states, only 12 of which contain national forests.

**State and private forestry cooperation**   The Forest Service cooperates with the states and with private landowners in forest-fire control, forest-pest control, forest management, and flood prevention.   This responsibility of the Forest Service is relatively much more important in the East where about 90 percent of the forest land is in private, state, or local government ownership than in the West where only about 18 percent of the forest is in such nonfederal ownerships.   The administrative structure for handling this function is therefore different in the two parts of the country.

In the western 17 states, Puerto Rico, and the Virgin Islands, the line of authority and responsibility for state and private cooperation runs from the chief to the regional forester.   The regional forester or a designated assistant regional forester deals directly with the state foresters.   The western regional foresters are thus responsible for both national forest management and state and private cooperation.

The eastern 33 states are divided into two state and private forestry areas, and the line of authority for the cooperative programs runs from the chief to the area directors.   The directors deal directly with the state foresters.   The eastern regional foresters have no responsibility for the cooperative programs.   In both parts of the country the forest supervisors and district rangers may work with state officers or private landowners on specifically assigned jobs, but such activities are incidental to their national forest management activities.

**Forestry research**    The research organization of the Forest Service is structurally independent of the other two parts of the agency's organization. Eight regional forest experiment stations conduct research on problems of local importance in their regions.    The regional experiment station headquarters is mainly an administrative office with much of the research work being done at universities and other strategic locations in the region.    Research on wood is centered at the Forest Products Laboratory in Madison, Wisconsin, although some wood research is done in the regional experiment stations.    The Institute of Tropical Forestry in Puerto Rico conducts research on tropical problems.    The line of responsibility for research runs from the chief to the directors of the experiment stations, Forest Products Laboratory, and Institute of Tropical Forestry with the deputy chief for research in a more or less line position in between.

In the Washington office technical subject-matter divisions (such as forest-protection research, forest-economics and marketing research) function in a staff capacity.    The experiment stations are organized by similar subject-matter divisions which for administrative purposes are grouped under assistant directors.    Technical guidance from the Washington office staff specialists is channeled to the station divisions through the directors.

This brief discussion indicates that the Forest Service is a rather elaborate institutional structure for executing policies concerned with many aspects of forest use in the United States.    Although this structure and pattern of activities has become highly institutionalized, it is not entirely rigid.    The recent establishment of the two eastern state and private forestry cooperation areas and the accompanying consolidation of two national forest regions shows that these institutions can change.    However, in general, the institutional structure for executing forest policies through the Forest Service is likely to remain substantially as it now is for some time.

## The Department of the Interior

The Department of the Interior was established in 1849 with its primary responsibility lying in the General Land Office and the Office of Indian Affairs.    When the policy of disposing of the public domain changed, the lands which were reserved for permanent public ownership were already under the administration of the Interior Department.    Although the national forests were transferred to the Department of Agriculture in 1905, a substantial part of the forest resources of the nation have remained under the jurisdiction of the Interior Department.    This department has therefore historically been and continues to be very important in the execution of forest policies.    Because of the location of its land holdings and the nature of its responsibilities, the Department of the Interior has always been heavily oriented toward the part of the United States west of the Mississippi River.    This is bound to affect its general outlook on problems and is an institutional characteristic of importance in forest-policy execution.

**Bureau of Indian Affairs**   The Indian lands legally belong to the Indians, but for many years the federal government has managed most of them in trust.   The area involved is significant because it is estimated that these Indian lands include some 16 million acres of forest land.   The situation is a cross between private and public management.   The major objective is to produce income for the Indian owners, but since the managing agency is a public bureau it is bound to take public interests into account more heavily than would a strictly private manager.   This bureau has the potential to effectively execute forest policy on some 2 percent of the nation's forest land.

**Bureau of Land Management**   This one bureau has under its jurisdiction about 21 percent of all the land in the United States.   These are mostly the remaining public-domain lands which have not been set aside as national forests or parks.   As might be expected, they are to some extent the lands that no one else wanted.   The Bureau of Land Management lists some 144 million acres of its holdings as forest and woodland.[11]   The Forest Service classifies only about 28 million acres of this as commercial forest land.   However, this commercial land includes the 2.4 million acres of revested railroad and wagon-road grant lands in western Oregon, which are some of the most productive forest lands in the country.
    The Bureau of Land Management is strictly a public land managing agency and has no responsibility for private forest lands or forestry research as does the Forest Service.   In addition, its activities are geographically restricted since only about one-half of 1 percent of the forest lands under its control lie east of the Great Plains.   Of the forest-land area under BLM jurisdiction, 80 percent is in Alaska.   Despite its more limited responsibilities, the bureau is obviously a significant factor in land use in the West (especially in Alaska) and plays a major role in the execution of some forest policies.

**Bureau of Outdoor Recreation**   The responsibilities of the Bureau of Outdoor Recreation lie in the area of planning, promoting, and facilitating the development of recreational facilities, and it does not operate any recreation areas of its own.   The Bureau administers the Land and Water Conservation Fund Act, which provides money for acquisition of recreation lands and waters.   It plays and will continue to play a very important role in the execution of policies concerned with outdoor recreation.

**Bureau of Sport Fisheries and Wildlife**   This is one of the two divisions of the Fish and Wildlife Service, the other one being the Bureau of Commercial Fisheries.   The Bureau of Sport Fisheries and Wildlife has broad responsibilities for the perpetuation and enhancement of fish and wildlife resources wherever they occur.   It cooperates with other agencies in research and in regulation of the taking of fish and wildlife.   In these ways it

[11] Bureau of Land Management, *Public Land Statistics 1967*, Washington, 1968, p. 132.

plays an important role in the execution of policies concerned with forest wildlife.   The Bureau also manages over 300 refuges and game ranges with a total area of some 28 million acres.   Much of this area is marsh and range lands, but a considerable amount of forest land is included.

**National Park Service**   This agency administers areas which are considered to be of national significance for their recreational, historical, and natural values.   Its primary function is to preserve these areas and at the same time make them available for the public to enjoy.   The Park Service is responsible for 29 national parks and almost 160 other areas (national monuments, national recreation areas, etc.).   These are scattered over 42 states and contain a total area of about 22 million acres.   A substantial part of this area is forest land.   Because of the restricted uses which the laws permit on these areas, the National Park Service is responsible only for executing some kinds of forest policies.   The fact that these Park Service areas are rather permanently "locked up" is an important institutional restraint on forest-land use in the United States, although most people would agree that it is a desirable one.

## Other Federal Agencies

A number of other federal agencies are involved with forests in one way or another.   We will mention here only two which are actively engaged in executing forest policies.

**Tennessee Valley Authority**   The TVA is an independent federal agency which in addition to developing the Tennessee River for flood control, power generation, and recreation has also promoted improved land use in the whole valley.   Since a large part of the Tennessee Valley is forested, the Division of Forestry Development has played an important role in the TVA program.   The Tennessee River drainage includes parts of seven states, and much of the TVA activity is in cooperation with these states.   Primarily concerned with private forest lands, the Tennessee Valley Authority is a unique institution in that it integrates forest-policy execution in a natural land area rather than within political boundaries, which are often rather artificial in terms of land use.

**Department of Defense**   Lands under the administration of the Army, Navy, and Air Force total some 29 million acres and are scattered over all 50 states.   These include substantial areas of forest land.   The primary uses of these lands are for defense purposes, but often these do not prevent their simultaneous management for other forest benefits.   Because of the area involved, these military lands can make a significant contribution to our supply of these various benefits.   The Department of Defense is therefore a land-managing agency capable of executing some forest policies, although its primary defense function places significant institutional restraints on its forestry activities.

## Forest Institutions in State and Local Governments

Every one of the 50 states charges some part of the state government with responsibility for forests.   In a few states like Kansas this is a very nominal responsibility, but in others the forestry agency is an important part of the state government.   Public forest ownership and management is not considered a major responsibility by most states, though in 1963 only two states reported that they owned no commercial forest land at all.   A few states are substantial owners of commercial forest land, the major ones being:

| | |
|---|---|
| Michigan | 3.7 million acres |
| Minnesota | 3.3 million acres |
| Pennsylvania | 2.7 million acres |
| Washington | 2.0 million acres |

Five other states—Florida, Idaho, Montana, Oregon, and Wisconsin—each own more than a half million acres of commercial forest land.

The local governments are not generally important forest-land owners. Seventeen states reported no local government ownership of commercial forest land in 1963.   Minnesota and Wisconsin are exceptions.   The counties own 3.4 million acres of commercial forest in Minnesota and 2.6 million acres in Wisconsin.

The states assume the primary responsibility for protecting private land resources and for assisting and controlling private landowners.   Most of this state responsibility for private forest lands is usually assigned to one state agency, and the state forests are administered by this same agency.   State parks are practically always administered by a different agency.   Only three states combine forest and park administration in one independent agency.   In many cases, however, the forest agency and the parks agency are both divisions of some larger agency.   Fish and wildlife are almost always handled by a separate state agency though fish and game, forestry, and state parks may all be set up as divisions in one larger state agency.

Forestry is an independent agency in one-third of the states, but these states do not agree on what to call it.   The most common names are Forestry Commission or Forest Service, but it is called the Forestry Department or Forestry Division in a number of states.   In 31 states, the forestry agency is a part of a larger state agency.   This is most commonly called the Department of Natural Resources.   Department of Conservation or Conservation Commission is also a common title, and in a number of states the name includes "development" as in Department of Conservation and Economic Development.

It is significant that two-thirds of the states try to integrate forestry with other land use and development matters by placing them under the same administration.   It is also interesting that only one state assigns the responsibility for forestry to the state Department of Agriculture.    The reason for this may lie in the fact that the kinds of policies and programs with which the state departments of agriculture are concerned differ materially from those of concern to the forestry agencies.    Or it may be that since the state agriculture departments are so firmly entrenched and powerful, it was feared that forestry in the same department would be dominated by the agricultural interests.    Most of the states do seem to feel that there are advantages to placing forestry in close administrative proximity to other resource agencies such as parks, water, fish and game, and economic development.

The state forestry agencies have been in existence for many years and have become quite institutionalized.    Rather elaborate fire detection and control organizations exist in almost every state.    A network of service foresters provides management assistance to landowners and primary operators.    Through their fire warden and service forester organizations, these agencies can reach landowners and other people of significance for forest policies in every part of their states.    State nurseries which operate on a continuous basis—and often on a very large scale—provide not only seedlings for the state's landowners but also a going machinery for executing policies of forest improvement through the development of superior trees. The state forestry agencies are probably in the most strategic position for executing most forest policies since they are closer to both the resources and the people involved than the federal agencies and are larger and more effective than county or other local agencies.

**Cooperative Extension Service**    In each of the 50 states and Puerto Rico the land-grant colleges have esablished extension services which cooperate with the Federal Extension Service.    The director of the state extension service is ordinarily the dean of the college of agriculture or reports directly to him.    Although part of the financing and a certain amount of technical assistance comes from the federal government, the extension services are considered to be state organizations.    The extension services function through county agents who are located in the individual counties and who often have a small staff to assist them.    Technical specialists, who usually are headquartered at the land-grant colleges, assist the county agents in the areas of their specialties and work through them in getting technical information to the landowners.    Forestry is one of these specialties.    In some states the extension forester has a number of assistants who share his duties.    The Extension Service is strictly an educational institution and does not provide other services nor engage in land management itself.    Because of its decentralized organization it provides a very effective institution for reaching farmers and other landowners with the ideas and knowledge needed to execute certain forest policies.

**State Agricultural Experiment Stations**    Each of the states has an experiment station attached to the land-grant college whose director is the dean of the college of agriculture or reports directly to him.    Many of these

experiment stations do some research in forestry, and much of their research on other agricultural problems (such as soils, entomology, diseases)
has carry-over value for forest problems.   Where the land grant college has
a forestry school, much of the agricultural experiment station's work on
forest problems is channeled through the forestry faculty, who are members
of the experiment station staff in their research roles.   This cooperative
relationship between the agricultural experiment stations and the forestry
schools has increased in recent years as the schools have expanded their
staffs and areas of interest.

**Forestry schools**   These schools at the university level educate the
people who spend their careers implementing forest policies and influencing their formation.   In addition to educating professional foresters, they
also provide specialized preparation for forest researchers and continuing
education to keep both practitioners and investigators up to date.   The
research and other scholarly activities of their faculties constantly add to
our fund of knowledge about forest-resource use.

Thirty-six of the states have at least one forestry school.   Because some
states have more than one, the total number of schools in the United States
is 48.   Thirty-four of these have been accredited by the Society of American Foresters.   But the other 14 are also educating people who will work
in forestry and therefore are an important part of the forest-education institution.   Forty-four of the forestry schools are state supported, the remaining four being connected with private universities.   The private schools
awarded 8 percent of the graduate forestry degrees in 1967, but only 3 out
of 1855 bachelor degrees.[12]   The state universities clearly play a dominant
role in forestry education in the United States.

Most of the forestry schools have active research programs in addition
to their teaching programs.   Forty of them receive federal-grant funds
for research through the Cooperative State Research Service.   Many
are also tied in with the state agricultural experiment stations as noted
above.

**Soil Conservation Districts**   These are units of local government specifically authorized by laws in the individual states.   Each district is run
by a local board of supervisors.   They function primarily to promote conservation practices.   The Soil Conservation Service assigns area and work-
unit conservationists to work with the districts, and these SCS employees
provide most of the technical planning and assistance to the landowners.
Most of the districts were originally given power to enact land-use regulations, but only a few have been enacted and none enforced.   The soil
conservation districts have not played a very large role in executing forest
policies, but they are part of the institutional structure which exists at the
local level and which might be used in the future.

[12] Gordon D. Marckworth, "Statistics from Schools of Forestry for 1967," *Journal of
Forestry*, April, 1968, pp. 333–339.

## INTEGRATING INSTITUTIONS

We have now seen that the institutional structure for executing forest policies consists of a large number of separate agencies. Some degree of integration exists when several of these agencies are parts of a larger governmental unit, as in the case of the Bureau of Land Management, the Fish and Wildlife Service, and the Park Service in the Department of the Interior. And yet we know that historically there have sometimes been not only failures in cooperation but cases of downright antagonism between bureaus in the same department (as in the struggle between the Soil Conservation Service and the Forest Service over responsibility for farm-woodland programs). The coordinating power of the secretary over the bureaus in his department is not as strong as it might appear.

Still, these many agencies do not all go off independently on their own chosen ways with complete disregard for what the others are doing. A variety of institutions have developed for integrating in one way or another the efforts of various groups of executing agencies.

**Grants-in-aid**   This most effective coordinating institution owes much of its success to the fact that it strengthens the agencies involved financially without taking from them control over their own programs. The states make grants-in-aid to local governments for other purposes like education, but in forestry this device has been almost entirely a case of federal grants to the states. Most grants-in-aid require a partial matching of the funds by the grantee and also specify somewhat the conditions under which the funds must be used.

The Weeks Act of 1911 provided funds for cooperation by the federal government with the states in the control of forest fires. These grants-in-aid are administered by the Forest Service and now go to all 50 states. Fire control is a state program administered by the state forester but partly financed by federal funds. The Forest Service does not attempt to dictate how these funds are used, but it does require reports and makes regular inspections. In the process, it influences the kinds of programs the states develop, and this has resulted in considerable uniformity among programs in different states.

The Clarke-McNary Act of 1924 authorized a grant-in-aid program to assist the states in providing tree planting stock for private landowners. Forty-eight states receive these federal grants.

Under the Cooperative Forest Management program, the federal government shares the cost of providing technical assistance to private woodland owners, loggers, and processors of primary forest products. Forty-nine states, Puerto Rico, and the Virgin Islands receive grants under this program. In 1967, the states more than matched the federal grant of 3.5 million dollars by putting 4.8 million of their own funds into this program.

The Forest Pest Control Act provides for federal cooperation with the states in the control of forest insects and diseases. The Forest Service now shares costs with about half the states in such pest-control programs.

Although grants-in-aid are basically a device by which one level of government provides funds to a lower level of government for carrying out certain activities, they serve a much broader function than that of financing. The granting government always specifies conditions which must be met by the grantees in order to receive the funds.    The two therefore become linked in a common program.    Although the ultimate control appears to rest with the federal government in forestry grant-in-aid programs, these all require matching state funds, and the federal government cannot carry out its desired program without state cooperation.    The states can and do influence the attitudes and ideas of the Forest Service, and the programs thus become truly cooperative in nature.    The Forest Service also serves a coordinating function between the states so that in effect all of the involved states and the federal government are working together in these programs.

Grants-in-aid may also exert a rather direct influence on the institutional structure of the grantees.    The Weeks Act program, for example, stimulated the establishment of a number of state forestry organizations in states where they previously had been nonexistent or ineffectual.

Commenting on the arguments for and against grants-in-aid, Dana says: "Whatever one may think of the relative merits of the opposing arguments, the system is apparently too well entrenched to make probable any material modification either in forestry or other fields." [13]    This view is strengthened by the development since 1962 of the program of the Bureau of Outdoor Recreation.    This bureau is charged broadly with encouraging and assisting other federal agencies, the states, their political subdivisions, and private interests in developing outdoor recreation resources.    As an effective device to help in carrying out these functions, the Land and Water Conservation Fund Act provides that federal funds derived from various specified sources are to be used by the Bureau of Outdoor Recreation for grants-in-aid to other public agencies to assist in buying and developing lands for recreational use.    In 1967, the amount of money available for such grants exceeded 100 million dollars or more than four times as much as the Forest Service had to spend on all of its forestry grant-in-aid programs.

**Interstate compacts**    This is a device which enables several states to work together formally toward a common end.    The formation of an interstate compact requires the approval of Congress since the Constitution specifically says that "No state shall, without the approval of Congress, . . . enter into any agreement or Compact with another state or with a foreign power. . . ."    The states have entered into such compacts for a variety of other purposes in recent years, but their use for forestry has been limited.

The first use of an interstate compact in forestry was the Northeastern States Forest Fire Protection Compact, which was formed in 1949.    The states of Connecticut, Maine, Massachusetts, New Hampshire, New York, Rhode Island, and Vermont were the original members, but membership is

---

[13] Samuel T. Dana, *Forest and Range Policy*, McGraw-Hill Book Company, New York, 1956, p. 342.

also open to any adjacent state or, with the approval of Congress, any adjacent Canadian Province.    The compact states that the federal Forest Service may upon request help in research and coordination, and the Forest Service is an active participant in the program carried on under this compact.

The compact creates the Northeastern Forest Fire Protection Commission as the action agency to carry out the provisions of the compact.    The commission consists of three commissioners from each of the member states and employs an executive secretary.    The purpose of the compact is "To promote effective prevention and control of forest fires in the northeastern region of the United States and adjacent areas in Canada."    The means proposed for accomplishing this are:

1.  Development of integrated forest-fire plans
2.  Maintenance of adequate forest-fire fighting services by the member states
3.  Providing for mutual aid in fighting forest fires and for procedures that will facilitate such aid
4.  The establishment of a central agency to coordinate the services of the member states and to perform such common services as the member states want [14]

The Commission has prepared a fire plan, holds annual training sessions, and publishes a quarterly called *Compact News*.    It appears to provide an effective means for enabling the states and the federal Forest Service to work closely in a joint plan of forest-fire control.

The second interstate compact in forestry was the Southeastern States Forest Fire Compact which was formed in 1954.    This was a compact among ten southeastern states and was patterned closely after the Northeastern compact.    The compact is administered by a commission, and the Forest Service has served as the coordinating agency for the commission.    The program has been similar to that of the Northeastern Commission.    Forest-fire compacts of a similar nature have since been formed by groups of states in the Middle Atlantic and South Central regions.

**Other integrating institutions**    A number of other organizations serve an integrating function in forest programs.    Relatively informal action groups exist in various regions.    An example is the Northwest Forest Pest Action Council which is composed of all persons in that region who are interested in the control of forest insect pests and diseases.    The meetings of these regional groups provide a place to exchange ideas and keep in touch with the activities of others.    Such groups also serve an action function by focusing attention on problems and encouraging coordination and cooperation.    The various conservation, industrial, and professional associations function both to bring people from various agencies together and also as promoters of integrated action.    Many forest agencies have formal advisory groups drawn from a variety of interests.    Some of these

[14] *Manual for Forest Fire Control,* Northeastern Forest Fire Protection Commission, Chatham, N.Y., 1958, p. A-4.

appear to serve only a nominal purpose, but others do exert an influence over the programs of the agencies they advise.

## SUMMARY

Forest policies in the United States are executed by an elaborate structure of private and governmental institutions.   No single agency or organization exerts a dominant control over the use of our forests.   This institutional structure is partly a result of our national economic and political philosophy and partly a result of historical accident.   Suggestions are frequently made for changing or reorganizing it, which their proponents claim would increase its effectiveness or efficiency.   These have always met with resistance from many quarters, and the overall institutions have not changed greatly in recent years.

The forest-related institutions developed their present fragmented form as a result of the complex and geographically diffuse nature of forest use in the United States and of the programs which influence and control that use.   The resistance to changing these institutions stems from a feeling that there were good reasons why they developed as they did and that it may not really be possible to achieve substantial improvements in their effectiveness.   This feeling is strengthened by the many conflicts in objectives and policies and our inability to decide what uses are ultimately "right."

Our approach to natural-resource problems is more sophisticated every year, however, and the forest-related institutions are not as disjointed and unrelated as they sometimes appear to be.   In fact, there is much evidence that the many parts of this institutional structure are becoming more aware of and synchronized with each other all the time.   The institutional structure is not static; it changes gradually in many small ways, and such a continuous evolution is necessary if it is to keep in tune with the similarly evolutionary changes taking place in forest policies.

# The Politics of Forest Resources

# 12.

In Chapter 3 we discussed in general and somewhat abstract terms the process through which forest policies are formed. In the intervening chapters we have explored in some depth the problems involved in forming policies and in establishing them as settled and accepted courses of action. We have also accumulated considerable information about the situation in the United States and the existing institutions which are involved with forest policies. Now we will try to see in more realistic terms how the political process functions in the formation of United States forest policies.

It is clear that we cannot hope to present in one chapter a complete picture of the political processes involved in the formation of forest policies. Whole books have been written about political activity in conservation policy during certain historical periods or in certain localities.[1] This book cannot pretend to be a thoroughgoing study of the politics of forestry in either its current or historical aspects. Such studies would be enlightening and useful and should be encouraged. Right now it may well be questioned whether any one person is completely aware of and understands all the political activity that goes on in the area of forest policy. The best we can do here is present an admittedly incomplete and perhaps even somewhat naïve picture of current forest-resource politics.

[1] See, as a few examples: Richard A. Cooley, *Politics and Conservation: The Decline of the Alaska Salmon*, Harper & Row, Publishers, Incorporated, New York, 1963; Samuel P. Hays, *Conservation and the Gospel of Efficiency: The Progressive Conservation Movement, 1890–1920*, Harvard University Press, Cambridge, Mass., 1959; and Donald C. Swain, *Federal Conservation Policy 1921–1933*, University of California Press, Berkeley, 1963.

## POLITICS AND POWER

As we have noted earlier, even in a democracy, policies are not really formed by all of the people.   On most policy issues—and perhaps on all of them—the attitude of a large part of the population is one of disinterest and apathy.   Very few forest policies have a direct and noticeable effect on the lives of many people.   They may have indirect effects, as in the case of a policy which would lead to future shortages of raw material for wood products.   But the average citizen will not get very much excited today about the possibility that he or his children might have to pay higher prices for or even do without certain wood products at some indefinite time in the future.

On many policy issues, most of the people are indifferent as to the outcome.   What proportion of the people in the United States personally cared, for example, whether a part of the North Cascades area in western Washington was made a national park or remained a part of the national forest?   On many other issues, they probably are not completely indifferent but do not feel the matter is of sufficient importance to them personally to make it worthwhile trying to do something about it.   They already have too many other really pressing problems.   Or they may feel that nothing they can do will change the outcome.   What can one individual do, for example, to affect the unsightly condition in which logging companies leave the forest when they complete their harvesting operations?

This does not mean that the mass of the people never have any effect on forest policies.   If a policy that affects them personally is not acceptable to them, they may resist complying with it.   The difficulty in establishing policies of not burning the woods in certain seasons, of camping and picnicking only in designated locations, and of not discarding trash and refuse at random on forest lands indicates that passive resistance by large numbers of people can prevent forest policies from becoming really effective.   When people are not truly indifferent to a policy issue they may be stimulated to some kind of action by propaganda or education or by the formation of a group which they can join or a program in which they can take part.   The large increase in membership experienced by the Sierra Club as a result of its dramatic newspaper advertising campaigns on wilderness and related issues indicates that much latent interest in these policies exists and can be stimulated into action.

In general, however, individual forest policies will be of vital interest to only a relatively small part of the people.   As Talbot says:   "There is no general public opinion in regard to the programs of the Forest Service or the Bureau of Reclamation.   There are many publics composed of substantial numbers of farmers and ranchers, private utility companies, hunters and fishermen, small town businessmen, and others who, concerned about the policies of those bureaucratic organizations, will try to influence those policies in varying fashion and with relative effectiveness." [2]   It is such concerned publics that are actively involved in forest-policy formation.

[2] Ross B. Talbot, "The Political Forces," in Howard W. Ottoson (ed.), *Land Use Policy and Problems in the United States,* University of Nebraska Press, Lincoln, 1963, p. 151.

## Direct Control of the Resources

It is obvious that those who have direct control over the use of the forests are in a position to influence strongly the forest policies of the nation.   In fact, so long as the rest of the people do not object, those who control the forest resources set the forest policies of the country.

Now unless all of the forests are controlled by one individual or one organization, the people who do control the forests are bound to have some effect on each other.   In a country with adequate forest resources, for example, they could not all decide to harvest all of their merchantable-size timber immediately.   The market just would not absorb this much timber at one time, and the most rapid general liquidation policy could only be one of gradually harvesting the merchantable timber as fast as the market would take it.   The tendency in such a case would certainly be for those in control of the forests to get together and work out a policy of orderly liquidation that would be of mutual advantage to them, or certain individuals might try to find some way to restrict the harvest of other people's timber in order that their own trees could be liquidated immediately.   This simple example brings out two basic characteristics of politics: compromise and a struggle for positions of power.   We will have more to say about both of them.

In many cases, even when those who do not control the forest resources raise no objections, there will still be conflicts between the individual desires of those who do control the forests.   Imagine a situation where two forest owners have properties which face each other from opposite sides of a lake.   One owner wants to develop his property for recreation and summer homes to take advantage of the beautiful scenery across the lake.   His neighbor on the other side of the lake, however, wants to cut all of his large trees and poison the rest, leaving the tops and dead trees to be disposed of gradually by the slow process of natural decay.   It is not difficult to imagine the efforts of the recreation developer to find some means of restraining the timber-cutting activities of his neighbor and the counter efforts of that person to retain his freedom to use his forest as he desires.

If we generalize the situation presented by these lakeside owners, it becomes apparent that those who control the forest resources will still determine the forest policies even though other people object to them unless the noncontrollers can somehow bring enough pressure to bear to make the controllers change their actions.   Many people may complain about the deleterious effects of chemical pesticides on fish and other natural fauna, but the policy will continue to be one of aerial spraying to combat insect epidemics as long as those in control of the forests feel that this is a necessary and desirable way of protecting the forests.   It will be possible to change this policy only if those who object to the broadcast spraying of chemical pesticides are able to achieve a position of power from which they can prevail upon those who control the forests to abandon this procedure.

Thus we see that those concerned with forest policies must seek to achieve positions of power in order to exert an influence on policy formation.

The strongest power position is to be in direct control of part of the forest resources.   This is what underlies the acquisition of forest lands by both public agencies and private owners.   But these direct controllers may also be controlled from other positions of power.   The politics of forestry is the activity through which numerous people are trying to attain positions from which they can influence or guide the formation of forest policies.

## FORMS OF POLITICAL ACTION

The direct controllers of forest resources fall into two broad classes: private owners and public agencies.   The ways of bringing pressure to bear on these two classes are somewhat different, though the political actions required to achieve a position from which such pressures can be applied may be similar in many cases.

### Influencing Private Forest Owners

The practices of private owners may be influenced by other individuals in the society through private actions or through resort to some kind of government action.   Many private owners are especially susceptible to economic pressures.   This is, in fact, the way that our market system operates to guide production policies.   If a forest owner were to insist on using all of his land to grow nothing but sumac trees he would soon discover that his crop was worthless in the market, and he would be strongly influenced to shift to growing something else that people wanted.   We do not ordinarily consider this market pressure as a political action but other types of economic pressure may be.   For example, people might be induced by an organized effort to boycott the products offered for sale by certain landowners who were using their lands in undesirable ways.   Wood-using companies have occasionally used a variant of this technique by refusing to buy timber from landowners unless they followed certain desired forestry practices.   In general, however, since most forest products are raw materials and thus not sold to the general public, economic pressures do not seem to be a very effective means for influencing forest owners' practices.
Other forms of social pressure may also be applied to private landowners.   Most people are concerned for what other members of their society think about them.   An organized campaign to demonstrate public approval or disapproval of certain actions by the landowners may therefore encourage them to continue these actions or to change to other practices.   On the positive side we find public recognition of "master farmers" and other "good" land managers, the certification of tree farms, and similar organized actions to show popular approval of desired policies.   On the negative side we find newspaper campaigns featuring "horrible" examples of misuse of the forests, condemnation by public figures, and in the case of other policies —though seldom in forestry—the use of extreme techniques such as picketing.   By organizing a campaign and mobilizing support from a variety

of interested sources it is possible to develop enough power to exert tremendous social pressure on private owners to conform to some desired forest policy.

Government actions to influence the practices of private forest owners have been discussed at length in Chapters 7 and 8. If people are not satisfied with what the private forest owners are doing now, either the existing public laws and programs aimed at private forest lands are not adequate or else they are not being enforced and executed satisfactorily. Through political action, therefore, the interested people must try to change the laws and programs or else the way in which the responsible government agencies are administering them. This means that these people must somehow achieve a position of sufficient power in government activities that they can bring to bear the pressure necessary to make the desired changes. The ways of arriving at these positions of power are the same as would be used in attempting to influence the actions of the government agencies which control forest lands. We will therefore first look at the problems of influencing these agencies and then at the means of achieving the necessary positions of power.

## Influencing Public Forest Managing Agencies

The public forest managing agencies are not as independent in deciding what to do with their forests as the private owners. Instructions (though perhaps rather general and vague) as to how the public forests are to be used have been laid down for them in legislative acts and sometimes in constitutions (as in the case of the New York Forest Preserve). At the same time, these public agencies are not affected as much by economic pressures from the market as are the private owners. They are, however, susceptible to social pressures of the same kind as affect private owners. It is hard to imagine a public agency being much influenced by positive expressions of acclaim and approval, though public administrators no doubt appreciate praise as much as any other man. But they are concerned for their "image" and do react to the negative pressures of public criticism and denunciation—very often, unfortunately, in defensive and not necessarily constructive ways.

One device for influencing public agencies is the so-called client organization whose membership consists wholly or largely of clients of a particular bureau. Western Lumber Manufacturers, Inc., for example, is an association of industrial firms which buy timber from the national forests in California. Through its Secretary-Manager it keeps in constant touch with the timber-sales program of the Forest Service. By calling attention to problems as they develop and working closely with the Forest Service in seeking solutions to them, it exerts a constructive influence on some of this agency's management practices. The National Parks Association functions in a somewhat similar role to influence the National Park Service.

The ways of influencing the public forest managing agencies through strictly private actions are rather limited. The most effective are those which get at them through the government itself.    These are the same ways that are used to reach the government agencies which influence private forest owners' actions.

## Stimulating Government Action

There are four major points at which pressures can be brought in an effort to stimulate government action—the bureaucracies, the elected or appointed executives, the legislatures, and the courts.    We will consider them in this order because this seems the most logical approach to understanding them.    But this does not mean that their relative importance is necessarily of this order.    Which pressure point is most effective depends on the particular policy involved and the kind of action that is desired.

**The bureaucracies**    In our present-day government, most of the people who staff the public forestry agencies are insulated or partly removed from overt political pressures by the federal civil service or state merit systems. They are appointed originally only after passing some kind of qualification test and once appointed can only be removed involuntarily as a result of serious failure to perform in a satisfactory manner.    The forest bureaucracies are therefore quite permanent and stable in nature, and there is no way of applying pressure to change their personnel abruptly.

It also is difficult to introduce new people with different attitudes or ideas into these organizations at levels of sufficient responsibility to change materially the actions of an agency.    Some important bureaus like the Forest Service fill practically all vacancies by promotion from within and seldom bring in people from outside in other than the lowest grades.    Of course, it would be possible to infiltrate any government agency by having people of a certain policy persuasion enter the lower grades by passing the examination and then work their way up to positions of responsibility in the hierarchy.    (To some extent this process actually took place in the Forest Service where for many years entering employees were largely restricted to professional foresters from a common educational background.) But it clearly would take a very long time to change the attitudes of a whole bureau by this approach.

This "protected" nature of the bureaucracies does not mean that there are no ways in which outside people can influence their actions with regard to forest policies.    They can be reached through other parts of the governments, and we will consider those possibilities when we discuss the executive, legislative, and judicial branches.    They also can be influenced in more direct ways.

Before considering these more direct means of influence it would probably be well to point out that the bureaucracies themselves are aware of and concerned about their insulation.    As a means of overcoming this, at least in part, some of the bureaus are making increasing use of administrative hearings in which interested outsiders are invited to express their views on proposed programs and thus to take part in the policy-making process.

One direct means of influence is "education" of the relevant officials of an agency in the desired viewpoints.   Suppose, for example, that the administrators of some forest agency have been almost exclusively timber oriented in their management of the public forests and have paid little attention to their recreational potential.   It may be possible to induce these officials through a variety of ways to become interested in or at least cognizant of recreation.   Literature may be sent them.   Interested individuals or groups may call on them.   They may be invited to speak at meetings, join recreation-oriented clubs, or serve as members of committees or study groups concerned with recreation.   The news media may criticize their attitudes openly or make slighting references to the quality of their management.   Concerned people could think of many other ways of reaching them.

Kaufman has referred to one variety of this approach as the "capture" of field officers by local populations and noted:

> The danger is really twofold.   On the one hand, there is the risk that field men, regarded by their chiefs as emissaries sent to live among local populaces and represent the agency to the people, become so identified with the communities in which they reside that they become community delegates to headquarters rather than the reverse.   On the other hand, there is the possibility that the field men, though devoted to their leaders, might be cowed by local pressures.[3]

Kaufman used the word "danger" because he was looking at this phenomenon from the viewpoint of the Forest Service's desire to maintain homogeneous attitudes toward policies throughout their entire organization. From the viewpoint of making government agencies responsive to the policy objectives of the people, it may be very desirable for government officers to be "captured" to some extent by the segment of the population with which they have intimate contact.

Although most bureaucrats cannot be hired or fired at will, they are subject to transfer, promotion, and assignment to specific responsibilities. Outside people may be able to exert an influence on some or all of these administrative actions.   If the timber buyers or other clients of a public forest are very unhappy with the way some local officer performs his duties, they may be able to present a sufficiently strong and well-documented complaint to his superiors that these will decide to transfer the offending officer to another location or other duties.   The possible unpleasant effects on them of such complaints brings pressure on officials to at least consider the ideas of outside people.   (More direct pressures such as the threat or actual practice of incendiarism have also been used on intransigent forest officers.)

Outside people may also be able to establish close enough rapport with the administrators of an agency that their suggestions and recommendations will be considered in selecting men for promotion or assignment to special

---

3 Herbert Kaufman, *The Forest Ranger*, The Johns Hopkins Press, Baltimore, 1960, p. 76.

duties.    Promotions and assignments can never be made mechanically and seldom in a truly objective manner.    By influencing the subjective judgments involved, it may be possible to encourage or facilitate the movement of officers with desirable ideas or viewpoints into strategic positions in the organization.    As might be expected, this situation also exerts pressures on the ambitious forest officer to deliberately foster good relations with people whose future support might be helpful in obtaining a promotion or desirable assignment.    Despite the dangers of the potential use of such arrangements for personal gain rather than public benefit, they provide a useful means for bringing the actions of public agencies into conformity with popular desires.

Many of the programs of any public agency depend heavily on cooperation by other people or organizations.    An agency may therefore be encouraged to develop or expand a particular type of program by offers of cooperation.    The cooperation of the large timberland owning companies and of the chemical pesticide manufacturers, for example, have had a continuing influence on public programs of aerial spraying for insect control. On the opposite side, programs or policies can be discouraged or even made impossible by the withholding of necessary cooperation by outsiders.    The federal effort to develop a national policy of public regulation of timber cutting on private lands encountered a serious handicap in the reluctance of many states to cooperate by developing state regulatory laws.    The effects of cooperation are not always so decisively for or against some action but may be equally significant in that working closely together in a cooperative arrangement gives the cooperators a continuing opportunity to influence the agency's actions in many subtle ways.

Finally, outsiders may find a place where they can exert an influence in the competition which almost always exists between agencies and between individuals within a single agency.    Where alternatives exist, they can throw their support to the one which appears most favorable or least unfavorable to their viewpoint.    The forest industries, for example, while basically opposed to public regulation of cutting practices on private lands, preferred to be regulated by the states rather than the federal government. They therefore actively supported the states against the federal government in the contest to see who was to do the regulating.    In many cases, probably nothing more than an implied threat to support the opponents is needed to obtain a reasonable attitude on the parts of ambitious administrators or bureaus.

It is perhaps desirable to repeat here that the kinds of political activity described above are not only legitimate but desirable in our form of government.    Unfortunately the word "politics" is frequently used in a disparaging way, and the application of influence or pressure on a public agency is somehow considered to be unethical.    Obviously such activities could be —and have been—used for unethical purposes, but this means merely that they must be scrutinized or perhaps controlled in some ways and not eliminated as effective means of policy formation.

**The elected or appointed executives**    The upper-level executives in the federal and state governments lack the insulation from politics enjoyed by the bureaucrats.    Because of the powerful influence they can exert on policies and on the activities of the public agencies, it is necessary that they be subject to removal if the people are not satisfied with their actions. The President and governors are elected, and they in turn appoint the secretaries of the cabinet departments and their assistants and the administrative heads of the various state departments.    These appointments are made only after consultation with interested parties and approval by the legislatures.    The President and governors can be removed at the end of their elected term, but the appointed executives can be removed at any time.

These highest-level executives can have a pronounced influence when they choose to personally promote certain policies or programs as Secretary of Interior Udall did.    They also exert a fair amount of influence over the actions of the bureaucracies which come under their administration.    We noted in Chapter 11 that the government agencies are not completely subject to the executive branch but have responsibilities to the legislative and judicial branches, which at times enable them to be somewhat independent of the executive who is nominally superior to them.    However, there usually are many means by which the executives can bring pressures on their agencies and influence their actions.

Thus there are two ways in which access to the elected or appointed executives can be used to stimulate government action.    One is by getting the executive to take some action himself, and the other is by getting him to bring pressure for some particular kind of action by the agencies under his jurisdiction.    Because of the position of the appointed executives, it may be possible to bring pressure on them from their superiors who usually were originally responsible for their appointment.    Thus a governor might be prevailed upon to instruct his conservation commissioner to take certain actions himself or to urge the bureaus responsible to him to take these actions.

In order to get a high-level executive to act on some policy issue, the outside parties must present a very convincing case or else be in a position to offer something of advantage to the executive or to threaten him with some unfavorable action.    Most forestry issues today appear to be relatively minor when compared with the serious problems of war, race relations, atomic energy, urban blight, education, and transportation, which demand the attention of the top government executives.    We are not likely to see very often a situation such as prevailed during Theodore Roosevelt's administration when the President of the United States personally was much interested in conservation and devoted a substantial amount of time to it. It will be very hard to get even a governor to give anything more than nominal support to an issue purely as a result of convincing factual arguments.    Outdoor recreation, pollution, and beauty are the only aspects of renewable natural-resource use that currently seem able to attract executive attention.

The appointed executives are more susceptible to being convinced than the elected ones mainly because they have narrower specific responsibilities and in the case of the Secretary of Agriculture or a state conservation commissioner actually have the forests as part of their area of responsibility.

The main kind of advantage or threat which can be presented to an elected or appointed executive as a stimulus to action is related to the maintenance in power of his particular administration or political party.   If some forest-policy issue were of sufficient concern to enough people in a state, the governor might be moved to favorable action on it by the offer of support or threat of opposition in a pending election.   Since in our form of government the appointed officials are usually political supporters or associates of the President or governor who appointed them they also have a large stake in future elections.

Clearly, one way to get action on an issue which the administration in power refuses to do anything about is to replace that particular administration with one which promises to take action on the issue.   This might be done by changing the leaders within the political party already in power or by defeating this party in an election.   Since there are constitutional limitations on how long one person can retain the office of President and also in many states the office of governor, opportunities do occur periodically to obtain a more sympathetic or active chief executive and as a result more favorably inclined appointed officials.

However, as we noted earlier, forest-policy issues are not likely to loom very large among those which will influence the choice made by the voters in an election.   Engelbert says that "Political parties and their spokesmen have found it both desirable and expedient in recent years to proclaim vigorously in platforms and speeches their dedication to the principles of conservation." [4]   But his historical evaluation indicates that both parties have contributed to the development of natural-resource policy and does not show that their attitudes toward these policies have had much, if any, effect on their success in winning elections.

He goes on to say that "Since 1930 the Democratic Party has been more successful in accommodating resources-development needs within its prevailing philosophy than has the Republican Party.   The Democrats have been more willing to use government to underwrite and operate extensive projects not undertaken by private enterprise.   Unless Republicans modify their approach, or provide politically acceptable alternatives to governmental intervention, there are likely to be substantial differences between the two major parties in the resources field for some years to come." [5]   If these differences are sufficiently large and have enough of an impact on specific policy issues, it may be worthwhile for the proponents of a particular forest policy to throw their support to one party in the hope that the general climate will be more favorable to their policy position under an administra-

[4] Ernest A. Engelbert, "Political Parties and Natural Resources Policies: An Historical Evaluation, 1790–1950," *Natural Resources Journal,* November, 1961, p. 224.
[5] *Ibid.,* p. 255.

tion by this party than it would under the other.    Naturally, all politicians are interested in attracting even small groups of people to their support if what is necessary will not run counter to getting the support of more potent segments of the electorate.    Support in elections may therefore be a means of developing favorable attitudes on the part of elected executives.    But it seems doubtful that forest policy issues will very often be crucial enough in elections for voting support to be used as a threat in forcing elected executives to take desired positions on these issues.

It may be possible to influence appointed executives to some degree by actions affecting their personal ambitions within the administration.    There have been and no doubt will continue to be struggles for power between executive departments whose outcomes might have an effect on forest policies.    The attempts during the 1930s by Secretary Ickes to change the Department of the Interior into a Department of Conservation and to concentrate within it all of the forestry activities of the federal government is a good example.    What effects there would have been on forest policies if such a reorganization of the federal departments had taken place is hard to say.    But at the time many people considered a transfer of the Forest Service out of the Department of Agriculture to be undesirable, and strong pressures were marshaled against the proposed reorganization.    President Roosevelt felt that "Forestry should be transferred as part of a plan to establish the place of conservation in a revamped governmental structure. His inability to carry out this intention offered proof that even a broad program of reorganization could not overcome traditional opposition to particular bureau transfers.    Ultimately, the Forest Service could muster such widespread congressional support for its position that Roosevelt was obliged to place political above administrative considerations." [6]

Probably it is not very common for interest groups to openly bargain to support an executive in his internal power struggles in return for promises of specific policy actions.    But such support is bound to improve future relationships with the executive, and open opposition might lead an uncooperative executive to take more conciliatory attitudes in the future. Even more important perhaps, as in the case of Secretary Ickes, is that well-placed support or opposition may keep or place power in the hands of that one of the competing executives who is generally most sympathetic or favorably inclined toward the forest-policy viewpoints which are desired.

**The legislatures**    The state and national legislatures are obviously important points of power in the governments.    The executive branch and the bureaucracies can do only what they have been authorized to do by the constitutions and the existing laws and then only to the extent made possible by the funds appropriated to them.    The legislatures, by contrast, can change or add to the existing laws, can initiate changes in or additions to the constitutions, and can raise money and allocate it to specific purposes. Their major actions are subject to approval by the courts and the chief

[6] Richard Polenberg, "The Great Conservation Contest," *Forest History,* January, 1967, p. 23.

executives (through the veto power) and can become effective only if they are carried out by the executive branches and the bureaucracies.   But they are in a very strategic position of power within the total governmental structure.

Through the legislatures pressure can be brought directly on those who control the forest resources (both private and public) or indirectly through public agencies which can influence or control the actions of the private forest owners.   A legislature m... be encouraged to pass laws requiring private owners to do certain things—such as make provision for regeneration after cutting timber—or not do certain things—such as start fires in the open without a permit.   Since a legislature has no means of enforcing such laws itself, it must instruct some existing government agency to enforce them or establish a new agency for that purpose.   In this respect the legislatures have the same limitations with respect to new laws that they have with existing ones.   But they do have the advantage over the executive and judiciary branches that they can change the existing laws and add new ones.

There are two main ways in which the legislatures can control the actions of the executive departments and bureaus—through legislation and through appropriations.   Pressure can be brought on the government agencies to take desired policy actions through both of these functions.   The legislature can instruct an agency to do or not to do certain things.   For example, in the Wilderness Act of 1964 Congress said:   "The Secretary of Agriculture shall, within ten years after the enactment of this Act, review, as to its suitability or nonsuitability for preservation as wilderness, each area in the national forests classified on the effective date of this Act by the Secretary of Agriculture or the Chief of the Forest Service as 'primitive' and report his findings to the President."

The legislatures may accomplish virtually the same ends by giving an agency some new authority or removing some authority from it.   The Cooperative Forest Management Act of 1950, for example, says:   "The Secretary of Agriculture is hereby authorized to cooperate with State foresters or equivalent officials . . . for the purpose of encouraging the States, Territories, and possessions to provide technical services to private forest landowners and operators, and processors of primary forest products with respect to the management of forest lands and the harvesting, marketing, and processing of forest products."   Congress had already given the Secretary of Agriculture authority to cooperate in providing technical services to farmers in the Cooperative Farm Forestry Act of 1937.   In 1950, it increased the Secretary's authority to include other private forest landowners and also processors of primary forest products.   Since the Secretary presumably was anxious to expand this cooperative program it was sufficient to authorize him and not necessary to instruct him to do so.

The legislatures can also affect materially the actions of the executive departments by providing new appropriations for new activities, increasing the appropriation for existing activities, or withholding part or all of the appropriation requested for existing activities.   Congress has, for instance, increased materially in recent years the appropriation for road construction on the national forests, though many people still feel that the amount appropriated is inadequate.    Except in the case of newly authorized programs, legislative appropriations are made in response to budgets submitted by the executive departments.    The most common result is for the appropriations committees of the legislatures to reduce the amounts requested. However, now and then legislatures decide to appropriate more money than was requested for a particular program.    Since the bureaus know they are going to have to return in the future with new budget requests, they are not likely to antagonize the legislature by refusing to spend more than they had asked for.

There are several other ways in which legislatures may bring pressures on government agencies to conform to desired policy viewpoints.    A legislative committee may be appointed to review or investigate the activities of a particular agency and to hold hearings where interested parties may testify.    The Comptroller General of the United States reports directly to Congress on reviews of agencies and programs conducted by the General Accounting Office.    A review and recommendations by the GAO is bound to influence an agency's actions.    Individual legislators also act in a go-between capacity to establish communication between government agencies and outside interests.    People who do not seem to be able to exert any influence directly on an agency often find that through their representative in the legislature they are able to get their complaints heard or to have consideration given to their views.    Since the agencies have to maintain good relations with the legislature, they are not likely to ignore a request or an opinion coming from a legislator, even though they are reasonably sure that in many cases he has little personal interest in the subject at hand.

The ways in which people can encourage a legislature to use some of the above means to direct or influence those who control forest resources are similar to those we discussed in the case of the executives.    Legislators might be convinced of the desirability of an action to the point where they will proceed to do something about it voluntarily.    They might be offered some inducement to act or they might be threatened with some unfavorable consequence of failing to act.

Since all legislators are elected—and except for the United States senators must stand for reelection at relatively short intervals—they are susceptible to election pressures.    In general, they represent constituencies which are more limited geographically than those of the elected executives, and therefore local forest-policy issues may be more important in their relations with the voters in their districts.    In heavily forested regions of the country, anything which happens to the forests may have significant impacts on local economies and voters give considerable weight to the attitudes of candidates toward the forests in choosing their legislative representatives.    The election process may therefore be a more potent means of bringing pressure on legislators than it is with the elected executives.

However, in urbanized districts and in regions where the forests are of minor economic consequence it is not likely that forest-related issues can have much of an impact on elections.   It seems very doubtful that any United States senator could be elected or defeated today solely on the grounds of his stand on any current forest-policy issue.   Of course, many elections can be decided by a relatively small block of votes thrown one way or the other, and any legislator facing a close contest might be moved by the promise or threat of a comparatively small organized group of voters to take actions they desire.   The financing of campaigns is a problem for all politicians today, and the financial support of some interest group may be more important than the number of votes they can promise to deliver.

An important characteristic of the legislatures is that most of the ways in which they can affect policies or programs require joint action.   Enough individual legislators must be favorably inclined toward a bill or appropriation item to outvote the other legislators who oppose it.   This means that it would be very difficult to replace through an election enough members of any legislature to change the overall balance between support for and opposition to a particular forest policy.   Electors take too many other things into consideration in deciding who they want to represent them in the legislatures.   The result is that the pressures must be brought on individual legislators to act as representatives of a particular interest group or policy viewpoint in developing within the legislature the necessary power to get favorable action by the entire legislative body.   We will consider the ways in which this necessary power might be developed later in this chapter.

In general, the process of influencing a legislature comes down to one of establishing good relations with individual legislators and encouraging them by a variety of means to work for desired policies or programs.   If these relationships can be maintained on a continuing basis, the particular interest group or policy viewpoint will have a representative within the legislature to act as their spokesman and work for their objectives.   Obviously, the more individual legislators with whom such relationships can be established, the greater the amount of influence that can be brought on legislative action.

**The courts**   The judicial branch of the government differs from the executive and legislative branches in that it cannot initiate policy actions but can only act on questions which are brought to it.   This does not mean that its influence on policies is trivial, however, since any public or private action is always subject to review by the courts and cannot be continued if they disapprove of it.

The courts, in effect, test any action which is brought before them against what society has decided over the years are the courses of action that are acceptable and that must be followed by the social group as a whole and by all of its individual members.   These agreed-upon courses of action are spelled out in the constitutions, in the statutory laws which have been passed by the legislatures and upheld in the courts, in the administrative regulations which have been developed in the executive branch and upheld in the courts, and in the common law as it has been determined and upheld in previous court decisions over the years.   A certain amount of interpretation is required in this judicial process, and in making these interpretations the courts do gradually modify to some extent the standards against which they test the actions brought before them.   This is not really a case of independent policy making, however, but rather an attempt to keep abreast of the current policy convictions of the society.

The courts can exert two kinds of influence on those who control forest lands and on those government agencies which are in a position to affect the actions of private forest owners.   They can forbid legislatures, government executives, bureaucrats, and private individuals to take actions which are prohibited by the constitutions or laws; or they can order these same people to take actions which are required of them by the constitutions or laws.   Other people concerned with a policy or program can therefore bring pressure on those who control the forests by complaining to the courts that the landowner or government agency in question is not complying with the existing laws and requesting the court to enforce compliance.

If a forest owner is setting fires at a time when it is prohibited to do so by the state laws, the state forester can ask the courts to make this owner stop burning.   The courts have the power to apply sanctions to those who do not comply with the laws.   Most fire and similar laws specify penalties such as fines or imprisonment for noncompliance.   If the state forester can prove that the owner did in fact violate the law, the court will fine or imprison him as a sanction to prevent him and other landowners from violating this particular law in the future.

If Congress should pass a law instructing the President to arbitrarily expropriate private forest lands without compensation to their owners, these owners could complain to the courts that this action of Congress was a violation of the Constitution.   If the court found that this law did in fact violate the Constitution, it would declare the law unconstitutional and thus null and void.   This would deprive the President of the power to do what the Congress had instructed him to do.

An effective form of political action, therefore, is to threaten to have recourse to the courts if certain actions are or are not taken.   In many cases the threat alone may be sufficient to get the desired effects without actually going to court.

Since the courts are in general the most independent of the governmental branches it is difficult to influence their actions.   However, judges and juries are human, and it may be possible to develop a sympathetic attitude on their part by educational activities designed to convince them that certain policies or viewpoints are in the public interest.   The enforcement of fire laws was handicapped for many years in some states by the unsympathetic attitudes of the public prosecuting attorneys, trial justices, and juries toward fire prevention.   As these people were replaced or became convinced of the bad effects of forest fires, enforcement became possible and fire-prevention policies were made effective.

## GROUP ACTION IN FOREST POLITICS

It seems plain from the preceding discussion that an individual person would have difficulty in using the political process to influence forest policies and programs.   Of course, individuals do play important and sometimes vital roles in policy formation and change.   But in order to reach positions of power or to exert a significant influence they need the backing and support of many other individuals.   We therefore find people of similar interests getting together and forming groups of sufficient size that they can influence policy actions.

These groups vary from loosely organized ad hoc units formed to deal with some current crisis to well-organized permanent associations capable of carrying on political action over long periods of time.   The activities of the ad hoc groups tend to be negative in that they are usually formed to try to stop the building of a proposed dam or highway or the cutting of some particular stand of trees.   But in some cases they have been quite effective in getting a park established or a new program inaugurated.   In any case, they typically try to rally to their cause the support of other more-permanent and more-experienced groups.   In the total picture, the well-organized permanent organizations are, therefore, undoubtedly the most significant in the political process.

Two kinds of group action are important influences on forest policy: that by outside interest groups and that by the staffs of government agencies. We will look at interest group activities first and then consider government-staff actions separately.

The outside interest groups used to be commonly referred to as "pressure groups."   This is a truly descriptive name, for a large part of their function is to bring pressures on those who are in a position to affect policies and programs.   But unfortunately the name "pressure group" has picked up the connotation of working for individual gain at the expense of the public interest.   While this is true of some interest groups, it is certainly not descriptive of interest groups in general.   Without such groups, our democratic political process would not function very well in developing policies which are in the interest of all the people.

Gulick recognized four major classes of voluntary forestry pressure groups: the conservationists, the professionals, the timber owners and lumber interests, and the organized grazing interests.[7]   Clawson and Held classified the groups whose major interest in the federal lands is in forestry or timber harvest as professional associations, such as the Society of American Foresters; semiprofessional, general-public associations, such as the American Forestry Association; and industry-sponsored associations, such as the American Pulpwood Association.   They also recognized grazing-interest groups and a large number of groups in the recreation, conservation, and general resource-use field.   They felt that the latter were not

[7] Luther H. Gulick, *American Forest Policy,* Duell, Sloan & Pearce, New York, 1951, pp. 40–44.

strictly professional in character, but rather semiprofessional or general-public in their appeal.[8]

The professional foresters, range managers, and wildlife managers are significant interest groups but have some peculiar characteristics as such. Gulick felt in 1951 that the professional foresters were the most important force in the development of forest policies in this country.[9]  Because of the location of professional foresters in the administration of both public and private forests, this is probably still true.  Foresters are generally in positions from which they exert direct control over the use of the forests.  But as an outside interest group attempting to influence other private and government controllers, they are much less effective than some other interest groups.

This is largely a result of the fact that the organized professional societies are made up of members with a wide diversity of interests and affiliations.  The Society of American Foresters membership includes people employed by federal, state, and local public agencies, private companies, and universities, as well as a substantial number who are self-employed. Individual members have primary interests in timber growing, recreation-area management, wildlife management, soil and water conservation, preservation of scenic beauty, or any of a number of other aspects of forest use. It is therefore difficult for the Society to take a stand or act as a pressure group in any controversial situation since its members are almost certain to be divided in their opinions.  As an interest group, the Society of American Foresters restricts itself largely to defending and promoting the interests of professional foresters, to promoting the increase of knowledge about forest resources, and to working for higher standards of resource management in general.

Some of the semiprofessional, general-public associations are similarly handicapped as interest groups.  The membership of the American Forestry Association, for example, includes professional foresters, wood-using industry employees, recreation workers, wilderness enthusiasts, and a great variety of other people who for one reason or another are interested in the natural resources.  It functions somewhat as a forum where rather diverse interest groups can get together and act on areas of common agreement. The policy issues on which the American Forestry Association is most active seem to be those on which it can find a consensus among diverse elements. It is more active as a pressure group than the Society of American Foresters but tends to stay aloof from the minor controversies and to take a more-balanced position on most policies than do many of the other interest groups.

The more specific conservation groups—such as the Sierra Club and the Wilderness Society—and the industry-sponsored groups are much more free to take strong stands on particular policies and to push hard for the

---

[8] Marion Clawson and Burnell Held, The Federal Lands, The Johns Hopkins Press, Baltimore, 1957, p. 138.
[9] Gulick, op. cit., p. 41.

policy actions they desire.   They usually work from some basic value judgment such as "wilderness experience is necessary for emotional balance" or "wood products are essential to man's future welfare."   They ordinarily do not feel obligated to develop a balanced opinion.   Rather they feel it is their duty to present the strongest possible case for their viewpoint, even though they recognize it is biased.   In most cases they have identified so closely with the cause or viewpoint they represent that they are honestly convinced that it is "right" and really would be in the long-run interest of other people also.   Because of all this, these groups are able to bring strong, continuous, and single-minded pressures to bear on the positions of influence in the governmental structure.

The most bitter controversies over forest policies develop among these latter kinds of interest groups.

> A . . . quality of group politics in the resource field is its intensity and inflexibility, suggesting attitudes more frequently associated with religion than with other spheres of human activity.   Perhaps this positiveness as to the rightness of a particular course of action reflects the scientific base of many resource proposals and is an expression of the tendency . . . of justifying programs and policies in scientific terms, overinterpreting data and overextending the conclusions which the data warrant.   Yet from this fact flow some of the most difficut problems of group politics.[10]

In such an intense struggle, it is very important that all interests be represented and that strong efforts be made to assure that all viewpoints have an equal chance to be heard.   Otherwise the result of the political struggle may be the domination of policy formation by the interests which are strongest economically or most adept at manipulating public emotions.

Traditionally, forest policies in the United States have been heavily influenced by the groups with economic interests in the resource.   As recently as 1965, statements like the following have been made in print:   "In many instances, it appears that the real decision makers in land-management policies are the interest groups involved: the farmers, stockmen, and timbermen." [11]   But in recent years, other interests have assumed significant roles.   Talbot described this situation clearly when he said that "in the area of public land policies, there are 'promotional' interest groups: those who do not have a direct economic interest in the area of their concern but do feel strongly that their goals should be promoted. . . .   As this nation becomes more metropolitan, these promotional groups, particularly the recreational and nature-loving varieties, will become more powerful in the arena of American politics." [12]

The staff of a government agency obviously has common interests and is organized in a way that enables it to operate as a group.   The United

[10] Norman Wengert, *Natural Resources and the Political Struggle*, Doubleday & Company, Inc., Garden City, 1955, p. 8.
[11] Emmette S. Redford, David B. Truman, Andrew Hacker, Alan F. Westin, and Robert C. Wood, *Politics and Government in the United States*, Harcourt, Brace & World, Inc., New York, 1965, p. 700.
[12] Talbot, *op. cit.*, p. 148.

States Forest Service has functioned most effectively as an interest group over the entire period of its existence.    It has access to the executive and legislative branches of the federal government and influences actions in both branches.    It also has developed close relationships with the states through which it can influence the actions of the state governments. Through the states it is able to influence local governments and also private forest owners.    Because the Forest Service is the one public agency charged with a general responsibility for the forest resources of the entire country, the maintenance of this access to positions of influence in other parts of the government structure is an important part of its functions.

During the first part of this century, the Forest Service was probably the most significant interest group influencing the development of forest policy in the United States.    Many of the forest policy ideas originated within the staff of the Forest Service and were brought to reality by its political strength and acumen.    Gradually other interest groups developed and achieved sufficient size and influence to dispute the field with the Forest Service.    However, it still remains one of the more potent interest groups in the area of forest policy.

The effectiveness of an interest group does not depend entirely on the fact that it represents a large number of people but rather that all of these people are involved in some way in promoting the interests of their group. Thus the group is able to bring pressures and influence to bear at many different places and many different times.    The staff of a forestry agency is usually dispersed geographically and thus in contact with people in many localities.    Through these "grass-roots" contacts it is often possible to bring the influence of numerous local people to bear on their representatives in the legislature or on the politically selected executives.    One of the problems in functioning this way as an interest group is clearly that of coordinating the viewpoints which the scattered members of the agency staff are promoting in their own localities.    Kaufman has described in detail in *The Forest Ranger* how the Forest Service has successfully accomplished this with its own staff.[13]

It is not possible to give in any detail here the many ways in which a government agency staff functions as an interest group.    Millett appears to have summarized it quite well when he said that "Planning is the usual way in which administrative agencies play some part in determining public policy.    An administrative agency undertakes to review the policies under which it operates.    In the process, it decides that other policies are desirable.    The agency must then seek to obtain such statutory authorization or higher executive sanction as it deems necessary in order to gain approval for carrying out the new policies.    This is administrative planning.    It is also administrative participation in the political process, because in the end it is the legislature and the chief executive who must agree that a change is desirable." [14]

[13] Kaufman, op. cit.
[14] John D. Millett, "Planning," in Fritz Morstein Marx, Elements of Public Administration, Prentice-Hall, Inc., Englewood Cliffs, N.J., © 1959, p. 115.

## DEVELOPING THE NECESSARY POWER

We have discussed at length the ways in which outside people might influence or bring pressure on governments to take actions on policies and programs which they consider to be desirable.  It is clear that other people will also be bringing pressures on the same points of influence and that frequently the objectives of the different interest groups will conflict.  Successful political action therefore not only requires overcoming inertia on the part of government but also overcoming the conflicting claims of other interests.  Many of these other interests are not competing for the use of forest resources at all but rather for the financial and manpower resources needed to implement the policies they desire in education, national defense, urban improvement, and many other fields.  It is necessary therefore to develop sufficient power to move government action in the desired directions.

In the political process it is usually easier to defeat a proposed change than it is to make a change.  This is facilitated in the national and state legislatures by the committee system under which all new bills must be studied and reported upon by the committee to which they are assigned before the legislature as a whole takes any action.  This means that a small group of legislators—such as the 15 members of the Senate Committee on Agriculture and Forestry—rather effectively controls the action of the legislature on a particular subject.  Under this system the members of the committees charged with legislation affecting forests, and particularly their chairmen, are in a very powerful position.

In commenting on techniques for defeating proposed changes, Clawson and Held say:

> Opposition is more likely to take the form of stalling.  This is particularly easy for the chairman of a committee; he may simply delay calling hearings or taking other steps, without refusing to do so.  It is also easy for an agency of the Executive Branch; it may delay reporting on proposed legislation, always with some good excuse for the delay.[15]

Clearly then, any way by which the members and chairmen of the relevant committees can be influenced to view a proposed change favorably or unfavorably is a potent means of developing power.

Even groups and the legislative and other political support they are able to develop will often not have enough power by themselves to obtain the actions they desire.  It is usually necessary, therefore, to form some kind of coalition with other interest groups and other politicians in order to develop this power.  In criticizing the development of land and water policies, Hardin complains that "The test is not the relative merits of alternative programs but rather the accumulation of enough political weight by adding enough interests into a general program to sweep all opposition

---

[15] Clawson and Held, op. cit., p. 150.

aside—the omnibus rivers and harbors acts are the best example." [16]    This is the process known as logrolling, where each of the parties involved agrees to support the other parties' programs in return for reciprocal support of his own program.

Hardin objects strongly to "poorly advised political procedures, wherein we fail properly to weigh alternatives of policy, we overstress local and particular interests at the expense of more general interests, and we elevate the necessary element of compromise into the highest form of the political art and thus make a fetish of logrolling." [17]    Certainly logrolling as it has been practiced in our legislatures has had many objectionable features and has often worked to the advantage of special interests rather than that of the people as a whole.    Still with the great diversity of interests in a country the size of the United States and the fact that most people are indifferent or apathetic about all but a few which affect them personally, it is hard to see how sufficient support can be recruited for most actions without offering something in return.    In theory the alternatives should be considered rationally and choices made on the basis of valid criteria, but this still seems more than can be expected from our present political structure.

An interesting example of the formation of coalitions to influence policy formation was the case of the North Cascades in the state of Washington. Most of the area involved had been in national forests, and the controversy arose over proposals to put parts of it into a national park and into national wilderness areas.    These proposals brought two government agencies—the Forest Service of the Department of Agriculture and the Park Service of the Department of the Interior—into conflict.    But outside interest groups were involved from the beginning.    Two ad hoc groups took the lead: the North Cascades Conservation Council in favor of the park and Outdoors, Unlimited opposed to it.    Joining a coalition with the North Cascades Conservation Council were outdoor clubs such as the Seattle Mountaineers, Audubon societies, nature-oriented organizations, and such national organizations as the Sierra Club and The Wilderness Society.    Joining with Outdoors, Unlimited were the hunting organizations, the logging and mining interests, the skiing interests, trail motorbike riders and four-wheel jeep clubs.    None of these groups individually had the power to control the use of the North Cascades area, but in coalitions they became very potent forces.[18]

## BARGAINING AND COMPROMISE

We have already noted the fact that people want many different things from the forests and that it is basically impossible for this resource—tremendous though it is in the United States—to completely meet all of these different

[16] Charles M. Hardin, "Land Policy and the Development of the West—in the National Interest," in Franklin S. Pollak (ed.), *Resources Development: Frontiers for Research,* University of Colorado Press, Boulder, 1960, p. 13.
[17] *Ibid.,* p. 11.
[18] Brock Evans, "Showdown for the Wilderness Alps of Washington's North Cascades," *Sierra Club Bulletin,* April, 1968, pp. 7–16.

wants at the same time.  Numerous conflicts over the objectives of forest use and of the policies to guide that use are therefore inevitable.  In this chapter we have seen some of the difficulties involved in trying to resolve such conflicts by overpowering the opposition.  As the distribution of political power and the knowledge of how to use it become more widespread among our citizens it grows increasingly difficult for any one interest group to achieve a sufficiently powerful position that it can direct policy exclusively in the directions it desires.

In 1957, Clawson and Held noted:

> As nearly as one can judge, political strength of the timber harvest, grazing, mineral development, and recreation-conservation-general-resource interest groups is nearly balanced today.  Each group is able to stop legislation or new administrative action that it finds highly objectionable, but at the same time no group is able to push through legislation or new administrative action that it wants but that one or more of the other major groups oppose.[19]

The situation has changed little since then unless it has perhaps become more difficult for a group to stop legislation or action to which it alone objects.  Under these circumstances it is clear that some other approach must be used in resolving policy differences.

Wengert points out that "a principal purpose of the political system is the choosing of goals, the reconciling of conflicts, and the compromising of differences."[20]  "Compromising" is clearly an important operational word here.  Since everyone cannot have everything he wants, some kind of compromise must be worked out under which each interest group accepts its share as being the best overall distribution that it can obtain.  No group is likely to be entirely satisfied and such compromises are probably always somewhat temporary in nature.  However, as we have noted frequently, all policies change with the passage of time, and it is therefore not unreasonable that the parties to a compromise should continue to work for changes in it.

As a result of the above, bargaining has become an important part of the political process in forming natural-resource policies.  Dahl and Lindblom explain succinctly why bargaining takes place:

> If leaders agreed on everything they would have no need to bargain; if on nothing, they could not bargain.  Leaders bargain because they disagree and expect that further agreement is possible and will be profitable—and the profit sought may accrue not merely to the individual self but to the group, an alliance of groups, a region, a nation, unborn generations, "the public interest."
>
> Hence bargaining takes place because it is necessary, possible, and thought to be profitable.[21]

[19] Clawson and Held, *op. cit.,* p. 141.
[20] Norman Wengert, *The Administration of Natural Resources,* Asia Publishing House, Bombay, 1961, p. 53.
[21] Robert A. Dahl and Charles E. Lindblom, *Politics, Economics, and Welfare,* Harper & Brothers, New York, 1953, p. 326.

All this certainly applies to the formation of forest policies. We may expect bargaining and compromise to become more and more important as the pressure on the forest resources grows and the conflicts inevitably multiply.

## IN SUMMARY

We have been working in this book with the definition of a forest policy as a settled course of action with regard to the use of forest resources which has been adopted and is followed by society. One problem with such a definition is the possible implication that policies somehow just develop within a society as a kind of natural process. In this chapter we have seen that this is generally not the case. Policies are formed as a result of complex social processes. And very important among these is the political process through which individuals and groups actively and overtly try to affect the formation of policies.

To a large extent, forest policies are determined by those who occupy positions of power, either as direct controllers of forest land use or as influencers of government actions. But the power of these people is limited by public resistance, and they are only able to enforce policies which the mass of the people will accept. In addition they face the countervailing power of other groups with different interests which try to outmaneuver them in the political arena. The inevitable result is that those in present positions of power must seek for compromises which will placate the public and the opposing groups but at the same time let them achieve what they consider to be the most desirable objectives as fully as possible. The resulting process is one in which leaders play a significant role but in which the society as a whole must be involved if the outcome is to be policies that are truly accepted and followed.

# Evaluation of Forest
# Policies and Programs

Our discussion of forest policies thus far has been almost entirely from an ex ante viewpoint.   That is, we have been looking ahead and asking:   How do people decide in advance what policies they wish to establish?   Which techniques will be most effective in implementing a policy that has been agreed on?   What kinds of arrangements should be made to execute the programs selected to implement a policy?   What political strategies will be most effective in influencing future policy formation?

Now policies obviously do become established, techniques are applied to implement them, programs are selected and organizations developed to execute them, and political strategies are adopted to strengthen, change, or eliminate them.   But just because people thought ex ante that these would be desirable or the best alternatives does not necessarily mean that this will prove to be true when we look back at them from an ex post viewpoint.   So it is extremely important that existing policies and programs be evaluated to determine whether they should be continued, modified, or done away with.

People involved with forest policies and programs are well aware of the need for this kind of ex post evaluation and have developed various ways of meeting their own needs in this regard.   But the literature on evaluation approaches the subject almost entirely from an ex ante viewpoint and is concerned with decision-making for future actions.   This chapter therefore has less of an existing base to build on than most of the previous ones and consequently will be somewhat incomplete and not entirely satisfactory.

However, the subject is so important for the future of forest policy that we will have to do the best we can with what is available.

## KINDS OF EVALUATIONS

In his study of forest policy, Gulick recognized four kinds of evaluations: financial audits, administrative audits or reviews, local criticism and review arising from interested citizens and from direct observers of the forest programs in operation, and general criticisms arising from outside professionals.[1]    A fifth kind of evaluation not mentioned by Gulick is that performed by ad hoc review commissions.

### Financial Audits

The financial audits are the most restrictive in scope of the various kinds of evaluations, although this in no way detracts from their importance. The basic purpose of a financial audit is to make sure that the funds appropriated for a particular program or project have been spent in the manner and for the purposes for which they were appropriated.   In effect the audit checks compliance against the budget which was approved and for which funds were allocated before the period of operation started.

In actual practice, however, financial audits can and do serve broader purposes.   This is brought out quite clearly in Hendee's description of financial controls in the Forest Service:

> The formalized system of financial management controls . . . insures that program objectives and quotas will be attained substantially as planned within the limits of funds available and in compliance with legislation and other regulatory authorities.   The controls provide for the timely and effective analysis of actual costs in the interest of increased efficiency, and facilitate future work planning.   The mediums of controls consist of current review and adjustment of financial plans; records of work accomplishments; accounting records; and performance checks.
> Financial plans are reviewed and adjusted, when necessary, to changing program requirements in order to secure program control on a continuous basis.[2]

Financial audits of expenditures by federal government agencies are made within the individual agencies and departments and also by the General Accounting Office.   The federal auditors also check on the expenditure of grant-in-aid funds by the states and other recipients and of the matching funds required in most of these grants.   All of the states have their own auditors who check the expenditure of state funds.

---

[1] Luther H. Gulick, *American Forest Policy*, Duell, Sloan & Pearce, New York, 1951, pp. 75–77.
[2] Clare Hendee, *Organization and Management Systems in the Forest Service*, Government Printing Office, Washington, 1967, p. 77.

## Administrative Audits or Reviews

This category includes a variety of evaluation techniques.    In general they are intended to determine what an organization is doing and whether it is meeting the responsibilities assigned to it within the authority that it has been delegated.    Like the financial audits, the administrative audits are designed to evaluate the execution of programs and the application of various implementation methods.    They usually do not attempt to evaluate the policies, programs, or implementation techniques as such but only the ways in which these are being carried out or used.

**Reports**    Many different kinds of reports are required and developed by the organizations concerned with forest resources.    Probably all forestry agencies prepare some kind of annual report of their activities.    Many federal agencies publish their annual reports and thus make it possible for all kinds of readers to judge what they have been doing.    Within the agencies, numerous reports are compiled regularly to show accomplishment on their varied activities.    Often these regular reports become stereotyped in nature and are not really very informative.    (There is obviously a need for a regular evaluation of reports and reporting systems.)    Most useful from the evaluation viewpoint are probably the special reports which all agencies require from time to time on aspects of their work or programs about which some questions have arisen.

A special kind of report which is used by the Forest Service and some other agencies is the official diary.    Field officers are required to keep a daily account of their activities with a record of the time actually spent on their various assigned functions.    From these diaries it is possible to determine how the field organization is using its time and to evaluate this distribution in the light of the agency's different responsibilities.

Since these kinds of reports are of necessity prepared by the people involved in the activities being evaluated, one could legitimately question how reliable they are as a basis for evaluation.    After studying the Forest Service, Kaufman concluded:

> It is almost inconceivable that manipulations of the records could long escape detection.    In any case the incentives to falsify reports are not very strong.
> . . . The penalties for occasionally inadequate performance are far less severe than those for misrepresentation: the risks of dishonesty are infinitely greater than those of honesty. . . .    Consequently, reporting tends to be highly accurate, and field officers turn in information that sometimes reveals their own weaknesses and mistakes as well as their competence and their triumphs.[3]

This is probably true of a closely knit organization like the Forest Service but may not be equally true of others.    There certainly must be a great temptation—particularly in the regular annual reports—to play up the agencies' triumphs and to relegate the mistakes to brief mention in obscure

[3] Herbert Kaufman, *The Forest Ranger,* The Johns Hopkins Press, Baltimore, 1960, pp. 129–130.

places or even to total omission.   Regular reports which are submitted by custom or tradition and which are not checked (or perhaps even read) by the person to whom they are addressed are not likely to be a very sound basis for evaluation.

**Budget reviews**   Practically all forestry organizations are financed by annual or, at best, biennial appropriations.   Each time they submit a budget for approval, it has to include the activities or programs which they wish to continue.   Federal agency budgets must pass the scrutiny of the Bureau of the Budget and the congressional committees on appropriations. State agency budgets must at least be studied by committees in the legislature, and many states also require advance approval by a budget or auditing agency.   There thus are repeated opportunities to evaluate all activities which extend over from one budget period into another.

Clawson and Held feel that, at least with regard to federal land policies, the evaluation which takes place as part of the budget process is nowhere near as effective as it potentially might be.

The whole process puts too much emphasis on the previous year, and is too slow to respond to changes. . . .   There is little direct examination of each budget in relation to need; the assumption is that what was arrived at last year was correct for that year, and that all that is now needed is to look at the changes from last year. . . .   The process . . . provides little systematic review, at any level, of past operations. . . .   At no point is there a careful economic and policy review of the effect of various programs at various levels, or a review of overall efficiency in attainment of goals.[4]

If this indictment is still true—as it undoubtedly is when we consider all levels of government—we must conclude that budget review is not now a very useful or effective means of evaluating forest policies and programs.

**Inspections**   Most forestry programs and organizations are spread over such large geographic areas that they cannot readily be observed and checked by those administratively in charge of them nor by concerned outside people.   Financial audits, reports, and budget reviews help but are far from adequate for reliable evaluation.   It is common, therefore, to resort to direct inspections of the activities as and where they are being carried on.

The Forest Service has developed a more elaborate program of inspections than any other forest-related organization in the United States. Hendee states:

The policy of the Forest Service is to conduct periodic inspections to assure proper administrative control of functions, operations and programs.   Inspections include studies, reviews, and appraisals to determine (1) the adequacy of established policies, procedures, plans, standards, regulations, and laws;

---

[4] Marion Clawson and Burnell Held, *The Federal Lands,* The Johns Hopkins Press, Baltimore, 1957, p. 157.

(2) the adequacy of compliance with them; (3) whether resources and other assets are properly safeguarded; (4) the degree of reliability of accounting and statistical data; (5) where recognition of good work is deserved; (6) ways and means of strengthening the services of people concerned; (7) follow-up action necessary to bring about needed corrections or other desired accomplishments.[5]

Except for the first two, these items are concerned with details of administrative management rather than policies and programs. Good administration is, of course, necessary in the execution of forest policies, but the evaluation of its details is relatively simple compared with the kinds of problems included in Hendee's items (1) and (2).

The most important type of Forest Service inspection is the General Integrating Inspection, which covers all Forest Service activities within a given territorial unit. Its purpose is "to examine and evaluate . . . the effectiveness of existing management and operating plans, objectives, policies, and procedures; to determine how well responsibilities . . . are being carried out; and to determine how well National Forest resources are contributing to the social and economic needs of the community and Nation."[6] Such inspections are made of each region and experiment station every five years, of each national forest every four years, and of each ranger district every three years. The General Research Inspection is similar but intended to determine the effectiveness of research activities within a given territorial unit.

General Functional Inspections cover all the functions, subfunctions, and special activities assigned to a responsible Forest Service line-staff officer. Their objective is to determine the effectiveness with which all phases of assigned responsibilities are conducted within an organizational unit. They thus attempt to evaluate the execution of a policy or program rather than the policy or program itself.

General Program Inspections are joint analyses by the Forest Service and a State of all cooperative forestry programs in the state. "The purpose is to examine the objectives, coordination of programs, planning, administration, achievement, legislation, staffing, organization, financing, and needs of the program."[7] If successful, these inspections should give a good evaluation of the cooperative programs which are intended to implement various forest policies. It is not clear whether these inspections make any attempt to evaluate the policies themselves or not.

As the Forest Service example shows, inspections are a useful technique of evaluation. But Kaufman noted that in the Forest Service "their *distinctive* function is to uncover deviation by field men from the behavior prescribed by the organization."[8] They are primarily an administrative tool and are likely to be less effective in dealing with the more basic questions about policies and programs.

[5] Hendee, *op. cit.*, pp. 31–32.
[6] *Ibid.*, p. 32.
[7] *Ibid.*, p. 32.
[8] Kaufman, *op. cit.*, p. 152.

**Administrative reviews and investigations**    These are really special kinds of one-shot inspections which are only made when something out of the ordinary is involved.    A special board of review may be constituted to study the reasons why some part of a program appears to have failed or why the organization did not function effectively under certain conditions.    The purpose of such a review is to uncover weaknesses or to discover ways of doing a particular job better.    There usually is no implication that there has been intentional misconduct.    By contrast, the term "investigation" usually is used when there is reason to believe that deliberate wrongdoing is taking place.

Such reviews may take place at many different levels and may vary considerably in their scope.    For example, a forestry organization may set up an internal review board to try to find out why a particular forest fire reached disastrous proportions.    Or a congressional committee may review a broad aspect of government operation as in the case of the Joint Committee on Federal Timber which heard testimony aggregating some 2,229 printed pages and produced a 54-page report on federal timber-sales policies.[9]

**Legislative committee studies**    Some states have interim committees of the legislature which make studies of particular state policies during the period between legislative sessions.    These interim committees report their findings to the whole legislature and frequently recommend changes in the laws or policies.    Some of the standing committees of the Congress perform similar evaluative functions for that body.

## Local Criticism and Review

Interested citizens and direct observers of operating forest programs are in a position to evaluate these programs and the policies they try to implement on the basis of local effects and results.    However, these are purely personal evaluations and the criteria on which they are based tend to place local and individual interests above broader public or national interests. The mere fact that a particular program or policy evokes a great deal of local criticism cannot always be taken as prima facie evidence that it is not desirable or effective.

The problem with local criticism and review is therefore one of how to bring it together in a way that it can be effective and also balanced with other opinions and viewpoints.    One way of doing this is through public hearings such as those held by the Joint Committee on Federal Timber. By holding hearings in a number of localities and inviting testimony from anyone who had an opinion or a criticism to offer, the Committee was exposed to a great deal of evidence about the weaknesses and strengths of the current federal timber–sales policies.

Another way in which local criticism can contribute to the evaluation of public programs is through appeals to higher authorities when a person feels

[9] Committee on Government Operations, *Federal Timber Sales Policies*, Government Printing Office, Washington, 1956.

that an action which affects him has been unjust or improper.    As Kaufman says:    "The right of appeal is guaranteed by custom, the Constitution, legislation, and regulations; citizens are not hesitant about invoking it. So no Ranger can ever be sure that the people with whom he deals in any connection will not appeal over his head when they are displeased with what he does, not even when the matter in question seems minor." [10]    The advantage to the appeals process is not so much that it keeps the local officials in line as in the fact that it forces their superiors to review and study the appealed actions in order to decide whether to back the local officer or to accept the complaint as justified and make some adjustments to meet it.

## General Criticisms Arising from Outside Professionals

Professional people who are outside of and independent of the organizations conducting forest programs and promoting forest policies should be in an especially favorable position to evaluate the programs and policies impartially.    For some reasons which are not entirely clear the professional foresters in the United States do not make a practice of publicly criticizing existing forest policies and programs.    We have already noted that the Society of American Foresters finds it difficult to take an official position on many controversial issues because of the heterogeneous nature of its membership.    But the pages of the *Journal of Forestry* and of other conservation publications are open to individual foresters' opinions, and it is rather strange that they so seldom express them.    It is not because of any unanimity of opinion among foresters—for quite strong differences do exist—but perhaps from some feeling of professional courtesy or a desire to avoid "washing the profession's dirty linen in public."

This avoidance of public criticism fortunately does not extend to many of the other professional conservationists and the employees of private industry.    So informed general criticisms are raised about many policies and have led to some soul-searching evaluations by those supporting them. It is too bad that this highly vocal and usually critical kind of public evaluation tends to be one-sided and that the professional foresters do not help to give it greater balance by taking a more active part in it.

There is one way in which the critical facilities of the outside professionals have been used effectively and that is in the form of officially appointed review committees.    An example was the Timber Appraisal Review Committee, which was appointed by the Chief of the Forest Service as a consequence of numerous complaints by the buyers of national forest timber.    This three-man committee consisted of two professional foresters —one a professor of forest economics and the other a valuation engineer for the Internal Revenue Service—and a professional appraiser and independent real estate broker.    After a 6-month study, which included interviews with dozens of people on both sides of the controversy, the committee

[10] Kaufman, *op. cit.,* p. 153.

submitted a 40-page report.  Of the 37 specific recommendations in this report, the majority either supported existing Forest Service policy or were accepted by them as desirable.  The Forest Service did not feel that it could accept three of the committee's recommendations, and the industry was not happy with some of them, such as the committee's refusal to accept industry's proposal that the profit ratio used in timber appraisals be based on the experience of a competing industry.  However, the overall result of this evaluation has been a definite improvement in the relations between the Forest Service and its timber customers.[11]

## Ad Hoc Review Commissions

These are special commissions appointed to review and make recommendations about policy in some special area.  A good example is the Public Land Law Review Commission which was established by Congress to make a thorough evaluation of the existing public land laws.  These laws had accumulated over more than a century and Congress felt it was time to review them in a comprehensive manner.  The Outdoor Recreation Resources Review Commission was given an even broader assignment—to review the status of policies concerning outdoor recreation in the United States and to recommend changes in and additions to these policies.

## THE PROCESS OF EVALUATION

The discussion in the preceding sections has dealt with the types of evaluation which we find in use today.  We have pointed out some of the weaknesses of these methods and particularly the fact that most of them appear better designed for checking on the administrative execution of programs and policies than for evaluating the programs and policies themselves.  It is at least possible that this is the best that can be done in the difficult area of evaluating forest policies.  But it will certainly pay to take a closer look at the processes and problems of evaluation in the hope that it might yield some clues as to how evaluations could be improved in the future.

The first and rather obvious question is: where does one start in making an evaluation?  Pretty clearly we have to start with a decision as to just exactly what it is that is being evaluated.  There appear to be four different kinds of things that might be evaluated in the broad forest-policy area, and these seem to fall logically into the following hierarchy:

Forest-policy objectives
Forest policies
Forest programs
Forest-related organizations

[11] Timber Appraisal Review Committee, *A General Review of U.S. Forest Service Timber Appraisal Policies and Procedures,* duplicated report, June 1, 1963 and U.S. Forest Service, *National Forest Timber Appraisals: A Statement of Forest Service Conclusions on the Recommendations and Suggestions of the Report of the Timber Appraisal Review Committee,* duplicated report, November 7, 1963.

Organizations function to carry out programs which are intended to implement policies which, in turn, are designed to achieve desired objectives. Although each level of this hierarchy is related to the other levels, it seems reasonable that one level might be evaluated without at the same time evaluating any or all of the other levels.    For example, a forestry organization might be evaluated without questioning the programs this organization is set up to execute.    This seems to be the pattern of much of the existing evaluation which we discussed earlier in this chapter.

Whenever we evaluate something we always do it in terms of something else.    That is, we evaluate it in terms of how well it does something outside of its immediate self.    We evaluate a policy in terms of how well it accomplishes the objectives that were sought when this particular course of action was accepted and followed.    We evaluate an organization in terms of how well it carries out the programs which it was set up to execute.    Each level has to be studied basically in terms of its relationship to the level above it in the hierarchy.

Now this seems to be all right until we consider the top level in the hierarchy: objectives.    In what terms do we evaluate a policy objective? This takes us back to the discussion in Chapter 2 where we discovered that many policy objectives are only desired because they will serve as means toward some further objectives.    Wherever such a means-end chain exists, a policy objective can only be evaluated in terms of how well it serves as a means toward the more ultimate objective.    If this process is pushed far enough, we clearly will find ourselves trying to make evaluations in terms of quite general and rather abstract objectives like freedom and security. Chapter 2 has already revealed the problems involved in such a situation. This is why the most seemingly insoluble controversies revolve around objectives.    At the lower end of the means-end chain, satisfactory evaluations of policy objectives are possible, but as we push farther toward ultimate objectives we find ourselves enmeshed in a web of value judgments and acceptable evaluations become very difficult or perhaps even impossible.

The other levels appear to be more amenable to evaluation.    Once an objective has been specified or accepted, it becomes possible to evaluate various policies in terms of their contribution to the achievement of that objective.    Suppose an objective of increasing the growth of timber has been accepted and a policy of complete exclusion of fire has been instituted to help achieve it.    We can now check the effects of fire exclusion and determine whether they increase timber growth or not.    If, as would be true in the case of longleaf pine, we find that complete exclusion of fire is actually detrimental to the best development of the forest, our evaluation will have shown that the fire-exclusion policy is not a good means of achieving the objective of greater timber growth.

Now this example leads us into a problem situation which may exist fairly often in evaluation efforts.    Suppose that in the above longleaf-pine example the state forestry agency had set up an intensive program of fire prevention, detection, and suppression and that as a result of this program, fires were completely eliminated in the area. We are asked to evaluate this prevention-detection-suppression program. According to our argument above, we must study this fire program in relation to the policy which it is intended to make effective. That policy is to completely exclude fire from the forests of the area. The state fire program has eliminated fires, thus perfectly implementing the accepted policy. The conclusion from our evaluation would have to be that this has been a very effective program; in fact, it is just about a 100 percent success.

Or is it? Remember that the objective of the policy was to increase the growth of timber in the area. The misguided policy of fire exclusion will not increase growth but instead will decrease it. The apparently successful program will therefore make things worse instead of better in terms of the objective of increasing growth. Evaluated this way we are forced to conclude that the program has actually been a detrimental one because it has successfully implemented a bad policy. It is in the same class with the cynic's definition of the high-speed electronic computer as "a device for getting wrong answers faster."

This kind of situation has some serious implications for evaluation. It means that it often is difficult to judge a program by the available information on its accomplishment. For example, the Agricultural Conservation Program reported that in 1966, in addition to many other accomplishments, it shared the cost of planting trees and shrubs on 181,000 acres, shared in the cost of improving 210,000 acres of forest trees, and shared the cost of other conservation practices on 1 million farms for a total of 187 million dollars.[12] Obviously the ACP was busy in 1966, but how do we evaluate the program from this kind of information?

The tendency which is certainly encouraged by the administrators of programs is to judge them in terms of the work they have done. The ACP program is supposed to encourage the establishment of conservation practices on farm lands. Since in 1966 it encouraged the planting of 181 thousand acres of trees and shrubs, the improvement of 210 thousand acres of forest, and many other desirable practices, the program must be accomplishing something. We might ask how much it cost to encourage these practices, whether more might have been accomplished with the same budget, and similar questions which we will consider in the next section on criteria. But at this point what we are interested in is the question: what does the program hope to accomplish by encouraging these practices, for it seems doubtful that anyone could argue that planting trees is good per se. In other words, what policy or policies is the ACP program intended to implement?

As a result of his study of public programs in North Carolina, Muench decided that the ACP program "can be seen to have two objectives: a stated resource-allocation objective of soil and water conservation and an income redistribution objective of reducing the disparity between farm and nonfarm per capita income . . . it is probable that when Congress appro-

---

[12] Agricultural Stabilization and Conservation Service, *Agricultural Conservation Program Summary Fiscal Year 1966*, U.S. Dept. of Agriculture, Washington, 1967, p. 2.

priates money under this act they have the latter point foremost in mind." [13]

Although Muench's "objectives" are rather clearly means to some more ultimate objectives, they do represent policies which the ACP program is intended to implement.   We rather generally accept policies of conserving our soil and water resources and of raising the incomes of the poorer members of our society to a point where they are more nearly in balance with those of the more affluent members.   If the ACP program is intended to implement these policies, an evaluation of that program must try to measure its effects on them.   If we can assume that the planting of trees and shrubs does conserve soil and water and that it also increases the productivity of the lands planted so that at some time in the future the owners will be able to realize greater incomes from them, then it appears that the ACP program is accomplishing something to implement the two policies.

But many questions are left unanswered.   Muench tried to evaluate the ACP program more completely in terms of these policies.   In relation to soil and water conservation, he points out that "cost-sharing can be obtained for planting trees on areas not subject to erosion" and asks:   "If it is assumed that timber production is not a goal of ACP, how can the relatively expensive practice of tree planting on non-erosible sites be justified?"   With regard to cost-sharing for such stand improvement practices as removal of defective trees and thinning of dense pine stands, he says:   "The question here is whether such removals increase the erosion-preventing and water retaining capabilities of the stand.   Probably not."   And in relation to income redistribution, he concludes, "If occupation and size of forest holding are acceptable as indicators of a landowner's income and asset position, then it must be concluded that ACP forestry practices are most useful in distributing income to those who least need it." [14]

This example is not given with any intention of defaming the Agricultural Conservation Program but merely because it illustrates some serious difficulties in evaluation.   If what we really want to do is increase the incomes of the poorer farmers, then ACP is probably not a very effective device.   But if we mistakenly think the purpose of the ACP program is to conserve soil and water, then its weaknesses as an income redistributor will not be apparent to us.   It is very important that every evaluation look far enough ahead toward the ultimate objectives to be sure that we are evaluating in terms of real results and not just surface manifestations.

Another example may serve to show the difficulties inherent in evaluating any large-scale government program.   The Timber Appraisal Review Committee complained that "A fundamental difficulty in appraising national forest timber is the lack of a clear statement of the objective which the Forest Service has in selling this timber." [15]   The Forest Service could not understand the reason for this complaint, commenting:

[13] John Muench, Jr., *Private Forests and Public Programs in North Carolina,* The American Forestry Association, Washington, no date (circa 1965), p. 33.
[14] *Ibid.,* pp. 44–45.
[15] Timber Appraisal Review Committee, *op. cit.,* p. 10.

It is surprising to have questions raised over objectives for National Forest timber sales. . . .   In January, 1963, Secretary's Regulation S-6 was amended in order further to emphasize that an orderly program of timber sales designed to obtain the regular harvest of National Forest timber at allowable cutting rates in accordance with timber management plans is one of the prime objectives of National Forest management.[16]

This statement by the Forest Service is a paraphrase of a part of section 2430.1 of the Forest Service Manual which gives the full text of the Secretary's Regulation.   It refers back to Secretary's Regulation S-3 (of the same date) regarding disposal of national forest timber according to management plans which says that:

Such plans shall:

1. Be designed to aid in providing a continuous supply of National Forest timber for the use and necessities of the citizens of the United States.
2. Be based on the principle of sustained yield.
3. Provide, so far as feasible, an even flow of National Forest timber in order to facilitate the stabilization of communities and of opportunities for employment.
4. Provide for coordination of timber production . . . with other uses . . . in accordance with the principles of multiple use management.
5. Establish the allowable cutting rate which is the maximum amount of timber which may be cut from the National Forest lands.[17]

It appears that the objective of national forest management is not "an orderly program of timber sales" as might be inferred from FSM 2430.1 but rather a continuous supply of timber for the citizens and the stabilization of communities and employment opportunities.   Since both of these objectives can only be attained by having the timber cut and processed into useful products, the Timber Appraisal Review Committee felt it necessary to point out that the Forest Service has a very large stake in the maintenance of a healthy and progressive timber industry.

In an attempt to meet the Committee's criticism, the Forest Service added to the Manual a section entitled "Objective," one paragraph of which reads:   "Adequate markets for timber are dependent on a progressive and healthy forest products industry.   In the long run, a successful sales program is dependent on a market generated by a healthy forest products industry." [18]   Although this represented an honest effort, the Committee was inclined to feel that the Forest Service had missed the whole point of its criticism and was still evaluating its own programs in terms of subobjectives rather than the real major objective.   Perhaps what this case brings out most clearly is the difficulty which any action agency experiences in trying to make an objective evaluation of its own activities.

[16] U.S. Forest Service, *op. cit.*, p. 2.
[17] *Forest Service Manual*, section 2410.1, dated November 1966.
[18] *Forest Service Manual*, section 2430.2, dated October 1964.

## CRITERIA FOR EVALUATION

It has become evident in the course of the preceding discussion that part of the difficulty in making evaluations arises in deciding what standards to use in judging the policy or program. We said that it is necessary to assess a program in terms of the policy or policies it is intended to implement. In a very simple situation it might be sufficient merely to find out whether the program being evaluated "works" or not. Suppose, for example, we are trying to implement a policy of thoroughly extinguishing all fires before leaving camp and picnic sites. To implement this policy we institute a program of putting up posters saying: "Prevent Forest Fires— Douse your Campfire" at all points where campers and picnickers congregate. If after some time, inspections show that most of the formerly careless campers are now carefully putting out their fires, we can say the program is working. If we find just as many abandoned fires as ever, we can say the program is a failure. But most cases of evaluation will not be such simple "yes or no" situations, so we need to consider what kind of criteria we might use in more complex situations.

**Effectiveness** This is certainly the most fundamental criterion for evaluating a policy, program, or organization. The first question in any evaluation is bound to be whether the thing being evaluated does what it was set up to do. This criterion will immediately separate out the absolute failures, as in the example of the preceding paragraph. But we do not usually consider as equally effective all of the possible ways of doing something that are not absolute failures. So we find ourselves with a second question: How effective is this policy, program, or organization for doing what it was set up to do?

Now what do we mean when we say that one program is more effective than another in implementing a given policy? Certainly, we mean that it does a better job of implementing than the other. But better in what respect? There seem to be at least two possible meanings of "better" in this use: (1) it does a more complete or thorough job or (2) it does the job faster or with less delay.

The first meaning indicates that effectiveness is a relative thing, and this is important to remember in evaluating policies or programs. Simon says "Attainment of objectives is *always* a matter of degree." [19] He probably is right, too, although it does seem that at least some minor forestry objectives might be completely attained. So we find ourselves evaluating a policy, program, or organization in terms of the degree of success with which it accomplishes what it is supposed to do. And this creates problems because we do not have a firm standard against which to test accomplishment.

As an example, it is inconceivable that any forest-fire control program will be able to absolutely prevent fires from burning over any land at all.

[19] Herbert A. Simon, *Administrative Behavior,* The Macmillan Company, New York, 1958, p. 177.

So how do we evaluate an organization which has restricted the area burned to 0.2 percent of the forest land under its protection? Was its program effective or not? It would seem that we would have to compare it with the results of similar organizations operating under similar conditions. But suppose that all of these other organizations are ineffective? In that case it probably would be necessary to construct some kind of model of the fire situation and to insert into this model reasonable and clearly attainable figures for the different variables in order to estimate what the potential accomplishment of an effective organization might be. The yardstick is obviously still going to be an imperfect one.

The measurement of effectiveness in terms of the time required to achieve a result also presents difficulties. Is a program that is reforesting the idle land in an area in five years more effective than one which would take ten years? Without a great deal more information about such things as the methods of planting, care taken in planting, quality and size of the planting stock, site preparation, and survival and growth, most of us would not care to try to answer that question. We certainly would hesitate to use elapsed time as a simple criterion of effectiveness in any but those comparisons where all other conditions are the same. In many cases, an organization or program can achieve speed of accomplishment by lowering other standards. This may be the desirable thing to do in those cases but we cannot assume that it will always be true. It is important, therefore, to take everything into account in comparing effectiveness.

This points up the fact that in discussing effectiveness we have been looking only at the output side of the picture and ignoring the input side. A fire-control organization with twice as much personnel, equipment, and budget will probably be more effective. But this does not necessarily mean that we should double our fire-control organizations. Let us see how we can bring the input side into the evaluation.

**Efficiency** When we consider the input side of any program or organization we are immediately reminded that it requires the use of scarce resources—both human and capital. These productive resources—as we well know—have many other potential uses, and in the interest of total human welfare we cannot afford to be wasteful with them. It is entirely reasonable, therefore, to evaluate organizations, programs, and even policies in terms of the amount of these scarce resources that they require or use.

The total amount of resources used is not by itself a very useful criterion, however. A state parks organization might, for example, operate very frugally, hiring few people and those at the lowest possible wages, providing only minimum facilities and maintaining these only enough to avoid their collapse, and making no provision at all for increased future demand. Certainly, we would not give this organization a very high score in any evaluation. Efficiency has to be considered in terms of the relation between benefits produced and costs incurred. The criterion as usually stated is to produce a given benefit at a minimum cost or to derive the maximum benefits from a given cost. Either way of judging efficiency may be useful in the kinds of evaluations we are concerned with.

As we noted in an earlier chapter, many of our forest policies are such that a certain amount of action toward a particular end is accepted and followed but not total action. It is our present policy, for example, to make a limited effort toward the prompt regeneration of cutover forest lands, but it is not our policy to promptly regenerate all cutover lands. The limitations are usually placed by the funds which we are willing to make available for organizations and programs to implement the policies. If the people of the United States were willing to provide the necessary funds, the federal and state forestry agencies certainly could develop programs which would reforest every acre promptly after it was cut over. Now in this kind of situation, the extent to which a policy is implemented depends on how efficiently the organizations and programs use the limited funds which have been appropriated for that policy. A useful criterion for evaluating such organizations and programs, therefore, is the amount of effective implementation achieved with the given annual budget.

In other cases the output is rather definitely specified and the intention is to achieve it completely. The accepted policy, for example, may be that no one builds a fire in the open during fire season without first obtaining a permit. The state forestry department has been charged with enforcing this policy. It is reasonable, therefore, to evaluate this department's permit program in terms of how much it costs to operate. If the permit program is not effective, and people are burning without permits, something is wrong with either the program or the department. If the program is effective, then the important question is whether it is efficient or not. Efficiency in this case would mean operating at least cost.

The criterion of efficiency requires the evaluation to consider alternatives to the present situation. The evaluation must ask: are there other policies or programs or organizations which would achieve the desired objectives more efficiently? That is, we not only have to consider whether an existing program might be operated at less cost but also whether there might possibly be some other program that would do the same job at a lower cost. The same question should be asked in evaluating policies and organizations.

While we are talking about alternatives, we must also remember that there are alternatives on the output side. That is, the resources used to implement a forestry program might instead be used for some other purpose of value to the people of the country. This means that we have to look at the input side of the equation in terms of opportunity costs. To take a simple example, suppose that a state forest and parks department assigns several of its employees to cleanup and maintenance work in a park. The improved recreational conditions for the park visitors appears to more than outweigh the salaries paid these employees. But now suppose that if these men were not maintaining the park they would instead be engaged in forest-fire prevention, detection, and suppression. The opportunity cost of using them in the park is the amount of fire damage that they would otherwise have prevented. This may be much greater than their salaries. In terms of opportunity cost, therefore, an evaluation might show that the department is making inefficient use of its resources by assigning these employees to park maintenance.

If an evaluation is to be meaningful, an attempt must always be made to determine the opportunity costs involved.    This is usually much more difficult than in the simple example above.    The opportunity costs of implementing a policy of increasing wood growth may show up directly in such forms as recreation opportunities foregone or indirectly in such forms as less-adequate educational or health facilities.    The difficulty in tracing the real costs of many forest policies has much to do with the great variation in attitudes of different people toward these policies.

**Spillover effects**    It is the nature of many forest-related actions that they produce other effects in addition to the ones at which they are aimed. These external effects may be desirable or undesirable.    In an attempt to increase the usable water yield from an area, a policy may be instituted of keeping the forest vegetation from producing its normal high canopy.    A program of cutting all trees back at periodic intervals may be instituted to implement this policy.    In addition to increasing water yield, this policy will have two spillover effects:    Deer and other wildlife species will increase because of the large amount of available browse produced, and the total usable wood yield of the area will be reduced by the amount which otherwise would have grown on the presently cutback areas.    In evaluating this policy we cannot look merely at the water yield but must also consider the values gained and lost as a result of the spillover effects.

We have become increasingly aware of spillover effects in recent years, especially of those which take the forms of various kinds of pollution.    As a result, some policies and programs which previously were considered good are being reevaluated.    An example is controlled burning to reduce fire hazard, control disease, prepare suitable seedbed conditions, or other desirable purposes.    In terms of effectiveness and efficiency, controlled burning has rated high and consequently has been widely advocated.    Now, however, questions are being asked about the inevitable air pollution resulting from such large-scale burning operations.    It is at least conceivable that future evaluations will decide that controlled burning is not an acceptable method to use in many places because of the spillover air-pollution effects.

Many spillover effects are intangible and difficult to determine.    However, as in the case of deterioration of the ecosystem, they may affect a very large number of people and must somehow be brought into evaluations of policies and programs.

## DO THE ENDS JUSTIFY THE MEANS?

We have now done about all that can presently be done with the subject of evaluating forest policies and programs.    It is clear that most of the present evaluation efforts are made at the administrative level and are concerned primarily with the efficiency of organizations and programs.

While such administrative evaluations are necessary and valuable in themselves, they do not come to grips with the really vital forest-policy problems.    By their nature they assume that the objectives or policies are worthwhile and that the only problems lie in how to achieve the objectives or to make the policies effective.    The danger in such a situation, of course, lies in falling into the trap of assuming that any organization or program or policy is justified if it is efficient and effective in reaching the objective. While most—if not all—foresters and forest administrators would balk at the philosophy that "the ends always justify the means" if it were presented to them in that form, they tend to follow this philosophy unwittingly in their day-to-day activities.    The objections that have been raised to the broadcast aerial spraying of DDT, the acceleration of erosion and clogging of streams in logging, the elimination of open areas vital to wildlife by solid reforestation with conifers, and similar practices indicate that those who directly control the use of our forest resources have often placed great stress on achieving ends and have uncritically accepted and used whatever means appeared to be most effective.

This is not intended as an indictment of the professional foresters and land managers, for the survival and continuing productivity of our forest resources are largely a result of their conscientious efforts.    But we will face increasing pressure on these resources in the future from many conflicting sources, and it will become more and more important that we evaluate and reevaluate all of our forest policies, programs, and institutions if we are to realize the greatest long-run benefit from our important forest resources.

# In Conclusion

# 14.

In the preceding chapters we have looked at forest policies from a number of different angles and have seen that their formation and execution are complex processes indeed. Before terminating our discussion, it seems worthwhile to try to pull together some of the ideas which have been presented and to see what guidance these might offer for future considerations of forest policies.

This analysis is based on the idea that a policy is a settled course of action that has been adopted by a group of people and is actually being followed by them. A statement or pronouncement that some particular course of action should be or will be followed does not of itself establish a policy under this definition. It is merely a policy recommendation or the expression of what some individual or particular group feels is the policy that should be followed. It will only become the policy of the larger society if enough of the members accept this course of action and actually follow it.

How many members is "enough" to establish a policy? Because of the great diversity among the people in a country like the United States, few forest policies will have enough direct effect on every individual to cause each one to consciously accept or reject the proposed course of action. Most people will be indifferent to what the policy is and can be led to follow any chosen course. But among those who are not indifferent there is likely to be a conflict of opinion. Enough of these concerned individuals must favor the proposed course of action that they can convince or coerce most of the other individuals into following it too. Compliance will seldom be 100 percent, but if the great majority of the people in a society are following one course of action, it can be said to be a policy of that society.

The choice of courses of action and their acceptance by enough people to establish them as actual policies is a gradual, incremental, and in some respects evolutionary process. Policies are not formed suddenly. What appears to be an abrupt policy decision is usually the culmination of a number of gradual changes in knowledge, viewpoints, objectives, and accepted criteria on the parts of many people.

But we must not make the mistake of visualizing the policy-formation process as some kind of "natural" or automatic phenomenon. People are involved at every step of the way, and as we saw in Chapter 12 they can find many ways of influencing or steering policy formation in the directions they desire. We cannot ignore this political activity, but at the same time we must not make too much of it. For although certain individuals and groups have had a great influence on the formation of some of our forest policies they have never had the free reign that is sometimes attributed to them. Without the tacit acceptance of the majority of the affected people, no one person or group could long impose an involuntary course of action on others. It is because this general acceptance has to be obtained that it sometimes takes so long to convert "paper policies" into real social policies.

At the same time we must not fall into the trap of assuming that since forest policies actually are formed in this gradual, evolutionary process, the result must necessarily be the best of all possible worlds. Unfortunately this process apparently can produce "bad" policies as well as "good" ones. Or at least it can result in policies which are less desirable than some of the possible alternatives might be.

Societies develop policies because they feel that following certain courses of action will lead to the attainment of desired objectives. But who specifies these objectives? The apparent answer in a democracy is that the people decide what they want, and this sets the goals for the society. Some have also argued that this is what happens in a free-market economy —the consumers control economic life. But economists have had qualms about consumer sovereignty on other grounds than just whether this really is the way the economy operates. There are many examples which indicate that if left to his own devices the average man will often make choices that work to the long-run disadvantage of himself or of other members of society. The reasons may be selfishness, greed, a very short-range viewpoint, or just plain lack of knowledge. In any event, what appears a desirable course of action to these individuals may be a very undesirable policy for society.

Most of us are susceptible to emotional appeals but emotions are not very good bases for policy choices. Resorting to emotion as a means of obtaining support for or acceptance of forest policies is a risky business. People may be carried along by their emotions to follow or demand certain policies without having any clear idea of the implications of these policies for the long-run welfare of their society. The highly emotional nature of the campaigns for wilderness, scenic beauty, open space, and pollution control, among other desirable things, might easily lead to the formation of policies whose unforeseen spillover effects could plague society for generations to come.

The proper response to these unpleasant possibilities is certainly not to jettison the policy formation process as it now exists; if such a step is even conceivably feasible.   Regardless of any doubt about the qualifications of the ordinary members of our society to make wise forest-policy decisions, substituting a dictatorship of scientists or "experts" may be little more than leaping from the frying pan into the fire.   For scientists and experts also have their built-in biases and emotions.   We need to make the most of their detached judgment and expertise, but we will do well to maintain most of the complex checks and balances of our present policy-formation process.   Our real need is not a new and different process but efforts to make the existing process more effective.

We are not at all clear, for example, about many of our objectives, the order in which we should rank them, and the choices we should make if conflicting objectives prove to be mutually exclusive.   We need to give more thought to the various criteria we use or might use in judging policies and programs.   It is entirely likely, for example, that the ranking of objectives or the choice between policies we obtain will depend on which particular criterion we use.   What do we do in a specific case if the economic criteria point to one choice and the ecological criteria point to another?   What if an economic criterion says that a course of action would be desirable but other social criteria indicate it would be "bad" for the society?

Part of our criterion problem is that we have only recently become aware that many different criteria can often be applied with relevance to the same situation.   These criteria are not new, but in the past there was a tendency for different segments of society to use different sets of criteria in making their judgments.   The inevitable result was conflict between the groups which were judging the same action with different standards, each being convinced that its own set of criteria was the only valid one.   Today there is rather widespread recognition that many different criteria may be valid in any particular case, and we face the difficult problem of how to use a set of multiple and sometimes-conflicting criteria.

In all respects we as a society now have more knowledge and understanding of the policy-making process and the problems inherent in it than we ever had before.   We are gradually moving from a traditional and emotional view of policy to an analytical one.   (This book is an example.)   We may expect this trend to continue and to accelerate as we learn more about how to approach and analyze the complexities of policy formation.

If our population and average income continue to grow as now appears probable, there is bound to be an increasing and changing demand for benefits from the forest resources.   Many of our present policies will have to be modified or even changed completely to remain relevant to the new conditions.   At the same time, our average educational level will continue to rise, and the mass media will become even better at communicating and interchanging ideas.   It appears reasonable, therefore, to expect the basic nature of policy formation to remain much as it now is but to anticipate substantial future improvement in the efficiency and equity with which the process operates.

# Index

# Index